I Never Cried In Rwanda

Cary Rasof, MD

This diary is the intimate and personal account of actual events in the author's life. The names of some individuals have been changed to respect their privacy and protect their identities.

The author assumes no responsibility or liability whatsoever on behalf of the consumer or reader of this material. Any perceived slight of any individual or organization is purely unintentional.

Warning: This document contains graphic depictions of violence and distressing themes related to the Rwandan Genocide. Reader discretion is advised.

2024
Christmas Eve

Thirty years ago, I celebrated Christmas Eve with friends at a table covered with a white, cotton Chinese bed sheet; tablecloths were at a premium in the aftermath of the Rwandan genocide. Snow was also at a premium in the heart of equatorial Africa. Christmas without snow didn't work so we worked hard and made some out of cotton balls that we snatched from the hospital's supply closet and upgraded all with tinsel from discarded foil packaging found in our surgical suite's trash bin. The décor was divine and exceeded our expectations, as was our feast replete with wine, salmon and Champagne, all in that order, as destitute, hungry peasants perused the landscape for a bean or two or three to make it through till tomorrow. If they made it, they would return to the field again in search of another bean or two or three. There was a great divide between us: the haves and the have-nots, the Whites and the Blacks, the professionals and the peasants, the rich and the poor. But despite the divides, we were all deeply connected and interdependent. We needed them and they need us. And together we were *One*.

Much of what was 30 years ago in Rwanda was beyond words. Nothing could adequately give voice to that pebble on our shared human path. It was easy for me to kick it to the side and continue down my yellow brick road, but what about the cracks and crevices left behind. I couldn't kick them down the road.

It has taken me thirty years to muster up the courage to share this diary with anyone on the outside of my inner world. What transpired in the aftermath of the Rwandan genocide was intended to rest in peace. So why do I open the gates and break my inner sanctum's seal thirty years on? Because we rest not in peace. As we wine and dine on wine, salmon and Champagne, people are still perusing the landscape for a bean or two or three. Thousands of people "disappear" in Mexico with drug lords at the helm; armed gangs in Haiti have left the country and population in ruins; Guatemala, El Salvador and Honduras are in freefall as people flee up north for safety only to be snagged by barbed wire and manhandled by border patrols, who are "just doing their job." Across the Atlantic, civil war, child slavery, sex trafficking, genocide, and religious persecution wages in Africa, the Middle East, South and Far East Asia.

Christmas has become a symbol of universal love for all people. This single day invites us to see not the differences that separate us from one another, but the similarities that bond us together. Christmas reminds us who we are and what we can create collectively for the greater good. Imagine everyone as one big family celebrating each other. Imagine our world without borders, free of racism, class distinction, or any other divisive division. How spectacular this would be!

From my heart and hands, I give you my diary on this auspicious day of love.

Mon cher ami,

There are no words to describe my sadness and deep admiration as I read your Rwandan Diary. Unlike your fortitude, I feel like crying as I learn of this massacre and how you bring it to life as painful as it must be for you. Every word you write brings a flow of all aspects of love, courage, dedication, and unwavering capacity to help and change such horrific situations as you did in your time in Rwanda. How fortunate that you were present and could relate those atrocities with such heartfelt compassion. I cannot continue reading since my tears obscure your magnificent text.

I thank you for giving me the honor of reading such a moving and inspiring story,

With love,

Lise

Human tragedy is untimely. It is never in or on time. The Rwandan genocide was not an isolated phenomenon in a small African nation, but rather a piece of the global puzzle, another thread in our human tapestry. It was not a single event with an unfortunate beginning and happy ending; it never ended. It just continues perpetually rebirthing itself until infinity, much as life itself tenaciously takes extraordinary measures to secure its own survival. Rwanda was a rerun, a scene acted before on many stages, a story told and retold, this time with a new cast of colorful folk with a backdrop of *mille collines* —a thousand hills. People have read this script before, seen a previous performance. The importance of bringing out this particular rendition is that it reminds us of our roles in the play and the urgency to change.

For Joseph

...that his story be told for always...

DEDICATION

I dedicate my diary to the children.
They are the true keepers of this world now.

They will carry history forward,
learn from it, and hopefully honor and preserve it;
in doing so, they need not re-enact it.

I pray that they have the wisdom and strength
to create a new history...
one of living love.

AUTHOR'S NOTE

I never cried in Rwanda. From the day I landed at the Kigali International Airport in September of 1994 to the day I departed in February of 1995, I did not shed a single tear. Naturally, I ask myself why. Am I insensitive, indifferent, or incapable of feeling? Am I the product of a stoic, machismo generation that said *real* men don't cry, or do I just find it hard to believe that man has the capacity to be so evil? Why didn't I cry in Rwanda? There was certainly enough to cry about.

When a gazelle is attacked by a lion, she falls to the ground and freezes. Immobile, she succumbs without a fight. Is she by nature so passive, or is this passivity a ploy used as a decoy to secure a few additional seconds to find some way to safety? Feigning death could perhaps give her one more chance to survive. After all, what great satisfaction is there in fighting a surrendered animal that is waving a white flag? Perhaps my passivity, surrender, and hear-no-evil, see-no-evil, speak-no-evil posturing was a way to gain a few additional seconds to find my own way to safety. Maybe my tearlessness was just a guise to hide my weakness, a harrowing attempt to disguise my helplessness, my own white flag to keep my emotional wreckage off the table and away from public scrutiny.

The body, heart, mind, and soul are our best friends. Like mothers and fathers, they sustain and nourish us, making sure we are safe and protected. They also guide and teach us and remain loyal, inseparable companions throughout our entire lives. My heart was a particularly good friend to me while I was in Rwanda. It did everything to stay intact against all odds and desecrations, bravely taking the brunt of the brutality with all its might and all its prowess as it stoically resisted breaking despite the heartbreaking genocide that I subjected it to. As a result of its sacrifice, I could love fully and be the best version of myself in order to serve the survivors of one of the most heinous genocides in human history. What you are about to read is indeed heartbreaking. I trust your heart will protect you too as you visit the aftermath of a genocide.

Why didn't I cry in Rwanda? I think I was so shocked by what I saw and experienced that my heart and soul couldn't mount a response commensurate with the magnitude of horror before me. It is difficult to explain, but it was as if my heart stopped beating because it had never experienced such tragedy and didn't know how to respond, so it didn't. It seems that my soul froze by a vision of something so atrocious that it had no choice but to go into lockdown to keep itself intact. Why didn't I cry in Rwanda? I may never know. What I do know is the helplessness, hopelessness and senselessness that I felt during my time there. What I *do* know is the inexplicable *freeze* I found myself in when face-to-face with man's very real inherent capacity to kill, slay, slaughter, butcher, and even exterminate his own mother, father and child.

The document you now hold in your hands is my personal diary. It is not a story with elaborate character development, an evolving theme, or a constructed plot. There are no chapters that neatly divide the ensemble or headings to help orient readers. Instead, this work is a collection of random thoughts and impressions, feelings and sorrows, slices of life—my life. And since we are all connected, your life—our life.

My diary is a sacred conversation between me and "My Dearest." It is a private and intimate dialogue that I started when I was 14 years old to help me cope with the bullying and loneliness that I experienced in my childhood. It was never intended to be shared with a wider audience. In fact, exposing so much of my personal life to the public is terrifying and leaves me feeling uncomfortably vulnerable. People can be brutally critical and judgmental. I don't want to be bullied or criticized, judged harshly or marginalized yet again. So why do I do it? Why do I parade these words before you and invite you to be part of this conversation? It is because today our world has never been so divided, our family has never been so polarized, and we have never felt so helpless and hopeless. Perhaps by being part of this conversation, you will find *your* voice, realize *your* power, and make a difference.

Transcribing this diary has been a labor of love. I say labor because it has not been easy. I buried this moment in my life, and bringing it back to mind has been excruciatingly painful, much like delivering a baby. Recalling Rwanda and bringing it back from the dead wasn't my plan or preference. But it had to be done because those who perished deserve to be heard and remembered. Their story must be indelibly inked in our history books to remind people of the *hazards of hate.*

I was told to let Rwanda rest. The event is over; the people are dead, and those surviving have moved on with their lives. I was advised to bombard the public with *happy*, because the world doesn't need more sadness now. I beg to differ. Rwanda is a story that needs to be told and retold. By telling this story, we are given a chance to right the wrong, a chance to change. As long as people are divided, Rwanda's story must be kept alive and embedded in people's memories. In this way, it might not happen again.

As horrific and appalling as the genocide was, is, and will always be, people will invariably come along and deny it ever happened. Others will come and attempt to rewrite history. In time, those who killed and those who lived will ascend or descend, and the public will no longer have the time or will to ponder the past. Generations will pass, and the human carnage will no longer be visible or available to serve as proof of what happened starting on the morning of the 7th of April, in the year 1994, and continued to happen for 100 days. Memorials, photos, books and diaries cannot do it justice but will need to suffice to keep the memory alive.

This diary is what I saw, lived and documented in near real time during the aftermath of the Rwandan genocide. It is real and cannot be denied or dismissed. Let its words serve as a testament and the testimony of a witness to the fallout of hate.

I give you my diary to remind you of the infinite needs next to you. I give you my diary to assure you that *you* are a key player in the puzzle of life that needs *you* to complete it. I give you my diary to experience history and change its course.

GRATITUDE

This book is a shared endeavor. It would not be in your hands now if it weren't for the generosity, kindness, and love of so many amazing people. I wish to acknowledge the angels who gave a hand, a shoulder, and so much heart to this work.

First and foremost, I would like to thank Cathy Terdich, my literary consultant, for so generously sharing her heart and soul to polish and perfect this work. Your devotion, encouragement, and unwavering belief that this document must be made public ultimately brought it to fruition. Bless you.

I would also like to thank a kindred spirit on the path, Jane Olivier, for adding varnish to the text to highlight and embolden it, to protect and preserve it. Jane, your capacity to care carries the breath of the breath, the thought of the thought, the beat of the beat. Through you 'just being,' I was carried over impasses and magic-carpeted over mountains. I pranam to you.

To the people of Rwanda, I offer my heartfelt appreciation for giving me the privilege to serve you. Caring for you gave my life purpose. Having your trust and faith was a real honor. And for this, I thank you.

To Anne Tolsma, Jane Morris, Linda Doull, and the many other humanitarian giants in the field, I reserve a special place in my heart. You came together to support and protect people struggling to hold on. You were unyielding in your resolve to serve desperate souls, so needing companionship and comfort, care and compassion. You came together from all corners of the world and created a family with one objective—to love. And you did. And you did it so well. I will always be indebted to you for being my friends and confidants, partners and co-creators, brothers and sisters. I salute you.

A special thanks to Anne and Tony Jones, Ralph Young, Taryn Sofaer, Thomas and Andreas Clauder, Olivia Wilson, Benjamin Fogel, Joe Ness and Tönnies Maack. Thank you for being there for me and for sharing and shaping my destiny in your own magnificent ways. Your dear friendship and support have given me the courage to step out onto fragile limbs and precarious cliffs and remain steady. With your shoulders to lean on and your hands to hold, I could never fall. I bow to you.

To my mother and father, Sharon and Marshall, I give gold medals, trophies and accolades shouted from rooftops and mountain peaks. You easily win first place for a job well done—bringing me into the world and keeping me safe every step of the way. You worked hard, lived conservatively, and saved your entire lives to make sure I had a good education, a roof over my head, and life experiences to prepare me for a meaningful life. Because of your generous support, I never had student loans to repay. Because I didn't have student loans to repay, I could make volunteer humanitarian service my life. So thank you! All words of praise fall pitifully short of what I feel for you and the respect I hold for all you have done for me. A son could ask for no better parents than both of you. Know you are deeply loved.

And then there is little Joseph. To you, my dear raisin in the sun, I apologize profusely for failing to protect you, for failing to find you a family, and for failing to reciprocate the unconditional love you gave me. You loved me, and this love was my *raison d'être*—my reason for being. And I let you down. The day I unwrapped your arms from my neck and shoulders as I returned you to your bed at the orphanage was the day I became a glass man, invisible to you. I am so sorry. Your life was hard—very hard—and I wanted to make it easy, but I failed. Please know that it is not in vain, dear Joseph. I do all in your name, and in this way, you live infinitely.

Finally, with great reverence, I wish to thank My Dearest for being there, here, now, then, and .... When there are storms, Your footprints are always in the sand. When there is a blistering sun, You come as a passing cloud to shade me. When torrential downpours flood the fields, You are the sun. What a perfect union we have. You once told me that *silence is Your oration.* Thank You for inviting me to Your lectures.

THE COVER

The cover miraculously manifested itself, as if predestined. I'm not surprised. Much of it is symbolic, touching sensitive chords at the core of my being. What appears as a concoction of colors with a person in the center is so much more.

Red is the blood smeared on church walls. Blood is also streaked and splattered throughout the entire country.

Yellow is the yellow brick road that was supposed to lead me to my idyllic life, my calling. "Follow the yellow brick road…" I find myself on the road that increasingly gets snared before my eyes. Doubt gets the best of me. Why am I here?

The figure on the edge of the yellow brick road is paused, stunned and lost. A shadow is seen behind him—*him* is me. It is this lack of light that follows me from countless mishaps, misunderstandings and errors that happened on my watch. The shadow is also violence and hatred—two dark forces that are anchors, paralyzing me in place, rendering me impotent and in perpetual self-doubt. I am but a shadow of vast apocalyptic human-orchestrated disasters.

My name is intentionally out of the limelight in a small font barely noticeable because I felt so diminished and ineffective in the whole scope of things. I felt insignificant and unseen, hardly a pixel on the screen of life, struggling with my hope of making a difference and confronted with the reality that I did not matter much.

I once met a very special person. He was someone extraordinary. When we parted ways, I asked for his address to stay in contact with him. He refused saying, "Forget my name and remember my story." That was nearly 50 years ago and I have never forgotten his story. In the same way, I am the author and the scribe. I assume my position and then fade away leaving my story behind. The less than visible name discreetly printed at the bottom of the cover is my way of saying, "Forget my name and remember my story."

PROLOGUE

Rwanda

Rwanda—the pearl of Africa—home to a divided people: Hutu and Tutsi. April 7, 1994, Hutus took to the streets and bludgeoned to death Tutsis and their sympathizers—friends, neighbors and family. According to official Rwandan government estimates, 1,074,017 Tutsis and their sympathizers were killed in 100 days. In other words, on average 10,740 people were killed every day during the genocide. After the killings had essentially cleansed the Rwandan landscape of the Tutsi people, humanitarian aid workers from around the world were invited into the country to clean up the mess and put the pieces back together again. I was one of those aid workers.

OPENING

Something exists because people give witness to it.
History repeats itself because people forget.
Genocide happens again and again because no one is left to tell.

The Rwandan genocide was an untimely endeavor. It was the culmination of a long-standing, brutal civil war that took place alongside other civil wars around the world—in Zaire, Burundi, Angola, Djibouti, Afghanistan, Tajikistan, Croatia, Bosnia and Somalia, to name just a few. Somalia's civil war was especially heinous, as it decimated the Somali people and left the country in absolute ruin. Hundreds of thousands of innocent civilians died from starvation, and many more were ravaged by disease. The international community was deeply affected by the Somali people's plight, and with an outpouring of love and compassion, they organized a massive humanitarian initiative to provide food to the people caught in the crossfire. And what came of the world's heart-filled efforts? Death and destruction. Somali warlords killed dozens of UN personnel and American soldiers, some of whom were defiled and dragged naked, with ropes tied around their necks through unpaved city streets for the world to see. And the world watched. The spirit of the world's goodwill was shattered. But what does this have to do with the Rwandan genocide?

Shortly after the Somali disaster, news of an impending genocide in Rwanda reached the West. No one in any political position of power wanted to commit professional suicide by intervening yet again in an interminable, unwinnable tribal war on a faraway continent where conflict and corruption had become synonymous with life itself. So the West stayed silent and looked the other way as Rwandans killed Rwandans.

After the killings had essentially cleansed the Rwandan landscape of the Tutsi people, humanitarian aid workers from around the world were invited into the country to clean up the mess and help put the pieces back together again. I was one of those aid workers.

INTRODUCTION

I'm lonely. I am 14 years old and have no friends. Bullied and beaten at school, I find refuge in my bedroom, where I spend most of my childhood. Loneliness greets and grips me daily. It needs me like I need it. It's very reliable and familiar. I can always count on it to be there for me. We are inseparable.

I want so much to have a friend. "Coincidentally," the diary of Anne Frank surfaces. To my amazement, Anne is also 14 years old, and is lonely in her room, and has no friends. To keep herself company, Anne created an imaginary friend, Kitty. What a good idea! I decide to do the same. I create an imaginary friend—My Dearest. And every night without fail, I convene with My Dearest, seeking refuge, companionship, counsel, solace, encouragement and much-needed love.

1979

Who am I? Unable to find a truly meaningful answer to this simple question, I quit college. Mom and Dad tell me that the real world can be brutal and that without a college degree, I will "amount to nothing." They have always given me very sound advice, but I am lost. My life is listless; my heart is heavy, and my soul is spiritless. I am only 20 years old, but I have no choice but to leave home in search of my *Self*.

My quest for truth takes me on a pilgrimage around the globe. I roam. My answers are surely inside that Egyptian pyramid, just over that Saharan sand dune, certainly playing hide-and-seek with me somewhere in the endless Siberian birch forests. I have to find truth and my life's purpose. Like a dervish dancer spinning around and around, I am here. I am there. I am everywhere: free and wild, fearless and careless, dazzled by abundance, awed by opulence, and entranced by the planet's perfection. The world is my playground. And I play. Everything is colossal. Everywhere is another miracle. Everybody is another sacred spirit to know. And I roam.

I am on top of the world. Or am I at the bottom of it? While gallivanting around Turkey, a curious thing happens to me. I see something. Is it a rat, a cat, a dog, or perhaps a squirrel? No, it is a child—a struggling, hungry child in a rubbish bin. What an awkward and shameful sight—a child sifting through slop, relishing tiny morsels of nothingness to fill a bawling belly. I'm immediately taken off guard by this little being, and my mind abruptly shifts from pilgrimage to abject poverty. Contemplating the Self cannot be more irrelevant. Instantly, my question changes from "Who am I?" to "How long has it been since this child has eaten?" The more I try to understand, the more questions surface. Why can I dine in fine restaurants expecting polite, professional service for a 15% gratuity, and he can't? Why is he poor and I'm not? What did he do wrong, and what did I do right? Like a ping-pong ball at a table tennis tournament, I am tossed back and forth, looking for something meaningful in this child's lot in life—some reason, some justification, some solution. Then, *out of the blue*, I realize *I* am the solution! As strange or extraordinary as this might sound, it is so. From a place deep within, I hear these words: "Become a doctor and help the poor." Before my next breath, I call home and tell Mom and Dad that I am going back to college to be a doctor.

Their initial response is not what I expected: "It's too long. It's too hard. It's too competitive. It's impossible to get into medical school," they say. "Be a lawyer. Be a teacher. Be an accountant," they continue. "You can't stand blood. You can't even eat tomatoes because they remind you of blood. You are utterly terrified of needles. Be an architect. Be a pharmacist. Don't set yourself up for failure!" And my reply is, "I know that medical school will be exceptionally hard. I know I can't stand blood. I know I can't eat tomatoes because they remind me of blood. And I know I am terrified of needles, but I have a *calling*."

And as intended, it comes to pass. Pre-med, medical school and residency are indeed brutally difficult; actually, becoming a doctor is the hardest thing I have ever attempted in my life. Yes, I need to go to summer school. Yes, I need teaching assistants, tutors and extra coaching from professors. And yes, I need to retake some exams, go through back doors, and sometimes totter on tightropes over treacherous terrain, replete with inclines too steep to ever do this again. But in the end, I graduate and hold my hand in position as I proudly swear the Hippocratic Oath in front of my proud parents and tear-filled professors. And true to my word to help the poor, I crawl closer to the cradle of our civilization in the heart of Africa.

__1993__

I finish my residency training in Family Practice Medicine at the University of Wisconsin. Exhausted, I need a break—a break from pagers, emergency rooms, dysfunctional labors, and all of life's incessant responsibilities. This can't be what life is all about. So I do a Buddha: leave everything familiar behind, and assume the guise of a homeless person. I want to know homelessness. I want to know poverty. I want to live it. I want to experience life on the other side. And I do.

Once again, I go gallivanting around the globe. I sleep in grottos and on park benches, in caves and under bridges. I go without meals and even without baths to know what that feels like, too. I can say with certainty that it is not nice. It is not nice at all. And I do not appreciate it. So I start bathing myself in the sinks at McDonald's, Mr. Chicken, and other friendly, unassuming fast-food joints. It is the littlest lot of comfort I afford myself. It feels good to bathe. It feels very good indeed. Living on the other side is not easy. Actually, it is downright degrading. How do you maintain your dignity with only the clothes on your back? How do you stay clean bathing in public restrooms? How do you refresh yourself living on park benches and under bridges? How do you get nourished, feasting on the harvests from dumpster dives?

It doesn't take long to lose interest in this experiment. Like Buddha, who also went from riches to rags and back between the two, I am fed up with living on the other side. I want my comforts back, along with apple pie and ice cream, too.

It isn't until I have a powerful realization, however, that I find the strength to retire homelessness. Real poverty is a lack of choice. My poverty is not real because I have *choice*—the choice to change, the choice to eat or not, the choice to be hungry or not. With credit cards in my pocket, stocks in my portfolio, money in the bank, parents with a home waiting to welcome me, and an MD after my name, I could only disguise myself as a homeless person. I could never truly be one. So, after one year of this nonsense, I go home and get a *real* job.

1994

I turn on my television set and immediately find myself hurled into hell. There is a genocide in Rwanda. People are fleeing for their lives, blood is hemorrhaging, and machetes are severing the Achilles tendons of tens of thousands as killers publicly parade their human conquests for all to see. Thousands of miles away, I recline on a soft sofa, comfy and warm, enveloped and secure, watching a world go wrong. Tears well up and stream down my face like raindrops in a heavy downpour of a thunderstorm. If these tears could talk, they would tell a story of inconsolable pain. My heart bleeds. I want to help. Something within tells me to go and wipe the tears from the innocence of the innocents. When I consider the danger, something else deep inside reassures me that I will be protected and taken care of, as the universe aspires to support me. When I question if I have enough to give to make a difference, yet another voice says, "If you trust that you are doing my life's work, how could you think I wouldn't provide for you? Haven't I always?" These few words change my life. Suddenly full of faith and free of doubt, I contact a respected humanitarian organization that specializes in medical care for disadvantaged people—Doctors Without Borders—and find myself on a plane to do my destiny.

What happened in Rwanda was raw and rude—too tender to talk about, too terrifying to bear witness. Fortunately, my diary became my guardian angel. It was a safe space where I could be me completely—proud and petrified, strong and weak, confident and everything but. It was a special place where I could bare my soul privately and intimately, a space where I could tell tales of the living, the dying and the dead. My Dearest was my lifeline, my confidant, my beloved. How astonishing that I abandoned my *soul's mate*, shoving it on a dusty shelf in my family's garage, to rot far away from anyone on the outside, far away from anyone who wasn't there, who wouldn't understand, or who wouldn't care. Intentionally left to disintegrate, hidden from public scrutiny, and denied a hero's welcome, the pages of random words and unbridled sensations were destined to remain irretrievable memories—out of sight, out of mind.

One day, while surfing my FM car radio, I stumble across a stunning interview with a man who served in Rwanda during the genocide, fighting for his life and the lives of others. Suffering from post-traumatic stress disorder following his service there, the kindred spirit takes his story, dusts off the cobwebs from its unseen form, and forms it, exposing everything unabridged from his heart to his soul. Listeners are completely transfixed by his story. To my surprise, people are truly interested in understanding humanity at its very best and its very, very worst. If this is actually the case and people want to listen and learn, and be ambassadors of change, then does My Dearest not beg to be a piece of the human puzzle that is as mysterious as the Big Bang? Does history not oblige me to fill in the blanks and gaps that are owned by voices silenced by slaughter? Is it not the right and responsible thing to do for the prematurely departed? And so, like the man on the FM radio, I dust off the cobwebs from my diary and give My Dearest an audience. It is said that one word can change a person's life forever. If anything I have written can bring about positive change, then let me tell you *our* story.

RURAL WISCONSIN

1 August 1994
Monday

My Dearest,

It is my first day at a new job in rural Wisconsin. I am running 40 minutes behind schedule because of numerous emergencies with patients. When I enter my next exam room, an exasperated patient waves a complaint form at me and says, "I know it's not you, doc, but I *gotta* fill it out." He's incensed that I'm late. Trying my best, doing my best, being my best is not good enough. Wanting to stay in good standing in my new job, I go beyond the call of duty to appease my disgruntled patient, pleading with him to forgive me for my tardiness. As I grovel at his feet, asking for his forgiveness, I recall the children on the other side of the world looking for a bean or two to chew away their hunger pangs.

What has gone wrong with American medicine? Patients look for mistakes and reasons to sue. Doctors, in turn, order expensive, extensive, and mostly unnecessary tests to protect themselves from patients. What has become of the honorable doctor-patient relationship? The once-revered and esteemed doctor has become the enemy, while the cherished patient seems to have become the victim.

I listen to my patients' lists of ailments. I can feel their pain and suffering. I can hear their cry for help. In most cases, my diagnosis for them is simply *loneliness*. What they want and need most of all isn't a pill but a friend—someone who cares, someone to share their life with. I wish I could cure lonely people. If only I could excise "I'm not good enough" and transplant "I'm good enough" in its place. If only I could reach out and hold my patients. After all, hugs are the best medicine for loneliness and the loathsome "I'm not good enough." Unfortunately, hugs are not allowed in modern medicine, nor is caring. The cost of each is prohibitive. Daring to care carries a fine that is simply too dear. And in the end, my hands are tied, my mouth is gagged, and my white doctor's coat feels increasingly like a straitjacket.

23

2 August 1994
Tuesday

My Dearest,

It is now night. Its quiet is good for me. After a hectic day, the calm is especially welcome, though I must admit I am a bit lonely in this rural Wisconsin town. The agency I work for provides housing for me in a modest residential hotel. It has the basics, including a television, which keeps me company. I haven't watched TV since childhood. Technology has surely advanced a lot since those days. The last time I changed a television's channels, there were only six of them: channels 2, 5, 7, 9, 11 and VHF. It appears these six channels have given birth to more than 60 stations. Another amazing development I discover is a small, state-of-the-art handheld remote control device. It can change the channels through the air. How incredible! What a nifty invention—just point, push, and the screen changes. It doesn't take but a few seconds to master the device and feel the exhilaration of traveling the world with my fingertips. I am like a child seeing fire for the first time. The lonely night is less lonely this way. Good night.

3 August 1994
Wednesday

My Dearest,

Rural Wisconsin can be isolating. I don't know anyone, so after work, I spend the rest of the day alone. The television, out of necessity, quickly becomes my favorite companion. It is akin to a contagious disease, and I've been infected. No matter how hard I try, I can't stop changing its channels. Turn it off, Cary. I can't. Then just walk away from it. I can't. It feels like I'm in a cage, unable to escape, *superglued* to a television screen, powerless to peel myself off of it. Gymnasts, sharks, surfers on Hawaiian waves—the entire world projected in full color in front of me. It's beyond sensational. I'm a kid again in a candy store. Why go to the store when I can have the entire factory. I think I have a serious case of *televisionitis*. Channel 1: children's cartoons; Channel 2: herds of antelope jumping in sync on the plains in the Serengeti; Channel 3: cooking lessons; and Channel 4: breaking news about someplace called Rwanda. What is Rwanda? Where is it? Whatever and wherever it is, something is going wrong there. Images of children crying and killers craving the flesh of friends and neighbors flash in front of me. Death—lots of death—saunters on the streets with no end in sight. The broadcast images are so horrific that I feel ashamed to be part of the human race.

During the news coverage of this Rwanda event, I notice in the background the flag of a well-known international medical organization, *Médecins Sans Frontières (MSF)*, which means doctors without borders in French. This organization provides emergency medical care to people in catastrophic situations worldwide. They appear to be well established there. This organization is always looking for doctors for their projects. I wonder if they could use any assistance in Rwanda.

What is a Rwanda? I've never heard the word before. If it is a place, from the pictures, I think it is somewhere in Africa, but it could also be in South America or the Pacific. I don't understand what is happening there. Newscasters say nothing about the reason for this violence. Their coverage only shows images—horrific images—and heart-rupturing scenes of death and destruction. People trudge on dirt and gravel roads, going somewhere other than where they had been. Where are they going? Why are they going? Tears come easily and turn to puddles as I sit stunned. The television screen has no mercy. It is relentless. People fall to the ground as others trample over them. Dead or alive, the people look dazed, with glazed eyes staring at nothing. I have to go there, to this Rwanda place. When I see the children with their purely innocent eyes and little, fleeing feet, I want to hold them. I want to protect them from everything bad, feed and shelter them, and give them love—lots of love. I want to listen to their stories and share them far and wide, so no one ever makes such stories again. It is hard to bear what they show on television. Do I not have a human obligation to go and help these people? Yes, I do. I'll go there, to wherever *there* is... to Rwanda.

4 August 1994
Thursday

My Dearest,

As soon as the alarm clock rings this morning, I grab the phone and call Doctors Without Borders at its head office in France. It is easy to push the buttons. It is less easy to organize my thoughts. What exactly am I doing calling them?

The phone is ringing…

"*Médecins Sans Frontières* [Doctors Without Borders]."

My heart thumps and misses a beat. I am tongue-tied.

"*Bonjour* [hello]," the receptionist continues.

"*Bonjour*," I stammer. "Uh, uh, I believe you are presently working in Rwanda. I am, uh, a doctor, and, uh, if you need any help, I am available." My words shoot out like baffled bullets that go off course in all directions.

"*Affirmatif* [affirmative]," the woman answers elatedly at the other end of the line. "*Docteur*," she continues. "Please give me your details and I will have someone contact you."

A lull follows as I struggle to answer her in French. All she wants is my telephone number, but I seem to be moderately mute, wrestling to find the right words in a foreign language I speak relatively well.

Hearing me dither, the woman patiently works with me to get my telephone number. She then repeats the numbers and says, "*C'est ça* [Is that it]?"

"*Oui, c'est ça* [Yes, that's it]!" I jump excitedly, proud that I managed to say my telephone number in French. A bit more confident now, I conclude our conversation with a striking "*Merci beaucoup* [thank you very much]!" Now I wait.

After the call, I prepare as I did the day before, decorating myself with a white lab coat and a stethoscope that somehow knows how to wrap itself elegantly around my neck, as if it were predestined to be there. I am at ease.

At the clinic, I mention to some patients and colleagues that I intend to go to Rwanda. Surprisingly, they aren't pleased or encouraging. Many are upset, saying it's irresponsible to put myself in harm's way. "There are plenty of underserved people in America who need medical care," they argue, and then remind me of Rwanda's machetes, corpses, and blood-splattered streets that brazenly dominate the world press at the moment. People's lack of support leaves me unprepared and speechless. I don't know what to say. Again, I am mute.

Fear can be a good friend sometimes, but it can also be a staunch enemy. I begin to wonder about Rwanda, my health, and the uncertainty of the work there. Should I not go? My mind races in all directions, looking for guidance and clarity. Am I not in a position to help the people there? Am I not obliged to assist those in need if I have the skills to do so? Is this not my calling? Money, comfort, pleasure, dreams, and life itself all seem unimportant compared to the needs of those aimlessly wandering souls in Rwanda. Oh, what to do?

5 August 1994
Friday

My Dearest,

To prepare myself for Rwanda, I read whatever I can find about the country and its people. Its facts and figures are both interesting and harrowing. The country is located south of the equator in east-central Africa. It is landlocked and shares borders with Tanzania, Uganda, Zaire and Burundi. It is quite small, about 3/4 the size of Switzerland, and only 32% of its land is arable. Its population is just 5,728,000, but because of its small size, it is the most densely populated country in Africa. Rwanda has an extremely high infant mortality rate of 130 deaths per 1,000 live births. In addition, 42% of the population is under 15 years old, and only 2.7% of the people reach an age greater than 67 years—not 27%, but 2.7%. The overall life expectancy is one of the lowest of any nation at 28 years, which is due, in part, to AIDS. Rwanda has one of the highest HIV prevalence rates in the world: 5.2%. This means that out of every 100 people, five have been infected with the human immunodeficiency virus, which leads to AIDS. This might not sound significant, but these numbers suggest nearly 300,000 people are currently infected with HIV, which has already killed millions of people. Other statistics continue along the same line of doom. For example, only 48% of the general population is literate, most households do not have potable water or electricity, and the gross national income per person is $150 annually, compared to $27,870 in the USA.

These figures suggest the country is in freefall and dying an agonizing death. Already on the brink of self-destruction, I can't imagine what is happening there now after the country was converted into a slaughterhouse. The situation appears to be so hopeless that I am starting to wonder if there is any point in me going there.

8 August 1994
Monday

My Dearest,

A representative from Doctors Without Borders called to tell me that my application has been accepted and that I am a "top candidate." I'm going to Rwanda. A somber resignation takes hold of me. Instead of being elated, I feel deflated. I am suddenly conflicted. Should I go? Will I get sick? Will what I see and do leave me psychologically damaged? Will what I learn and come to know leave me an outcast in a once-familiar world? Will unsightly scars cover my naïve and unscathed heart, leaving it broken or permanently impaled with pain? And what of my innocence? What will become of it?

Will Rwanda be the definitive test of my faith in some organizing power that I believe is ultimately responsible for everything in this conundrum we call life? Or will I decide my faith is all an irrational figment of my imagination, and life is just random chaos, sometimes in and sometimes out of sync? And one more question: If I should pass a dying child and circumstances force me to step over him or her, what will become of my faith?

Am I doing the right thing by going to Rwanda? If I follow my enthusiasm, then I know I am. If I listen to logic, then I know I am not. Do I have the capacity to make a difference? Do I have the intelligence to know right from wrong and the discernment to determine who should live and who should die? Then there is my family. Is it right to abandon the most important people in my life? And then there is my health, not to mention the possibility of being in an accident. What future will I have if I am physically maimed, mentally deranged or brain-dead? And what about simple comforts like water and electricity, clean food, a postage stamp, telephone, toilet, and a safe place to lay my head at night to dream? I am beginning to have reservations. Fresh out of medical training, young, eager, willing and yearning to serve, I have a wonderful career and life ahead of me. Am I sacrificing it all for naught?

When the receptionist from the headquarters of Doctors Without Borders called me and said I was a "top candidate," did she mean I'm over the top?

9 August 1994
Tuesday

My Dearest,

There have been times in my life when I suddenly grind to a halt and resemble a piece of petrified wood—hard and immobile. This usually occurs when I am faced with extreme adversity. It is at these times that I look back at the best in my life and selectively forget the worst. Sure, my life has been filled with its share of turmoil, but the thought of losing this precious, time-sensitive gift brings to mind many reasons to hold onto it and hold on tight. Sure, living life can be tough, but now being so close to losing it, I find myself tenaciously clutching onto it. The bad times were not so bad, and the good times were so good that it is worth fighting for more of both. In my life, the grass was always greener on the other side. No matter where I was, I was driven to be on that greener grass over there. But now, at this very moment, I find myself happy right where I'm at.

29

Rwanda could possibly be the end of my life. Part of me calmly claims that I am being melodramatic and overreacting; another part invites me to take responsibility and do the right thing. But what is the right thing to do? I don't know. I do know that I can help people in need. When? Now. I also know that I can go to the front line in Rwanda and do something meaningful. I have been trained to do this. I have not been trained to flee from my fears and shirk my responsibilities. When I first saw those images on television of people dying in pain without anyone bending down to comfort them, I saw myself there, nearly in the flesh. Was this a prophetic vision of my future? If there is some organizing power anywhere out there, then I must believe the organizer will look after me. I need a sign—yes, a sign. My Dearest, give me a sign. And when the sign comes, make it loud and crystal clear! I don't want to miss it.

10 August 1994
Wednesday

My Dearest,

Doctors Without Borders called to confirm my departure. I will be briefed in Paris with the rest of the team on August 29th, which is only 19 days away. Then, if all goes well, we will depart for Rwanda on September 1st. They refer to their Rwandan activity as a "*mission.*" It sounds so official, almost clandestine, as if we are undercover agents assigned to save the world. My fear and reservations are overshadowed by gratitude and a deep sense of purpose. After a decade of grueling and painstaking medical studies, I am finally going to live my dream.

This mission will surely change my life in a profound way. It will put me head-to-head with humanity and force me to take a good look. At this point, I don't believe in evil. People can do evil things, but I don't think they are intrinsically evil. Evil is the absence of love. As I see it, everyone has the capacity to love; therefore, there are no evil people. Will I return with something to add or subtract on this subject?

With a departure date finally scheduled, I find myself more settled and enthusiastic about going. There is even a little excitement creeping in, which overshadows my fear. With a firm date of departure, it somehow feels inexplicably right to go to Rwanda. With confirmation of my departure, however, I quickly become a full-fledged adult and do what adults do: worry.

11 August 1994
Thursday

My Dearest,

Am I going to die in Rwanda? Is this trip a round-trip or a one-way? And if it's a one-way, how do I prepare for it? Who do I say goodbye to, and how do I say goodbye? What do I give to whom and when? I have never been in such a situation before.

My to-do list is almost as big as my medicine kit, which accounts for the bulk of my luggage. It includes mefloquine 100 mg to be taken one week before departure for malaria prophylaxis, Fansidar if I get malaria, and quinine in case I get a resistant strain of the disease, which is known to kill many foreigners. Antibiotics, anti-inflammatories and antifungals are part of my personal weaponry, along with other lifesaving necessities like insect repellents, mosquito nets, and water purifiers. I also have appointments for the hepatitis B, tetanus, typhoid, cholera, yellow fever and polio vaccines. In addition to all these vaccines, I need to resign from my new dream job, learn everything possible about Rwanda and the conflict between the Hundis and Titzis (or is it Hutzis and Tutus?), and read up on the many infectious diseases that are found in abundance there but are rarely found in the West.

Am I going to get sick? Will I be maimed or mentally impaired? And if I should, by chance, be maimed or find myself mentally impaired, will I accept my disabilities and go on living, or will I choose to die in order to put an end to my misery? What am I doing?

12 August 1994
Friday

My Dearest,

After work, I drive back to Illinois to spend the evening with Grams and Gramps. I am so happy when we are together. They are a lifeline for me, so whenever possible, I visit them to replenish my happiness. How lucky I am to still have them in my life. After so many years, our love for each other has not changed. I know change is an essential part of life and that everything must change at some point, but perhaps a little exception can be made when it comes to my grandparents.

This evening, I have come to realize that this illusory thing we call time is not on our side anymore and that it is rapidly running out; our together time is coming to an end. Once I leave for Rwanda, I may never see my beautiful beloveds again. Grams, at 86 years old, still makes the world's best oatmeal, and Gramps, at 87 years old, still sews my clothes better than a Singer sewing machine. I love them so much. I love to love them, and I love to be loved by them. Leaving my precious grandparents for an extended period of time will be difficult—very, very difficult.

13 August 1994
Saturday

My Dearest,

One night in a dream, I stumble across a bottle on a beach. Upon opening it, a genie emerges and says, "I will grant you one wish. What do you want?"

Without hesitation, I say, "Give me happiness!"

Genie chuckles affectionately. "Happiness? You can't give someone happiness. Happiness is different for everyone. No, I can't give you happiness, but I can give you what will make you happy. Tell me what will make you happy," Genie prods.

To answer this question takes a lot of thinking. So I think and think, and then think some more. What makes me happy?

When am I the happiest? After some time, I realize that I am the happiest when I am serving others, whether it is leading a blind person through a crowded intersection, helping an elder put on a shoe, petting a puppy, playing with a child, or just giving roses to strangers on a street corner. Serving makes me happy. So I say, "Genie, let me be of service!"

And so it has come to pass. Day after day, I am presented with countless new opportunities to serve. Why my happiness comes from serving others, I don't know. What makes me fight for the poor, block the bullies, and right the wrongs? I don't know, either. What I do know is that it feels good to do *good*. It feels great to care and ecstatic to love.

14 August 1994
Sunday

My Dearest,

While on a pilgrimage to India, a guru gave me a personal lesson: "Your job is not to change the world, but to serve it with love." To date, I have failed to find the deeper meaning in her words. But I'm not giving up. I believe the truth behind this pearl will be revealed to me in Rwanda.

15 August 1994
Monday

My Dearest,

I still have not told Mom and Dad about my departure. I don't want them to worry prematurely. My plan is to tell them a few days before departing. Grams advises me to share the news with them now so they can prepare themselves. She has a point, but I am reluctant to say anything because they will discourage me from going and fill me with more fear than I already have. There is still an internal battle raging inside me about going to Rwanda. I am so conflicted that any opposition to me going could easily sway me from boarding the plane. I must avoid being challenged by anyone right now. The easiest way forward would be to say nothing.

16 August 1994
Tuesday

My Dearest,

I heed Gram's advice and tell Mom and Dad about my decision to go to Rwanda. To my utter amazement, they are both supportive and encourage me to go. Maybe they have also been touched by the plight of the people there and send their son as their emissary. Having their blessings means a lot to me. I am not a parent and so I can never truly understand how it feels to have a child leave on a dangerous mission to an obscure African country in the middle of a genocide. It must be excruciatingly painful for them to let me go.

18 August 1994
Thursday

My Dearest,

I am horrified by the ongoing news reports from Rwanda. The atrocities people orchestrate and commit against other people are beyond belief. One report describes a man jumping on another man's back until his spine splits in two. Another report tells of people being raped, castrated, dismembered, hacked to death, and burned alive. Such grotesque displays of human barbarism incapacitate me. What good am I in such conditions? How can I block someone's blade from severing a trembling man's carotid artery? How will I stop a machete from lacerating someone's Achilles tendon? In my medical training, we were taught a little about a lot of things, but my education did not include therapies or antidotes for barbarism, hatred, violence and human slaughter. I still really want to go to Rwanda and do something meaningful, but realistically speaking, in the big scheme of things, what can I really do, and what difference can I possibly make?

When I think of making a difference, an inspiring story I once heard comes to mind. There is an old man walking on a beach after a torrential storm. The wind and rain had stranded thousands of starfish on the shore. As they lie nearly lifeless on the sand, the old man is overwhelmed by sadness for the starfish and decides to save them. Working furiously, he picks up one starfish after another and feverishly hurls them back into the sea. A young lad on the same beach sees the old man working frantically to save the starfish. He laughs hysterically while watching the frantic elder struggle.

"Old man," the young lad chuckles, "are you crazy? Do you see how many thousands of starfish have washed up on the shore? What difference do you think you can make?"

The old man looks at the young lad, picks up yet another stranded starfish, and says, "I can make a difference to this one," as he hurls it back into the water.

19 August 1994
Friday

My Dearest,

As my time at the clinic comes to an end, the staff make a going-away party for me. On my desk are gifts, notes, and a handmade card signed by everyone wishing me well in the next chapter of my life. People share special words with me, and I am profoundly touched. It is hard on the heart, bonding with exceptional people and then having to leave them behind. Fortunately, I can bring their blessings and memories with me to Rwanda and continue to have a part of them in my life wherever I go. I've been in these people's lives for just a brief moment, yet there is something very real and familial between us. It is as if we've known each other for decades. Throughout life, we go in and out of each other's lives, leaving some friends behind and taking others with us forever and always. It's all good.

With a heavy heart, I pack up my things in Wisconsin and make my way across the Illinois state line. While the border between the two states is not visible, crossing it has a visibly piercing effect on me. Leaving the familiar past behind and embarking on something unfamiliar and still unwritten is like closing one chapter and opening another. I wonder what will happen now in my book of life.

Home would not be home without a visit to see Grams and Gramps. When I arrive, they are already waiting at their front door with open arms to welcome me. As is our tradition, we sit around their little, round and white kitchen table under a ceiling filled with fluorescent lights and talk for hours, making the moment magical. Their capacity to love me is astounding, and I bathe in the sweetness of the sensations that come from just being with them. It is already 2:30 in the morning, and we are just now ready for bed. Gramps says, "We are so fortunate to have such a wonderful grandchild."

I correct him and say, "I am more fortunate to have such wonderful grandparents." In my heart, I say, "Good night and pleasant dreams, my loves. Please be here when I return!"

25 August 1994
Thursday

My Dearest,

A week has passed since leaving the clinic, and while it was hard to say goodbye, I haven't had a chance to look back. At this point, there is no going back: I'm leaving today.

Saying goodbye to Grams and Gramps is an assault on the soul. They are old, and this may be our last goodbye. Why is life so raw and unrefined? While Gramps encourages me to follow my heart, Gram's penetrating eyes pierce my heart as they plead with me to reconsider and stay. As I kiss her goodbye, she looks at me intensely and says without words, "I may not be here when you come home." As I hug her, I say, "You promise to be here when I return!"

"Okay, okay," she answers as she pushes me quickly out the door, not wanting to show any weakness as I am about to fly far away from the nest.

My Dearest, let it be like old times when I return. I know they are both in their eighties, but let there be just a little more time so that when I return, I can hug them and have a bowl of oatmeal once again at their little, round, white kitchen table.

I am surprisingly withdrawn from everything around me and noticeably apprehensive about the unknown in a foreign land. Although I will absolutely go to Rwanda, I go with half a heart.

Mom and Dad take me to the airport. Dad stays in the car, stoically holding back his tears. Mom bravely walks me to the terminal building, hugs me, and cries like a baby. I wonder what a mother feels when a child leaves, perhaps forever. I reassure her that I will come back, but we both know there is that unmentioned chance of that other possibility.

Mom and Dad drive away. I stand alone, staring blankly at nothing among hundreds of people in the airport terminal.

26 August 1994
Friday

My Dearest,

5:41 AM—somewhere over the Atlantic …

The sky is brilliant with stripes of red, pink, yellow, orange and purple, along with shavings of royal blues. How can the world be so striking in the sky and so putrid on the ground?

Touchdown … Paris!

I adore Paris; I always have and I always will. It pulsates with passion and possibilities. I am beyond ecstatic to be here and nearer to my final destination. After settling in, I make my way to the office of *Médecins Sans Frontières* for the briefing I'm scheduled to have with the other team members who will be accompanying me to Rwanda.

"Bonjour. Je m'appelle Docteur Cary [Good morning. My name is Dr. Cary]," I say timidly to the receptionist.

"Qui êtes-vous, Monsieur [Who are you, sir]?" the woman responds.

"Dr. Cary," I reply.

"Qui [Who]?" she impatiently repeats. *"Vous n'êtes pas*

dans l'ordinateur [You aren't in the computer]." Then, in perfect English, she says abruptly, "Come back tomorrow."

I have a déjà vu of a wizard in an emerald city who tells a sweet little girl to "come back tomorrow!" I begin to rage inside. Come back tomorrow? Come back tomorrow after I just flew thousands of miles over my own rainbow?

Aggravated, I struggle to hold my tongue and maintain my composure. Apparently, there is not going to be a briefing, and there is no team accompanying me to Rwanda. I still do not know my posting or the objective of the mission I agreed to join over the phone just days ago. It appears that the logistical frenzy in Rwanda has left the Parisian office in disarray, and heads and tails are no longer on opposite sides of any coin. Unable to hide my disappointment, the receptionist reassures me that all will become clearer once I reach Rwanda.

Next to me at the reception desk is a woman from Belgium who has also just arrived. She receives the same news and looks as disappointed as I am. The two of us look at one another as if asking for permission to reconsider while we still have a chance. I conclude this minor obstacle is only one more test of my resolve. I am going to Rwanda regardless of any ditches and glitches along the way.

31 August 1994
Wednesday

My Dearest,

A good day. After waiting for what felt like a lifetime, the receptionist finally confirmed my mission and presented me with a flight ticket. I am now 33,000 feet in the air en route to Nairobi, Kenya, where I have a connecting flight to Kigali, the capital of Rwanda. Just a few days ago, I was bombarded with deplorable images of people dying in an unknown country on the other side of the world, and now I will be there within a few hours. What will I find there? An author once referred to Africa as the "heart of darkness." Is it so?

I have not adequately prepared myself for what I am about to do or witness. There was not enough time, and besides, is enough preparation even possible in this situation? I know nothing about the conflict leading to this slaughter, the history of the people, or the politics of the place. I don't even know where my assignment is or what I will be doing.

We cruise at a speed of 600 miles per hour. My mind races a tad faster. I have never met a murderer. And I have never treated anyone whose next assignment was to maim, torture and slaughter. I don't know if what I am about to do will help or hurt, promote or demote peace. Will the life I "save" be worthy of life itself? Will the life I rescue go out to take yet another life? I've been trained to respect and save life at any cost. How much is one life worth where I am going?

1 September 1994
Thursday morning

My Dearest,

Touchdown ... Nairobi!

Jomo Kenyatta International Airport is truly the real deal—something resembling a World War II or sci-fi Hollywood production projected on the big screen. United Nations troops, too many to count, scamper about the tarmac as confident logisticians walk with intention, going here and there. There are also dozens of prehistoric bomber-look-alike transport planes dominating the runways in random, haphazard con-figurations, some ready for takeoff while others wait to be filled to the brim with supplies destined for Rwanda. People are among the cargo, some with extensive field experience, while others stumble about without a clue. Everyone has their specific assignments and agendas. Missing are tour guides and tourists; leisure travelers are not welcome. This is not their time or place.

My first impressions of East Africa are many, with more I'm sure on the way. The native Kenyans are attentive and friendly. They smile easily and have penetrating eyes that can easily pierce the most hardened. Many of them are strikingly attractive and have a natural elegance and confidence that fit them well.

The sun here is unbearably hot, ruthless and unforgiving. It singes and parches the delicate, white skin that envelopes the stray and incongruous White man, who historically overstayed his visit here.

I'm told elephants and giraffes graze around the grounds on the outskirts of the airport. The only animal I am able to see is a picture of an elephant on the departure tax sticker attached to my passport.

I'm completely exhausted. On my papier-mâché globe at home, Rwanda was just on the other side of the Atlantic Ocean. It was just around the corner, not more than a quarter of a turn away from Chicago. How deceptive an ornamental globe can be!

All access to Rwanda is strictly prohibited, except for UN peacekeepers and a number of aid workers from humanitarian agencies that provide expertise, financial resources, logistical support, medical services, as well as food and non-food items. All commercial flights into the country have been canceled because of political turmoil and social unrest there. Airlines are reluctant to restart commercial services for now because of the risk to passengers, crew members and aircraft.

A Dutch aid worker at the airport tells me he was nearly murdered on a number of occasions while on humanitarian assignments in Africa. This is exactly the information I don't need at this time as I head deeper into the interior. Why would anyone want to hurt this man who has come from so far to help the people here? Am I missing something? As a child, I believed that if I left mosquitoes alone, they would leave me alone. Dad said it didn't work that way. I just knew he was wrong, so I held tight to my right to believe what I knew to be true. Somehow that innocence remains alive and well in me as I naïvely continue to deny the darker side of our species.

Boarding...

My time on the tarmac is cut short as I am shuffled onto a plane that, from the outside, looks as if it was stolen from a museum for antique aircraft. On the inside, its innards remind me of a gigantic hollow bullet. There are no windows, aisles, seats, cushions, or anything else resembling an airplane. There are also no stewards, stewardesses, or anyone else resembling an airplane crew. And there is no option for pre-booking since there is no help desk, customer relations, or airline toll-free phone number. In all fairness to the aviation company, there are wooden planks affixed to the floor for unassigned seating.

It is over 100 degrees in this flying hellhole. The heat is stifling. Sweat gushes from every pore of my body, and I am totally drenched. Where is the overhead ventilation system? There is none. Where is the air? There is none! The airlessness is suffocating, and we haven't even taken off yet. This corroded contraption was not made for human cargo.

Takeoff...

The reverberation of the aircraft's motors on the walls of this uninsulated metal cabin mimics an MRI machine at full throttle. I am forced to cup my hands over both ears and press hard to dampen the deafening sounds. The plane bounces on the tarmac like a kangaroo with a torn tail and two severely broken legs. Up, up, down. Up, up, down. Are we going to make it? It seems the fuselage refuses to let go of the ground. It begs to be retired from this and any other flight in the future, but the pilot ignores its request and pushes full speed ahead. Can't we honor this seasoned veteran's wish to be permanently earthbound and wait for an alternative flight? Most probably, this aircraft was retired from service decades ago but resurrected from the dead to assist in the airlift for this specific humanitarian crisis.

Up, up, down. Up, up, down, up. At this point, I have no option but to expect the worst and hope for the best.

Miraculously, we are airborne. But are we? Five minutes into the flight, the heat in the cabin is hotter than a raging inferno. Beads of sweat begin to pour from my forehead and burn my eyes. My back is soaked with sweat, and my shirt sticks to my skin, which sticks to the wooden planks that pretend to be seatbacks. The uncontoured benches must have been bleachers from some defunct football stadium that was destroyed for failing to meet basic standards for human use. There is nothing remotely friendly or functional about them. We sit upright with boards behind our backs that don't know they are supposed to recline, and seat belts around our chests and waists that only serve as straitjackets to keep us in place. I wonder if these belts aren't purposely designed to prevent passengers from jumping out the windows. Oh, I forgot—there aren't any windows. Perhaps the belts are in place to prevent people from jumping out the door to an untimely death. The conditions on board are so unbearable that it could be argued that death would be timely.

RWANDA

When I first heard the word "Rwanda," I had no idea it was a country. My initial ignorance would be best left unmentioned, but I'm not alone, as few people around the world have heard of the place. Even fewer understand the very conflict that led to the genocide that occurred. Let me share what I have heard and read about this small country, its people, and its people's conflict. Before I begin, however, it is important to understand that Rwandan history is unclear and contentious, and that any conclusions drawn from transcripts of scholars and experts in all fields are bound to be hailed by some and condemned by others. Furthermore, sensationalism, prejudice, bias, sentimentalism, gray areas, and contrary interpretations, take their own twists and turns, leaving anyone even remotely touching the subject of the country's history overly exposed and vulnerable to public criticism.

Speaking of history, one could argue that the word itself implies "his story." In other words, there is an objective and a subjective perspective on past events. Stories can be told and retold and morph into more flamboyant renditions or new and improved versions. Therefore, I am not going to add to the mishmash by analyzing, synthesizing, interpreting, or judging any part of the Rwandan people's past or present. The more prudent approach is to invite people to do their due diligence by making their own way through the testimonies, historical records, and the maze of madness that ultimately led to the near extinction of a people. Despite my decision to step aside and put the responsibility of seeking the "truth" in the hands of readers, I will share, at times, some details I gleaned from the popular press and also from casual conversations in the field. Forgive me if the facts and figures I note conflict with or even contradict versions already in circulation. Forgive me for presenting anything that is incomplete, flawed, or inaccurate. If anything I have written is deemed inappropriate or offensive in any way, I apologize in advance. My intention is not to judge or criticize, sway or influence, or direct the narrative in any particular direction. I solely wish to support those who live, honor those who died, and document the *hazards* of *hate*.

When examining the genocide, it is important to note that not all Hutus were complicit in the slaughter of Tutsis. There were many Hutus who protected Tutsis and risked their lives doing it, too. Furthermore, while the aim of the genocide was specifically to eradicate the Tutsi population, there were also thousands of Twa and moderate Hutus who were slaughtered. When looking back at the event, I contend that no one was spared. Every Rwandan citizen was touched and affected in some way by this tragic event.

I also wish to emphasize that I am not a historian and that this diary is *my* personal experience of the aftermath of the Rwandan genocide. It is my hope that by showing the hazards of hate, people will restrain themselves from going off course in the future. And then maybe we will have a chance to do what we've come to do—love one another.

RWANDAN HISTORY AND CONFLICT

Rwanda is one of Africa's smallest countries but has one of the continent's biggest human conflicts. The conflict itself is complex and convoluted, but at the same time, it is simple and straightforward. At the core of the conflict is an identity crisis. Who are the Rwandan people? Where did they come from? Are they one homogeneous people, or are they a mix of different ethnicities from faraway lands? Anthropologists, sociologists, archaeologists, geneticists, academics, and even politicians have done their utmost to answer these questions, but to date, no one knows for sure. What is for sure is that ethnicity is at the very core of decades of intense hatred that ultimately led to the Rwandan genocide.

There are many theories about the origin of the Rwandan people. Two popular theories worth noting are diametrically opposed and contentious. The first theory maintains that the people of Rwanda are all one homogeneous group whose ancestors were the original inhabitants of the territory that today is Rwanda. The second theory espouses an alternative reality. According to this theory, the Rwandan people are comprised of three distinct ethnic groups: the *Twa*, the *Hutu* and the *Tutsi*. I personally call this partitioning of the people *The Great Divide*. The theory goes like this: The Twa, also known as "Pygmies," are believed to have been the original inhabitants of the region, dating back thousands of years. These people were forest dwellers and sustained themselves by hunting and gathering. The Twa are easily distinguished by their relatively short stature, typically less than 5 feet. The Hutu are thought to have migrated from Central Africa sometime between the 5th and 11th centuries. They are considered to be of Bantu ancestry and have physical features to support this supposition: stout constitutions, dark skin and wide noses. These people were skilled farmers. The Tutsi are thought to have originated from the Horn of Africa, purportedly the region around Ethiopia, and immigrated to the area around the 14th century. These people have tall statures, light skin and narrow noses. They were skilled pastoralists.

Opponents of this latter theory discredit it because all three groups share a common language and religion, have the same traditions, and are genetically similar to one another. They claim this serves as proof that the Rwandan people are essentially the same—one people from the same family who shares the same blood. Proponents of this latter theory have their own rebuttal with credible arguments to support their claim that the people of Rwanda originated from three distinct ethnic groups. Regardless of the claims, assertions, and suppositions for and against either of these theories, *The Great Divide* has led to a people divided.

Before the so-called *Great Divide*, ethnic division was not a dominant issue in Rwandan society. According to historical records, people more or less got along, intermingled and intermarried. And life was good. During these times of social harmony, people prospered and multiplied. Some farmed and lived off the land; some were pastoralists, raising predominantly cattle, while others hunted and gathered what they could from the forests. Eventually, as the population grew, some of the pastoralists took charge and established a ruling monarchy, and a small kingdom. In this way, the people of those times were organized and governed. And life went on this way for several centuries, at least, until the White man came for an extended stay on the continent.

In the 15th century, European expansionism was born and grew rapidly as greed drove colonists deep into the interior of Africa. The first countrymen to arrive on the continent were the Portuguese, followed by the Spaniards and Dutch in the 1500s. In the 1600s, the Danish, French and English made their debuts, followed by the Belgians, Italians and Germans in the 1800s. Over a period of five centuries, Europe captured and claimed most of the African continent and its vast natural resources, including gold, diamond and ivory, as well as men, women and children, who in large numbers became slaves. Along with colonists clamoring for wealth and power came many religious enthusiasts who sought to spread the gospel, populate their parishes, and increase their global influence.

They believed that the gospel would definitively "civilize" the African "heathens" and, in turn, "save" them. And so, Africa was *born again*. From the cradle to the cross, Africa was slowly and steadily crucified.

Rwanda's crucifixion started around the late 1800s, when Germany took control and attempted to colonize the African Great Lakes region, which, in part, included Ruanda-Urundi, Their sovereignty was short-lived, however, when they were defeated in World War I and lost control of the territory. The League of Nations made Ruanda-Urundi a protectorate and entrusted Belgium with its governance. This landmass was later divided into modern day Rwanda and Burundi.

Overall, the Belgian colonists worked cooperatively with the existing monarchs, though at times they dominated them and made sure they complied with their demands.

For a foreign nation to dominate a region and its people living thousands of miles away, there needs to be a strategic plan, keen coordination, and meticulous administration. With the odds of success clearly against them, how do a few hundred Belgian loyalists establish dominance over a vast population of several million? The answer is *division*. For an alien power to subjugate a united and sovereign people, they must divide them. After all, a people divided will always be defeated. A divided people are weak and easily dominated. Colonial powers knew this all too well; hence, for Belgium to successfully control the Rwandan people, it needed a level of division and dissonance within the population. Once such fracturing is achieved, the people will have no choice but to succumb to colonial rule. And this is how it all went down.

The division of the population came shortly after Belgium first took control of Rwanda. Subscribing to the theory that the Rwandan people were comprised of three unrelated and distinct ethnic groups, the Belgians separated the population along strict ethnic lines. Using people's physical attributes, they systematically categorized and methodically divided the population. Accentuating people's differences gave credence to the notion of separateness in Rwandan society.

The dissonance within the population evolved naturally as a consequence of dividing the people. In addition, Belgian favoritism toward one group over the others fomented disdain and jealousy, which further fractured the people. The Belgians were most impressed by the Tutsis. Physically, their tall, majestic stature and Caucasoid features set them apart from the other natives. Economically, their skills as pastoralists gave them greater wealth, and socially, they were among the ruling class that made up Rwanda's monarchy. The Tutsis were thus considered superior to the rest of the population and most suited to serve Belgium's colonial interests and ambitions. As *superior* subjects, the Tutsis were given better housing, education, and employment compared with the rest of the indigenous population. Furthermore, they were placed in positions of power and authority over their Twa and Hutu neighbors, a dispensation given in exchange for their loyalty and cooperation in supporting Belgian rule.

The Twa and the Hutu, on the other hand, were considered *inferior* subjects and were left marginalized and neglected. In some cases, they were denied education, forbidden to own land, and often forced into hard labor. Belgian favoritism toward the Tutsi minority, along with its neglect and abuse of the Hutu majority and Twa, created a rift between the natives. One could argue that establishing a hierarchy within the Rwandan population was intentionally done to divide the people and undermine any social cohesiveness.

The Great Divide was made even greater in the early 1930s, when Belgian rule further degraded the population by obligating every Rwandan citizen to carry a personal identity card that included their ethnicity. Those with short statures were labeled Twa; those with dark skin and wide noses were Hutu; and those with light skin and tall statures were Tutsi. But what happened with people who didn't physically fit the standard Twa, Hutu, or Tutsi descriptions? For people whose physical appearances were indiscernible, as would be the case with offspring from intermarriages between Twa, Hutu and Tutsi, the Belgians used the number of cows in people's possession to categorize them. Those who possessed less than ten cows were considered Hutu, while those who possessed ten or more cows were considered Tutsi. By accentuating people's differences, the colonists robbed the nation of a national identity. As a result, the Rwandan people lost sight of who they were and how they were all interconnected.

Belgium's "divide and conquer" method of governance to keep a stronghold on the population worked. Its declaration of a superior and inferior class within the Rwandan population did manage to create dissonance. The categorization of the people did divide them. The preferential treatment of one group at the expense of the others did create rivalry. And over time, hardship gave rise to hard feelings, domination gave rise to resentment, and class distinctions gave rise to social unrest. And yes, this all did pave the way for colonial dominance. But it also led to the colony's ultimate demise.

In time, the population became so polarized that political reform was the only recourse left to subdue an increasingly disgruntled population. Such political reform came shortly after World War II. After decades of despots and dictators, wars and casualties of war around the world, the international community trended toward more democratic rule worldwide. Rwanda was no exception. The inequitable treatment of the Hutu was no longer sustainable or acceptable. As a result, the United Nations, along with Belgium and the presiding Tutsi king, agreed to increase Hutu representation in government.

In the early 1950s, the momentum for political reform accelerated with a push for independence and the cessation of Belgian occupation. Unfortunately, people in political power were slow to honor their commitments, and citizens lost faith and hope in the political process. True reform would require the power of the people united. Miraculously, this happened in November 1959. After several decades of domination and denigration, the majority Hutu population rebelled against Belgium's rule and fellow Tutsis. Thousands of Tutsis were killed, and hundreds of thousands fled for their lives, leaving their homeland behind. Hutus took control of the country, ousted the existing Tutsi monarchy, and elected their own political figureheads, who accordingly declared Rwanda's independence in 1962.

Over the next three decades, political and social turmoil continued in and out of the country. Exiled Tutsis engaged in repeated guerrilla warfare across borders, hoping to return to their homes and regain their power. Hutus countered their insurgences, leaving countless deaths on both sides. Until the early 1990s, the Hutu-led government in Rwanda was able to fend off Tutsi incursions, but this was about to change.

Since the Hutu revolution in 1959, exiled Tutsis never lost sight of their long-held dream of returning to their homeland and reclaiming their lives. This was particularly true of the Tutsis exiled in Uganda, where in the 1980s they established an organization called the Rwandese Alliance for National Unity (RANU) to address the issue of their repatriation. When their call for change went unheeded, they reorganized themselves into a rebel army called the Rwandan Patriotic Front (RPF). In October 1990, the RPF invaded Rwanda and engaged the Rwandan Armed Forces (FAR) in a civil war.

The Rwandan civil war raged, and death and destruction ensued on both sides for two years. In an attempt to end the violence, the international community used its leverage to assertively push for peace in the region. Pressuring the Hutu-led Rwandan government to seek reconciliation with exiled Tutsis, the presiding Hutu president, Juvénal Habyarimana, acquiesced and began moderating policies in favor of Tutsi repatriation. This eventually led to a ceasefire between the Rwandan Patriotic Front and the Rwandan Armed Forces in July 1992 and subsequently a peace agreement known as the Arusha Accords in August 1993. To bolster the peace process and ensure its success, the United Nations Security Council established an international peacekeeping force called the United Nations Assistance Mission for Rwanda (UNAMIR). Its mandate was to assist in the implementation of the Arusha peace agreement and support the transitional government.

The Arusha Accords were intended to unite Hutus and Tutsis and to establish an equitable power-sharing between them. Unfortunately, a number of Hutus in and out of the government vehemently opposed the peace agreement, which they felt was only a harbinger of Tutsi domination again in Rwanda. With dissent in the government ranks, Hutus with more extreme ideologies established the *Interahamwe,* a far-right Hutu paramilitary group. This radicalized group of extremists, rogue militants, and dissenting members of the president's core administration took matters into their own hands and masterminded a plan to definitively secure their own political dominance. Their plan guaranteed a future without Tutsi interference in the country's internal affairs. Their plan was called GENOCIDE.

Speaking of genocide, it is fitting to reference the largest genocide in human history—the Holocaust—since the basic architecture of both genocides was similar. On January 20, 1942, several nazi officials gathered around an oblong dining room table in a majestic villa in Wannsee, a posh locality on the outskirts of Berlin. Their agenda for the meeting was to finalize plans for the systematic extermination of a proposed 11 million Jews. They called their malignant plan "The Final Solution." (Note: The word "nazi" has been intentionally left uncapitalized to strip it of any respect.)

The Interahamwe orchestrated their own *final solution*. To bolster support for its implementation, the paramilitary group needed to mobilize the more moderate Hutu population to join them in their fight to achieve complete annihilation of their enemy—the Tutsis. But how do you turn peace-loving people into murderers? The Interahamwe knew the answer to this question: fear. And they knew the words to use and the actions to take to fan the flames of fear. They spoke of an imminent, lethal Tutsi invasion and warned of renewed Tutsi domination in the country. They also spoke of imminent revenge killings by Tutsis, whose ancestors were slaughtered decades earlier by Hutus in 1959. It didn't take long for this propaganda to ignite millions of Hutus to join the cause. Everything was now in place and ready to go.

And so it came to pass. On April 6, 1994, while President Habyarimana was flying back from a meeting in Tanzania where, ironically, he was addressing the cessation of ethnic violence in Rwanda, his plane was shot down. The Tutsis accused extremist Hutus of assassinating the president to incite violence and get more Hutus to join the extermination campaign against them. Hutu extremists, on the other hand, claimed that the Tutsis were responsible for the president's assassination in order to retake the country. Decades later, no one knows for certain who shot down the plane.

Regardless of who was responsible, the response to the tragic event was immediate. The orchestrators of the genocide instructed Hutus to take quick and decisive action to prevent a Tutsi takeover. They ordered Hutus countrywide to bear arms and protect themselves from the Tutsi invaders, whose objective, they claimed, was to reconquer Rwanda and exterminate the entire Hutu population. The radio became the orchestrators' mouthpiece, and through its transmission their venom spewed: If you don't kill them, they will kill you! Broadcasts were incendiary and encouraged the total annihilation of every Tutsi citizen. "Kill the *inyenzi*!" they blasted. The word *"inyenzi"* means "cockroaches" in Kinyarwanda, the national language of Rwanda. It is a derogatory term used to dehumanize Tutsis. "Kill the children," they commanded. Those at the helm of the genocide believed that if the Tutsi children were allowed to live, they would avenge their fathers' deaths in the future. In this way, the children would continue the cycle of destruction and Tutsi domination. So, the instigators instructed the Hutu population over the radio to "kill them! Fill the graves! They are only half full! Kill the children! The children—kill them!" And so it was.

As if under the spell of some demonic force, thousands of Hutus took to the streets and started massacring their Tutsi neighbors. Men, women, and children were brutally tortured and mutilated. Babies were smashed and crushed to death, and pregnant women's fetuses were excised alive. Anyone sympathizing with the Tutsis or opposing the master plan to ethnically cleanse the country was also slaughtered. And in this way, hatred hurled humans back to the Dark Ages. This killing spree lasted for 100 days, during which time a million people were murdered. These deaths were celebrated over the radio by the génocidaires, who proclaimed victory: "Let us rejoice, friends; cockroaches have been exterminated." One might ask, where was the United Nations Assistance Mission for Rwanda (UNAMIR) while this killing spree was taking place? They were there on the ground. So what did they do? Nothing. Why? Because their official mandate was to assist in the implementation of the Arusha Peace Accords, not to stop a genocide. Could they have done something more than nothing? Yes. Then why didn't they? That's a good question. Many have asked this question and wait for a good answer. For years, people have been trying to understand the reason behind the international community's refusal to intervene.

Speaking of the reluctance to intervene, it is again fitting to reference the Holocaust. In 1942, at the peak of World War II, the United States State Department and its allies were informed of Germany's genocidal ambitions to rid Europe of all Jews. Extermination activities in concentration camps were disclosed, and allegedly upwards of two million Jews had already been murdered. Concerned parties implored the allied forces to bomb the railroad tracks used to transport Jews to their death in the killing camps. What was their response? There was none. They looked the other way as an additional 4 million people were gassed and then incinerated.

Could the allied forces have bombed the tracks to disrupt the transport of Jews to the gas chambers? Yes. Then why didn't they? That's a good question. Many have asked this question and wait for a good answer. For years, people have been trying to understand the reason behind the international community's refusal to intervene.

Back in Rwanda, after over a million Tutsis were either butchered, tortured, or burned to death, what happened? In an unexpected show of military force and prowess, the Tutsi-led Rwandan Patriotic Front overwhelmed the Interahamwe and the Hutu-led Rwandan Armed Forces, as well as thousands of Hutu civilians, and took control of the country. Defeated, the génocidaires, along with millions of Hutu civilians, fled the country. Then what happened? This is where *my* story begins.

1 September 1994
Thursday afternoon

My Dearest,

Touchdown ... Rwanda!

We made it. I'm elated that this hollow hellhole delivered us safely. There is excitement and thrill. When the aircraft door finally opens, a barrage of blinding light streams into the dark, windowless fuselage, causing my eyes to involuntarily shut. I have a sense of being freed after a grueling internment. Freedom! Once my eyes are acclimated, the first thing I see is a soldier. In fact, the airport has more soldiers than civilians. UN peacekeepers decorated with powder blue berets scurry about, while chiefs of staff, project coordinators, and heads of missions walk to and fro, each with their orders and particular agendas. To my surprise and utter delight, someone holding a dossier and *Médecins Sans Frontières* T-shirt is standing on the tarmac. Could he be waiting for me? I was told in France that the infamous T-shirt emblazoned with a red stick figure streaking across the words *Médecins Sans Frontières* is my ticket into, out of, and around Rwanda. The MSF logo is well known and credits one of the most prestigious and respected medical humanitarian organizations in the world. This solitary mark on the front of a piece of cloth supposedly grants me diplomatic immunity. If it is so, this T-shirt will become my skin, my protector, and my life.

I am so relieved and grateful to be warmly welcomed by someone from the organization who knows of me. Given the debacle in Paris, I am more than delighted to find someone who cares and is assigned to protect me. If I were the Queen of England, I would knight this good-deed doer. King, queen, prince, duke or dunce, he is my knight in shining armor.

My personal knight introduces himself as Peter and assures me conditions in Rwanda are stable. I am immediately at ease and finally able to exhale. He then leads me to a vehicle that is proudly decorated with the same logo that is printed across my T-shirt. The vehicle, he explains, is specially equipped with all the most modern bells and whistles to guarantee our safety: a sophisticated communication system, landmine-proof chassis, and diesel fuel tank to ensure that if we are bombed, we will not be set ablaze and incinerated. Apparently, diesel does not burn. I am reassured the organization has thoroughly done its homework to protect its staff. This feels good, and I seize the moment to convince myself that I am immune to any violence or danger in this country.

Kigali ...

I hop into the front seat of this luxury limo, and off I go with my chauffeur. Near and around the airport, things look calm and peaceful. I see no signs of civil unrest or warfare. The ride from the airport to town, however, changes my first impression. Rwanda is the most densely populated country in Africa, yet its principal city, Kigali, is a veritable ghost town. There is no sign of life anywhere. Nothing moves. Nothing is. A haunting sensation overcomes me, similar to the eerie sense of calm that precedes the touchdown of a tornado.

A spine-chilling hush pervades this place, as if something unprecedented happened here. Unfortunately, no one remains to tell the story. I felt this hush once before. It was inside the gas chambers and next to the doors of the ovens at Dachau, a nazi concentration camp 20 minutes from Munich, Germany. Again, no one remains to bear witness to what happened there. Only the lingering scent of burned human flesh impregnated into the concrete walls remains to tell the story. The story of that genocide will live forever in the oration of the hush. Will we never learn?

Kigali is now just undisturbed dust, filth and refuse. Its silence says more than words. Not a single person in a city of hundreds of thousands walks the streets. The city resembles a makeshift movie set, staged somewhere in the Wild West. There is even tumbleweed rolling across the road. Where are the people? Something is strangely amiss.

On the evening news back home, I saw images of mounds of bodies and collections of appendages rotting around the city. They were indistinguishable from slabs of animal carcasses in a slaughterhouse. Were these images that caused me to shed a tear, quit my job, and risk my life real or imaginary? Were the images fabricated by a media desperate to boost public ratings? I ask Peter if the televised broadcasts of the genocide were a hoax. He glares sternly at me. I think my choice of words and the tone of my question gave him the impression that I deny the extermination took place here. With a sigh of resignation or perhaps as an act of defiance, he says, "I'll take you there." "There?" Hmm. Where is "there?" I wonder, but I dare not speak another word.

Unable to read this man accurately, I am ill at ease and uncertain about going anywhere with him. I sense he has a sadistic darkness in his generosity to show me his playground. It appears he is breaking protocol and about to trespass into areas that are deemed unsuitable for foreign nationals to see. My once-upon-a-time knight quickly loses his regal standing as I strip him of his 'k'. From now on, he is *Night*—a dark force.

I sit in complete silence as Peter drives deeper into the abandoned city. Something in me needs to see what is not intended to be seen or shown to me. Something in me needs to see with my own eyes what my mind categorically wants to deny. As we drive by street after street, I suddenly become irrationally anxious and consider canceling this unpleasant excursion. Perhaps there is good reason the government makes certain areas off-limits to foreigners. Maybe there are sensitive places that would soil the soul and leave it irreparably injured. So what's the point? After all, the crimes have already been committed, and I can't do anything to reverse even a single death. I start to prepare myself emotionally for what this man is about to show me. Fortunately, there is only silence between us. If I am about to see signs of torture and death, then this silence seems most fitting to show respect to the people who perished.

Peter stops the vehicle in front of a huge open field. The landscape is barren, and the earth is charcoal black. The soil has notably been freshly tilled and groomed to be more presentable. Peter inclines his head and, without saying a word, invites me to exit the cabin and proceed alone on foot through the field. All this is in complete silence. I reluctantly open the door and stand unsteady in front of an open space of nothing. Not knowing what I am doing or what I am supposed to see, I look back at Peter for some cue or direction. He just stares at me. So I start walking through the field. The silence is harrowing. Anticipation and fear of the unknown make me uncomfortable, but I continue to wander around the empty landscape. Initially, I scan the ground for something odd or unfitting. There is nothing noteworthy. I scrutinize the terrain more carefully and see absolutely nothing, except, of course, the open field of black, manicured earth. As I continue to look for something remarkable, I notice something curious. There is a smoldering fire with only embers remaining. The fire has already consumed its meal, leaving only ashes and residual smoke behind. My eyes shift their attention to another curious finding. There is a lone piece of paper that rests alongside the ashes. The paper is intriguing because it is spotlessly white, pristine and without a single wrinkle or fold. One could argue that the flame itself made an executive decision to preserve it for future generations to see. I pick the unobtrusive piece of paper off the ground and find a handwritten list of names with their personal details. In any other context, this would not be significant, but in this particular field, it is inextricably linked to an important part of Rwanda's history. Prior to the killing sprees, government officials and heads of villages were asked to identify and record the names and particulars of every Tutsi resident destined for destruction. The lists they compiled were essentially people's official death sentences. I hold in my hand possibly one of those lists. How do you kill a child? They don't know hate yet. How do you murder an infant who has yet to taste something other than their mother's breast milk? How do you stomach the gurgling of a slashed throat or the gasping of someone begging for one last breath of air? How do you remove the life from a life that never made it to a single digit? How do you erase a human being simply because the word "Tutsi" has been inscribed on an identification card?

My rational and skeptical mind can easily discount this piece of paper as something other than what I know it is. Part of me wants to set it ablaze. It could easily become a part of the mounting mound of ash that has already claimed other valuable treasures of truth. But then, there is another part of me that feels this piece of paper is a critical piece of history that must never be forgotten. After some thought, I conclude this piece of paper deserves an audience, so I fold it up, put it in my pocket, and return to the driver's side of the vehicle.

Peter sits patiently in the driver's seat; there still has been no exchange between us. I say nothing, but my body language shouts, "Why are we here? What do you want me to see?"

Finally, he breaks the silence and says with an authoritative one-word imperative, "Look!"

Again, I scan the same expansive field of nothingness.

"What? I see nothing but dirt," I say curtly, with a startled indignation at his breaking the silence.

Peter steps out of the vehicle and takes my hand as a father would take the hand of a child. He walks a few steps with me.

"Look!" he commands.

I do. And suddenly, I see, inches in front of me, a human arm, recently severed from the shoulder, sliced clean and precise, like only a chainsaw or the blade of a sharpened steel machete could cut. It just lay there, motionless, frozen in time. Horrified, my torso is abruptly taken by some paranormal force that twists me from behind without my permission. Seconds later, my head and torso spontaneously twist in the opposite direction. I seem to have lost control over my body and perform as if I am some sort of dummy under the direction of a ventriloquist. Not only does he move me, but he expulses words from my mouth.

"That's a doll's arm. That's a doll's arm," I blurt out over and over, like a broken record or an obnoxious parrot. "That's a doll's arm! That's a doll's arm," I repeat.

Without reflection, intention or purpose, I start walking the field, stumbling, moving aimlessly, going nowhere, repeating the same words: "That's a doll's arm! That's a doll's arm!" I say again involuntarily, as though something has taken hold of my tongue. For several minutes, I continue stumbling about, repeating the same words over and over. From the outside, it seems like I am having a mental breakdown, but in actuality, I feel my heart and soul are just trying to flush themselves clean.

What did I gain by violating my fragile innocence? How can I apologize to my heart for breaking it with this image of a savage amputation? This violation will haunt me for the rest of my life. It wasn't necessary to come here and see what I was not supposed to see. It wasn't right. I played with fire and got burned. Cary, what were you thinking? Why did you need proof that the genocide was real?

Spiraling out of control, I have to take control and stop the self-flagellation. Seizing the moment, I vow to bury the doll's arm, un-record its history, and save others from the same violation. I do manage to steady myself for about a moment, but once again, I lose control. Whose mother was it? Or was it father? What did he or she say, do, and feel at the moment of *slice*? How long did this beloved son or daughter suffer? Was anyone nearby to hear her cry, and did anyone come to his rescue? I can't stop my mind from asking countless questions.

I can't stop racking my brain to understand how and why. Why am I so disturbed by the sight of a severed arm? After all, I am a doctor, and I have seen many amputated limbs in anatomy class in medical school. I have even assisted with amputations in surgery during my residency. Why am I so distressed by this arm? I am distressed by it because it was part of a person who was part of a family, that was part of a community, that was part of a village, someone's loved one, someone's mother or father or child. I am distressed by this arm because it is proof of human hatred and the evil of man, both things I refuse to believe are real. Anything that threatens the foundation of my being and the belief I have of man's intrinsic goodness puts me in a state of paralysis.

Peter and I return to the vehicle. There is not a single sound outside, inside, or between us. I am elsewhere in thought, trying to process what has just happened to me. By the time we reach what will be my home here in Kigali, everything is blocked out and tucked away in a hidden file somewhere, only to be accessed and retrieved with an authorization code. I make sure to discard the code, at least for a little while.

The residence ...

I am given a tour of the MSF shared living space in Kigali. The house has all the amenities and comforts of a house back home, including a home-cooked meal waiting on the kitchen table for me. I am eager to meet the other expatriates in the team. ("Expatriate" or "expat," for short, in this context, is a term used in the humanitarian world to refer to a foreign aid worker who comes from one country to reside and work temporarily in another country.) Everyone seems preoccupied when I am introduced to them. No one greets me or extends a hand to welcome me. Perhaps they, too, are processing terrible images that they have seen, or maybe they are missing people they love. It is hard to know why they behave this way. I have heard expats often lock themselves in impenetrable, protective bubbles to process the difficulties that they experience. Given this, I think it's best to eat lunch by myself and keep to myself.

After lunch, I wander around the compound and find three Rwandan natives preparing our next meal. I speak with each one of them, shooting question after question in all directions.

"Why weren't you killed? What did you do when you first saw your family dismembered on your return home? How do you cope with realizing that you no longer have any family?"

In retrospect, my questions were insensitively timed and downright inappropriate. But while the little boy in me felt sorry for being so intrusive, he needed to know. He needed to deeply understand. Our Rwandan staff are the only interface between what happened here and me. The staff graciously attend to me and answer all my many questions, either directly or indirectly through their stories. One of the women says she was away at work. When she returned home, she found her mother, father, and seven siblings chopped to pieces in a pile on the floor in her front room. Another staff member shares that he was one of 40 survivors out of 6,000 people he watched get slashed to death in front of him.

I listen to their stories, stunned, clearly in a state of denial. "You're having a bad nightmare," I say without any reflection. "Your mom and dad will be home around dinnertime," I add, like a babbling inebriate, unable to accept the truth just yet.

I am in a time warp, a sort of pseudo-comatose state. How can people kill and torture other people? One day, I could not find my favorite bicycle. It was gone. I figured I had somehow misplaced it, so I bought another one. In time, that bicycle became my favorite bicycle, and again, in time, that bicycle was gone. I had no choice but to buy another one. I did this 15 times because my bicycles kept *going gone.* As ludicrous as this may sound, it never occurred to me that people would steal my bicycles, so it never occurred to me to lock them up. I never even had a lock. Why would I buy one to prevent people from stealing things that belong to me when people wouldn't intentionally do mean things to others? Similarly, I cannot believe people slaughter other people. So again, I say to these three seriously traumatized victims of genocide that none of it is real. Nightmares are never real. Everything will be better in the morning. This is what doctors are supposed to say, no?

I realize if I am going to be of any value to the people in this country, I must accept the harsh reality of what happened here. Otherwise, I have no role to play in anyone's healing. What is our role in Rwanda? A cynic might say we are here to assuage our guilt and apologize for abandoning these people when they needed us most. After all, the United Nations did receive advance intelligence of the premeditated plan to murder all Tutsis in Rwanda. And what did they do? They did nothing. And what do they do now? They send their heartfelt condolences and some humanitarian aid… after the fact.

The dinner bell rings. I welcome the home-cooked meal, but I feel awkward feasting on food while our guard is alone outside and hungry. He patrols the garden through the night to secure our safety, putting his life on the line for us. Shouldn't we look after him? Doesn't he deserve to be looked after? He says nothing and will not complain, but I know he is hungry.

As the team eats dinner together, no one talks. I wonder if this is a European cultural norm or a French preference to maintain distance and anonymity. I find myself out of place being the only American in the team. It would be nice to converse a bit, but I don't feel comfortable being the first one to break the silence. After all, I have only just arrived, and I think it is best to remain as unobtrusive as possible.

After the meal, I offer to clean up. My offer, admittedly, is not without a hidden agenda. I plan to save the scraps and leftovers to pass on a feast to the guard outside. The expat in charge of our team tells me to throw the leftovers away. Right, well, that's just not going to happen on my watch. Throwing food away when our neighbors are nearly starving to death? No way! People are holding on for dear life by a thread here. With these leftovers, their grip can hold on a little longer.

In the kitchen, I quietly prepare a plate of goodies for the guard. Making it is easy; bringing it to him is not. Transferring the goods will require some stealth and skill. First, there must be complete darkness. Second, everyone must be asleep. This takes time, but I have lots of it if, in the end, the guard gets his feast. Like a praying mantis, I wait in the shadows. When the coast is clear, I dart out the back door and fling the plate of food like a Frisbee at the man who humbly puts his life on the line to protect us. I intentionally have no eye contact with him, as I pretend to have nothing to do with this illicit drop-off. My charade is silently loud and convincing: "Mum's the word!" He quickly understands and smiles a smile of gratitude.

After the guard completes his meal, he washes the plate and leaves no sign of our illicit transaction. Without proof of our crime, we both feel safe again. Only he and I—and his belly—will know our secret, our covert operation. Once safe and sound, I take a moment to ponder a disturbing internal debate raging within. Why do I have to *sneak* food to the man who is protecting us? Why can't I bring him a plate of food honorably? Why isn't feeding him part of our human ethos?

The expats in the team seem to avoid the local staff as if they have some infectious disease. Somehow, I fear being kind to them would, in some way, jeopardize my position in the team. It's as if I would be chastised for caring. Is this because they don't know to what extent the Rwandan staff participated in the genocide? I need more time to understand these people and their mindsets. We are all touched differently by what we see, and we each have our own particular ways of coping with adversity. Perhaps the uncertainty, instability, and precarious political situation in this country weigh heavily on them and, as a result, they are guarded and on guard. I think maybe a bit more compassion and patience are in order for now. I certainly can manage this, at least until tomorrow when I leave for my final destination—a health center in a remote, rural town called Mabanza, several hours down the road somewhere.

I am exhausted and I need to sleep, but I cannot because I share my bed with a field, a list of names, and a doll's arm.

4:38 AM. A mosquito just bit me. Did I just get malaria?

MABANZA

2 September 1994
Friday morning

My Dearest,

On the road ...

My back and body are breaking as the driver maneuvers his way over an atrociously impassable dirt road. Both my hands grapple for anything stationary to prevent me from cracking my head open on the ceiling as the truck bucks like a bronco over potholes deeper than canyons. I am unable to see much of the countryside because my eyes are riveted on the driver, who struggles to control the vehicle on this terrain. Are we going to a remote rural town, or are we going to our deaths?

Finally, after four punishing hours, we arrive. Mabanza will be my new home. Few people make this journey, so I guess there will not be many visitors coming for tea and crumpets. Speaking of food, a wonderful home-cooked meal awaits my arrival—a perfect housewarming gift!

After lunch, I'm given a tour of the house. It is modest by Western standards but palatial compared to the typical huts sprinkled around the country. Surrounding the compound are exquisite gardens that host a symphony of serenading crickets as the mountains envelop us majestically. The house staff are like the mountains—magnificent. Kindhearted, hardworking and truly committed, they care for me as if I were one of their children. They know I am from a distant place and seem to have an unspoken agreement with Mom and Dad to protect me. How can this be? This is the beauty of Africa.

For the grand finale, my Rwandan "parents" show me to my bedroom and make sure everything is in order. Everything exceeds my expectations. I am happy, so they are happy.

With lunch deep in the belly, introductions made, and the tour complete, I am eager to see the area and meet the local people. Before I take my next breath, I'm off down a narrow dirt footpath to explore the town. Sadly, my first impression is not a good one. The place is filthy, its people haggard, and the surroundings look like a no-man's-land for anyone on the run. Thousands of people camp out anywhere they can find a spot, either outdoors on sidewalks or inside pieces of cardboard that are somehow freestanding. The more privileged seem to have commandeered hallways, carports and storefronts in gutted, vandalized or vacated properties that were most likely owned by Tutsis prior to the killing sprees. None of these "abodes" have windows or electricity, but they are a welcome upgrade from the all-too-common paper, twig, grass, cardboard and "cardboardless" accommodations most live in under the stars.

People's "kitchens" are small, handmade, dug-out holes in the dirt, which they fill with leaves that burn briefly to make a façade of a fire. These fires cook when there is, of course, something to cook, which is not often. It appears that no one has eaten, bathed, or slept for days. The situation is critical. Something has to change in these desperate people's favor, hopefully soon, because everyone teeters on malnutrition, which is winning this battle.

Children from the West would take this opportunity to set up their dollhouses and prepare a make-believe meal in their make-believe kitchens with make-believe cutlery to serve these very real, hungry people. I can't help but wonder where the people pass their previous meals; there are no toilets, and there is no toilet paper. And how do they wash their hands afterward? There are no sinks or spigots, and there is also no water, for that matter. But frankly, I don't think handwashing is very high on anyone's list of priorities at the moment.

I leave the downtown area and continue along another dirt path to the hospital. I am told the staff already know of my arrival, and everyone is pleased to finally meet and welcome me. I can't wait to meet them too. They will be my extended family for the next many months.

The "hospital" is basically a glorified collection of concrete blocks without any amenities. The building was previously an elementary school that was converted into a health center to meet the medical needs of the displaced population. As any school would be here, it is simple and far from being even basic, but it is to be my second residence for a while. When the hospital staff see me poking my head around a corner, they know immediately who I am and why I have come. Could it be my skin color that so readily gives me away? There is nothing white around here except me and a few lab coats. Thankfully, it does not matter. The people are exceptionally kind and willing to do whatever they can to help anyone in need. Everyone has a smile on their face and gigantic hearts that welcome me affectionately. I'm so blessed to be here.

After touring the hospital, I visit an area where displaced people live. It is essentially a refugee camp, or should I be politically correct and say a camp of refuge? For the record, a "refugee" is a person from one country who crosses another country's border seeking refuge from devastation and possible extermination. A person who flees from devastation and death within their own country is called a "displaced person." In my opinion, the distinction is unimportant. Displaced people and refugees are both caught in the crossfire, somewhere between hatred and war. Both seek refuge to survive.

The living conditions in this camp are appalling. People live under plastic tarpaulins that flap in the wind and do little to protect them from the elements. It is bitterly cold, and no one has proper clothing. Everyone shivers. Their clothes are just fragments—more like figments of an active imagination. The people have no other option but to wrap themselves with their arms to keep warm. A few have blankets, most have no shoes, and no one complains.

As I walk around the camp, I see a young boy lying on the ground sweating, short of breath and feverish. He is severely dehydrated and seriously ill. I find his mother and, with the help of a translator, ask about his condition: "Is your child drinking, and is he able to keep fluids down?" She says she doesn't know because she has not been giving him fluids. "Why?" I ask. She says, "I don't have a cup." I invite her to take her child to the hospital for immediate care.

The children find me a fascination, as if I'm from another planet. Most have never seen a white person before and wrestle among themselves to get close to me so they can get a good look. They fight to touch my skin, feel the hair on my arms, and shake my hands while proudly practicing the one White man word they know in French, "*bonjour.*" When I smile and say "*bonjour*" back to them, they giggle, tickled that they could communicate with me in some way. They are precious, filled with life, and exude pure love. Can't we hand Rwanda over to these little ones and watch them make it a better place? Surely, they would find real solutions to the miserable mess we adults have made for them. Children know no hate at their young age. They learn how to hate from us.

And while I'm on the subject of the children, I must pose a question to the *One* upstairs. Why has there been such neglect and inattentiveness toward this continent? Little has changed here over the millennia. It seems time chooses to stand still in this corner of the world compared to other corners. When will Africa have its time to bloom and blossom, to grow and flourish? I was taught in school that Africa is the cradle of civilization. Our mother came from here. She birthed us in these very fields, and far beyond her borders we thrive. Why do so many children here in Africa stay warm in the womb and never make their debuts? Why do so many children here stay close to the cradle without ever leaving their cribs? And why do so many find themselves at the base of a vertical mountain that forbids passage? What am I referring to? Infant mortality. Africa has the highest infant mortality rate in the world, with Rwanda leading: 130 infant deaths per 1,000 live births, compared to the United States: 9.2 deaths per 1000.

After my visit to the camp, I return to the hospital and work late into the night. When I finally leave, I am not at ease. It feels wrong to return home, given the amount of work that still needs to be done, but I also have to eat and sleep. I could easily lose myself in the unending needs of these people. They are so gentle and generous of heart, yet so frail and vulnerable. I'm grateful to be here and be of service to them.

As I eat dinner, there is a knock at the front door. A man has come to the house complaining of abdominal cramps. I guess I haven't left the hospital after all. The man is not in obvious distress, so I have time on my side. But I must admit, I'm not sure what is going on with him. It is difficult to take his history because he doesn't know my language, and I don't know his. Without a translator to help me, there is only one thing to do: play charades—the next best thing.

Question number one: "Do you have diarrhea?" I squat and then repeatedly brush my hand briskly from my backside to the ground to indicate a continuous flow of watery diarrhea. He immediately understands, smiles, then shakes his head from side to side. Okay, the gentleman has no diarrhea. Then, for question number two: "Do you have gas?" I recruit help from my trusty lips and cheeks and simulate an imaginary flagrant fart—a *faux pas* in my circle, but an essential part of the doctor-patient relationship here. Again, he shakes his head from side to side. Okay, he has no gas. So far, I've ruled out diarrhea and flatulence, and I am quite pleased with myself. Question number three: I first squat, then grunt and grimace, pretending something is stuck. He nods excitedly, with great relief and satisfaction that a diagnosis has finally been made. Voilà! I've got it. Constipation! I proudly blurt out, "You have constipation!" That's an easy one, or so I think.

On a small piece of paper, I write a note for him to give to our assistant who works at the hospital dispensary: "This man needs some glycerin suppositories, a laxative, and an enema. Advise him to eat lots of fiber and drink copious amounts of water."

One of my housemates is a seasoned nurse with a lot of experience working in Africa. She is considerably amused. "They don't have these things here," she says.

"Oh," is about all I can offer. So I write another note to the hospital assistant: "Tell him not to eat cheese or white rice."

This amuses the expatriate nurse even more. "They don't have these things here either," she points out. "Cheese and rice are only for the rich!" Okay. I write a more appropriate note: "Tell him to eat more raw foods."

Once again, the nurse chuckles. "I guess they don't have that either," I say, quicker than she can add her own two cents.

With such a limited pharmacy and impoverished kitchen, I give the man a condom to disimpact himself. Disimpact is a medical term we use, which in layman's terms means to scoop oneself out. I then fill a bottle with hot water and place it on his belly. He doesn't seem too happy with the bottle or my prescription. The gentleman wants an injection because that's what the local doctors supposedly do here. And, of course, he wants biscuits as well, because that is what White people are known to do—give biscuits. It doesn't take too long for me to understand the challenges people have living here in Rwanda. Seriously speaking, what is this gentleman supposed to do with dietary restrictions, senseless advice, a condom, a hot water bottle, and a biscuit?

3 September 1994
Saturday

My Dearest,

The sounds of the morning are sweet. The birds and the bees, insects, and maybe monkeys come together in a concerto that rivals Bach, Barber and Beethoven. Even the dew seems to play its part in this orchestral magnificence.

My Rwandan parents have prepared breakfast along with one gallon of water, my daily allotment for bathing. The other team members already have their water boiling on the stove. When I first arrived, I thought it was a waste of fuel to heat our bath water. It didn't take long for me to join the morning queue for a free burner on the stove. The morning cold at 6,500 feet above sea level is penetrating and doesn't befriend anyone. A bit of comfort in these challenging conditions is a necessity, not a luxury.

After breakfast, I bundle up and set out for the hospital along the narrow dirt footpath that runs through the field next to our compound. It is chilly, and the wind is fierce. Masses of people stare at me with big, round, curious eyes. The white part of their eyes is brilliantly white, like the color of newly fallen snow. The people in this area, for the most part, have coal-black skin, but today it is white from blowing dust, which makes them look indistinguishable from Italian pizza makers who have just doused their dough with flour.

People are constantly on the move. They shift much like the wind on a windy day—here, there, anywhere and everywhere, except back to their homes. The danger of insurgents attacking them at any moment is more than real and constant. If they manage to steer clear of insurgents, there are always loads of lethal landmines next in line, flexing their muscles. When people finally find a safe and hospitable place, they quickly set up camp to rest and recover. Mabanza appears to be a place where people come to congregate. This makes sense. There is a hospital, security, aid workers and food.

Speaking of food, anything edible is quite hard to come by in these troubled times. Fortunately, international aid agencies distribute daily rations to people on the go. Rations include 500 grams (1 pound) of cornmeal per person. Unfortunately, Rwandans do not eat corn; traditionally, corn is only fed to livestock, and therefore, it is not fit for human consumption. Most people refuse to eat it. Beans would be better and more nutritious, but there are no beans on the international donor menu. Even if beans were sold at the market, it wouldn't matter because no one has any money to buy them. You might ask why starving people would refuse to eat food that is given to them for free. The answer is simple: the locals don't know that there are two different kinds of corn: field corn and sweet corn. In many countries, field corn is used to feed livestock, whereas sweet corn is used for human consumption. Sweet corn is not grown in Rwanda, so the people are unfamiliar with it. Eating animal food is not an option for them.

Back at the hospital…

When I arrive at the hospital, I am given an orientation and a more thorough tour of the facility. I am surprised to see a modern convenience that has miraculously made its way to Mabanza in wartime—a refrigerator. I am impressed.

"I see you have a refrigerator," I say excitedly.

"Yes, we have a refrigerator," the nurse boasts, taking great pride in it. "But we have no gas to make it work," she adds.

As we visit the patients, the same nurse says, "We have many cases of dysentery. Many die of it."

There is currently an epidemic of Shigella in the area, and the hospital is filled with patients infected with this lethal pathogen. Shigella causes dysentery, which ravenously claims its captives by rapidly bleeding them to death. This disease is treated with a short, five-day course of a very strong antibiotic called ciprofloxacin, which is truly a lifesaving drug. This antibiotic is plentiful up north in Europe, to the east in Asia, and across the Atlantic, and sits impatiently on pharmacy shelves begging to be bought. All it needs to be liberated from its captivity is a customer, a doctor's prescription and money. Here in Africa, the situation is different. This medication is too expensive, difficult to access, and in very short supply. I can write plenty of prescriptions, and there are more than enough "customers," but none of them has any money. We treat all patients for free, but by the time they come for treatment, they are usually too far gone. Despite all these problems, we try, though most die regardless of our heroic efforts. Why is it like this in Rwanda? Hatred. Hatred leads to prejudice, which leads to division, which leads to disunity, which leads to war, which leads to poverty, which leads to disease, which leads to death. These are all the *hazards of hate.*

P.S. Flashbacks of that doll's arm return without reprieve. That solitary human appendage comes and goes, and goes and comes, over and over again. It has taken on a life of its own and is overtaking my mind. Go away! Go away! Go away!

4 September 1994
Sunday

My Dearest,

I wake up. Outside, it is calm and quiet. The air is piercing cold. I go out back and huddle close to a few sticks of wood our cook uses to make a fire to heat some water. Two small birds, crimson and brown, come and peck at some crumbs on the ground. Our chicken squawks and enjoys eating some of the same crumbs for her breakfast. The wind is assertive and rushes through the amber embers, sending flecks of fire in all directions. They are like fireflies that dazzle and fascinate me for a while. Ash floats around like snowflakes. I'm at peace.

My peace and quiet is unfortunately interrupted by news that the Rwandan Patriotic Front has just arrived to the area. They moved their army here late last night. According to the United Nations, this is forbidden. Is the military preparing for an armed conflict? I am told to be vigilant.

There is no telecommunication system here, but the spoken word passes from person to person faster than the speed of light, CNN, BBC, or any other satellite broadcasting station. It is astonishing how fast information can travel. But are the mouth-to-mouth transmissions true? Reliable sources of news are in short supply, and oftentimes, inaccuracies and falsehoods are the mainstay of the people's press. There is one source, however, that tells no lies—commodity prices. Believe it or not, the most accurate reporting of current events comes from the prices of commodities. When prices of goods at the market suddenly rise and people start selling their meager possessions to acquire means by any means, something bad is bound to happen. As rising barometric pressure portends an imminent storm, armies bring storms of their own, often with thunder and lightning too.

As news of the army's arrival spreads, tempers flare and temperatures rise. Where do we go if we are suddenly under attack? Where is there to hide—under someone's cardboard cottage? Our evacuation protocol obligates us to stay in our compound until safe passage is secured. We are such easy targets. Not only are we not *camouflageable*, but we have all and everything anyone would want—equipment, cars, money, phones, medicine, and more money. After all, we are a people of plenty of plenty. But not to worry, we have the T-shirt. Yes, the *Médecins Sans Frontières* T-shirt we proudly wear with its little logo will give us diplomatic immunity and guarantee our safety. Uh-huh. Right! While the international community's strength and determination are powerful allies and assets here, they are outranked and overpowered by machine guns in the hands of those who don't follow protocol, let alone know what the words "diplomatic immunity" mean. The white skin that once unrolled the red carpet and afforded us access and privilege is now to our detriment. An escape through this untamed and untrimmed terrain is impossible. Where do we go if we are attacked? I never got this far in my preparation when I was packing for Rwanda.

Fortunately, I am distracted from my preoccupation with security forces by the attending nurse, who comes to the house and asks me to examine a child on the ward. She says the patient "isn't doing too well." We quickly make our way to the hospital and enter the "ward," a euphemism for what is nothing more than a space with four walls, a ceiling and, for everyone's comfort, a floor. The ward is basically a warehouse without the wares. It has minimal lighting and no facilities, toilets, water or furniture, except for some haphazardly placed metal bed frames that are missing mattresses and linens. The children on the ward are in a pitiful state. They look like emaciated cadavers being strangled by intravenous tubing and accosted by bags of fluid that drip desperately, trying to save their flailing lives. Everything about these slivers of flesh and bone screams exhaustion. Mothers and sisters, no bigger than the patients themselves, are the children's caregivers. They sit next to their loved ones, waiting for a miracle. Everyone is barefoot, disheveled, unbathed, hungry, and wrapped in rags. The so-called "nurses" are mostly people from the street who were randomly selected to assist with patient care. Some of them can read… kind of, and among them, a few have basic mathematical skills. There is no system in place for the staff to attend to the patients; beds are unmarked, patient records are illegible, and progress sheets are scantily done, if at all. But the staff's hearts are good and bigger than big. They want to help; they want to give; they want to learn and grow; so, in the sheer madness of it all, there is magic.

The child I am called to see looks exhausted and breathes shallowly. His eyes are glazed over, and he is disengaged from everything around him. It is difficult to assess the severity of his status because, relative to all the children in the hospital and out in the village, he looks the same: ragged, worn, out of place and out of time. The child has repeated hand movements and is barely moving air. Is he convulsing? I stand at the side of his bed with my hands at my sides, much like a soldier at attention or a psychiatric patient confined in a straitjacket. I can't act or react. I want to do something, anything, but what? Stop the seizures? Do a tracheotomy? Inject epinephrine? It is too late. Nothing I can do will make a dent or a difference. Without any other option at hand, I listen to his chest with my stethoscope and watch his labored breathing get shallower and shallower. The child's mother is reassured when I auscultate him, but there is nothing more to auscultate. He is dead. When her son's fate is sealed, Mom cries silently to herself.

When death comes and gobbles up its next meal, the other patients in the room nonchalantly go on with their daily affairs as if someone has just gone to relieve themselves in the public bathroom. Death is so common in their lives that witnessing it at any time or in any place doesn't faze them. It is just a part of life, as is their daily ritual: wake up, wash a bit, look for something to eat, see someone die, cry inside, fetch water, sell a potato, go to sleep. And so it is.

I need to understand why this child died. There has to be something in his medical records to explain why this beautiful baby being died so young. He had a simple case of diarrhea. He shouldn't have died.

I review his records and discover that he wasn't given his "medication"—ORS, which stands for oral rehydration salts. ORS is a simple mixture of sugar, salt and potassium. The nurses forgot to give him his cocktail of sugar, salt and potassium. Again and again, they forgot, and the little boy was too weak to make much of a fuss and remind them. Mom thought her child was resting comfortably in his bed, so she said nothing to the busy people scurrying about the ward—nothing until nothing was left.

I feel alone, a foreigner in a foreign place, unequipped for this medical nightmare. If I were a magician and this were a dream, I would give it a happy ending. But this is not a dream. This is a nightmare. No one improves. The patients just decay before my eyes, rotting like spoiled meat. And when they are no longer, they are discarded somewhere, out of sight and out of mind. "*C'est la vie* [This is life]," I am told.

It is disturbing how all this suffering and death affects me. It doesn't. I think I may be in shock, conscious yet at the same time unresponsive to the horrors happening around me. I seem to observe everything and then immediately disengage without getting emotionally involved. Do I dare acknowledge or call attention to this callous creature I have become? I used to be so compassionate, so connected and caring. There has to be something wrong with me now. It would be good to share this concern with someone in the team to get some clarity and understanding, but exposing this heartlessness would leave me too vulnerable and open to stern, public criticism. What kind of doctor have I become, shrugging my shoulders when faced with a dying child, cowering before death, and resigning to its power without a peep or a fight? This is not me. This was never, ever me. This is inhuman, yet this is the person I have become. Am I in denial, shock or depression?

I finish my work at the hospital and return home to have dinner. To my surprise, the other team members open up and generously share personal accounts of their own insensitivity and idiosyncratic indifference when things here go horribly wrong for them. It soothes me to know I am not alone in this. Perhaps we are in the process of digesting the meals of misery we are constantly being fed here. Perhaps our emotions are just hiding for a while, packaged in places deep inside, somewhere in a concealed crevice, waiting to emerge later, in due time, when it is safe to feel, safe to cry.

5 September 1994
Monday

My Dearest,

I am an ant standing in front of a sequoia forest—too small to see the bigger picture, too insignificant to matter. This isn't the *Land of Oz*. This is the *Land of Odds*. Things just don't add up here. In the West, for example, when faced with death, people call out the National Guard, bomb, nuke, or whatever it takes to save a life. Here in Rwanda, on the other hand, when people are neck-and-neck with death, they quickly surrender to it without a fight. When death knocks, they passively accept their fate. If a loved one dies, they close the book of life and return to their daily routine, sometimes to a field to plant potatoes or to the market to sell a basket of tomatoes.

Today, death doesn't knock. It bashes down the door. Since my arrival, I have been engaged in a fierce competition with death, but today I have no choice but to admit defeat and submit. It is a very humbling experience to be defeated. Years of medical training did not prepare me for what has been thrust on my shoulders and dumped in my lap here. Give me a moment to vent. There are more than 60 people on the ward who need to be seen this morning. It takes me 11 hours to complete all the medical evaluations. While rounding on the patients, I encounter problem after problem. Problem number one: There are no protocols or provisions for malnourished children, which means once they enter the hospital, they leave dead. Problem number two: Two children arrive; both are severely anemic and need transfusions. We have no blood. Problem number three: A dehydrated child with dysentery and a prolapsed rectum from many bouts of diarrhea comes in breathing rapidly and shallowly. He is also severely anemic, has a pulse of 160, and holds on to life by a cobweb's thread. He has practically no blood or fluid left in his little, bony body. I cautiously give him fluid to hydrate him. Two hours later, he dies. Did the fluid dilute his blood too much and kill him, or was he too far gone to be saved? If the fluid killed him, did I do something wrong? After all, I wrote the order. Standing fully clothed, I am naked before my own tribunal. What is my defense, and who will defend me? The little boy was dying. He needed fluid. He needed blood. We didn't have blood. We had fluid. So I gave him fluid. Did he drown from it? And if he did, did I drown him? Who will hold me and tell me it's okay?

After work, I return home convinced I'm a failure. My mind is not my friend. It berates me. I could have done this, should have thought of that, and would have, if only…. I am exhausted. I need some downtime and some space to settle. I need to hold my heart and rock it for a while, give it some TLC—tender, loving care. Some comfort food would be nice, too. But how can I recline and dine in this comfortable house knowing that just next door people have no food to eat?

Tonight, I must give myself permission to do something unambiguously nice. I need to do something with a guaranteed happy ending—something I can control and know irrefutably that I helped someone in need. Many people eat to comfort themselves. I am a bit different. I comfort myself by feeding others. So after dinner, like in Kigali the day I arrived, I offer to clean up. The team likes the idea. Little do they know what Dr. Cary is up to. As before, I wait until everyone is asleep. Then, like a mouse scouring a kitchen for something to eat, I raid every pot, pan, bowl, cupboard, and crevice for some meaningful morsel that will put some stomachs at ease for one more night. Done! With supplies in both hands, I sneak out to the hospital with leftover rabbit and chicken for the marasmic patients. The problem I have now is that I don't have enough for everyone, and giving only to the neediest will be difficult.

The night is dark. Since there is no electricity, people burn candles, kerosene lanterns and twigs, which give glow. As I am nearsighted, this glow is not bright enough for me to make my way unattended down the footpath to the hospital. But I have no choice. I have to go. It is the right thing to do.

For people who are able to see in the dark, it must be an unusual sight to see a White doctor quietly tiptoeing through the darkness, carrying pots of food in each hand. As I enter the ward, people appear baffled. Night visitation is not a common practice, and it is uncharacteristic to see foreigners out after curfew, which is strictly forbidden, I might add. Eyes from all directions are on me. I scan the ward and smile at everyone to affirm this is a friendly visit. They are reassured. It doesn't take long for the people to figure out the reason for my visit.

I walk around the ward, pensive and deep in thought. I can feed only a few of the weakest of the weak. But why give food to people who will die regardless of this tidbit of kindness? They are already at death's doorstep. Why not give the food to people who have a chance to leave the hospital alive? But then, why not give the sickest of the sick a bit of pleasure and kindness just before they die—a last supper? Is it better to feed men, women or children? I conclude the women because children need healthy moms, or they don't stand a chance. But if I feed the men, they can then work and feed their wives and children. Without a healthy father, the women and children don't stand a chance. I should feed them all, but there isn't enough food for everyone. To give or not to give—this is the question. Oh, what to do? I'm not God, and I'm not supposed to be the gatekeeper at the pearly gates.

I walk among the patients lying in their beds and get more confused by my thoughts and questions, which become more numerous and convoluted. The patients slowly understand my dilemma. I hold two pots of food, standing in a hospital ward with 30 hungry people. Even without basic math skills, people can calculate with precision that there is not enough for everyone. One woman dares to break the silence by pointing to one of the pots, claiming her child is the neediest. This is the case in her loving eyes, but her baby is much heftier than others nearby. One man, seeing the pots, cocks his head to the side and, pretending to be frail, says, "I'm hungry." He is the most robust in the group. He lies near a man who is in a pitiful state and needs the meal most of all, but I can't give him food and ignore his neighbor.

It takes me two arduous hours to find the "right" people for rabbit and chicken tonight. Once my decision is made, I dole out the delicacies. Watching the few chosen patients devour the rare feast is beyond words. It is simply indescribable. The feeling I have is that of a relieved father who finds food for his starving children. How can feeding people bring me so much joy? One man, a mere skeleton, has three portions. He is so hungry, he even eats the bones. Seeing this poor man's sunken eyes, emaciated arms, peg legs, and daunting head movements in slow motion is too much for me. Seeing him in this pitiful condition makes me go off-kilter for a moment.

When the patients finish the meager offerings, they say in unison, "*Murakoze* [thank you]!" No one needs to thank me. They get what they desperately need and deserve, and I get what I desperately need and deserve—to love.

6 September 1994
Tuesday

My Dearest,

A severely malnourished child with dysentery was left on the hospital steps this morning. I'm not sure if he will make it until tomorrow. The woman who abandoned him told us his mother was killed. What is this woman's relationship to the child? Actually, she is his stepmother. "It's not mine, and I don't want it," she said as she disposed of him, as if he were a bag of trash, and then walked away. I took particular notice of how she called him an "it," completely devoid of any affection or connection. Either we feed "it," or we let "it" die. How does it feel to have your stepmother throw you away?

A Letter Home

Dear Mom and Dad,

I'm not sure if you will receive this letter, for miracles are rare nowadays, but if you do, understand you are witnessing a miracle. If you now hold this letter in your hands, know it had to be hand-carried to Kigali, which is four hours from where I live, down a dirt road that is so impassable only four-wheel-drive jeeps can successfully pass. Once in Kigali, someone else had to transport it by hand to someone on a United Nations cargo plane to Nairobi, where yet another person had to take it to Paris, where Médecins Sans Frontières forwarded it to its destination—you. If you write me, the entire transport chain goes in reverse. As you see, miracles do happen.

Contrary to your fears of me suffering, I am surviving and even thriving in Rwanda. I'm so grateful to be here. Médecins Sans Frontières is the crème de la crème, and it feels almost prestigious to be one of their doctors. They are impressively organized, give us excellent logistical support to facilitate our work, and provide a staff of three people to cook, clean and look after all of our needs. We are more than comfortable and extremely fortunate. There are four expats in my team, and we live in a small compound adorned with a tropical garden, flowers and bugs—lots of bugs. And if you permit me to boast, we have more crunchy cockroaches than you'll ever see in a lifetime. But don't worry, they are diligent and hardworking, constantly on the move, and don't mind me freaking out.

Our hospital is filled to capacity with people suffering from cholera, pneumonia, malnutrition, dysentery and dehydration. These diseases are the byproducts of hate. How so? If there were no hate, there would be love—just love. If there were just love, there would be no division, jealousy, corruption, haves and have-nots, war, poverty or diseases. Speaking of diseases, a child suffering from pneumonia died as I was listening to his lungs. After the child took his last breath, his mother cried a few tears, then went on her way back to the field to find food for her other children. When I left the ward, my nurse said,

"That makes two today!" It wasn't even noon yet! Death is so common that the staff don't bother to tell me when patients die.

Most of our medical staff are people without any formal medical training, but they have big hearts and do their best. There are practically no qualified medical personnel left in the country because most were exterminated in the genocide. Was this because the educated people were mostly Tutsis, or because educated people had influence and posed a risk to those intent on cleansing the population? After all, educated people have the wherewithal to mobilize the masses to rise up and bring down even the most powerful regimes. Whatever the reason, there are only a few medical professionals alive here.

Since I am talking about extermination, I must say that the stories I hear of the horrors of the genocide cannot be humanly possible. Something other than human beings carried out the atrocities. In fact, the stories are so outlandish that it is easy to dismiss them all as fabrications of frenetic and disturbed minds. But if the tales I hear are fictitious, then how are they being told and retold by different, unrelated people from all corners of the country?

Our house cleaner once had a mother and father and seven younger siblings. She went home one day in April and found her entire family chopped into pieces in a pile in her front room. She now has no one left. Others speak of their piles of skulls left behind for loved ones to see, touch and hold—memories of the good times before.

Prior to the genocide, about 14% of the general population was Tutsi. Today, there are practically none left. It is as if a species has been exterminated and is now extinct.

I don't mean to be the bearer of bad news, but it is quite cathartic and therapeutic for me to write about the things I see and feel here. In this way, I send them far away from me, and the burden of their weight is lifted from my shoulders. Thanks for letting me vent.

I love you, Cary

7 September 1994
Wednesday

My Dearest,

The sun is still far from changing guard with darkness, but I can't sleep. Instead, I lie restless in bed as my mind races in all directions. What causes abdominal bloating and lower extremity swelling? Where are the books MSF promised me? In Paris, they assured me I would have a substantial reference library at my disposal. It never arrived. I am working solo without the support of other physicians to discuss cases and get second opinions. There are no specialists to consult, and I'm out on a limb alone. My patients are severely sick with pathologies that my medical school professors disregarded because, in their words, such illnesses are "unicorns, red herrings and zebras." In other words, "Forget about them; you will never see them." Well, here in Rwanda, unicorns, red herrings and zebras are the norm.

I think of the little one who died shortly after I hydrated him. He was already in death's fangs, but I wonder if the fluids accelerated his death. Without blood, did he have a chance? Did I have a chance? Did I have a choice? In medical training, we are taught, "If it's not broken, don't fix it." Well, it was broken, and I had nothing to fix it with. And now I agonize over the child's death.

I also agonize over the little boy whose parents abandoned him on the hospital steps. He lies alone in his bed without anyone to comfort him. The nurses do manage to occasionally give him a cursory glance as they pass his bed, attending to other patients, but other than that, he is ignored. He is only two years old, severely malnourished, and still doesn't know how to walk. We don't have the personnel or time to care for him, but I can't abandon this boy. Yesterday, I went to his bed to hold him, but he had such profuse diarrhea that I could not risk being contaminated by stray fecal matter. I have to remain healthy. If I get sick, I won't be any use to anyone. So I didn't hold him. And he lay there, miserable—a bony skeleton on a metal mattress, without his mother or father to love him. It broke my heart not to hold him. And it breaks my heart now as I think about it.

My mind seems to be driving independently of the driver—me. It feels as though I'm its passenger, or should I say its prisoner? With death so common all around me, I can't help but worry about my own health and safety. I have only been here a week, and I am obsessed with contracting some fatal disease. Every pain, sneeze, itch, yawn, cough, or clearing of my throat becomes a preoccupation: Do I have tuberculosis, pneumonia, or perhaps a parasitic infestation? Every mosquito bite creates utter pandemonium: Did I just get infected with malaria, and if I did, will the dreaded disease paralyze me from a stroke, leave me permanently comatose from cerebral edema, or put me six feet under ground? I play Russian roulette with my life as I refuse to take malaria prophylaxis. The package insert in the box of pills says it causes retinal problems and baldness. It's the baldness I worry about. The few pieces of hair I still have on my head, I'm keeping.

Speaking of heads, I begin to wonder if I will keep mine. The people who committed the massacre are alive and well somewhere beyond the borders of this country. It is inevitable that they will eventually come back. Their mission to kill all Tutsis has not been achieved; a number of them are still alive! Their carefully crafted genocide needs 100% annihilation for it to be successful. When will these killers come back, and when they do, will they hurt humanitarian aid workers for treating Tutsis they so vehemently abhor? Why are the Tutsis so hated? In the movies, the good guy always triumphs, and the villain is always defeated. I believe this is called a "Hollywood ending." I'm afraid this Rwandan tragedy will have no ending.

My mind shifts its attention back to how I can safely sneak our leftover food to the hospital patients. If the team finds out, they will forbid it. Until they find out and forbid it, however, it remains fair game. The other expatriates have been on many previous missions, so they have more experience than I do. Perhaps they have good reasons to throw leftover food away while people starve outside our gates. As this is my first mission, I may be somewhat naïve and uninformed, so please enlighten me. How does feeding the garbage can make sense?

My mind continues to munch and crunch on everything past, present and future. The night passes this way until dawn yawns and intrudes on the darkness with its early light. Our chickens peck about near my bedroom window, and a goat's desperate bleating is driving me crazy. I need some stillness and some sleep. I need to stop the mind chatter, but how? Where have all the sheep gone? Come, so I can count you and fall asleep.

All of a sudden, an atrocious gasp and gurgle dash all hope for even the minutest speck of stillness. It is just too much. I run out back and see two men with knives straddling a goat whose head is half-cut off. Blood gushes like a geyser onto the ground as the animal suffocates in his own blood. The poor animal's eyes are wide open. Looking into his eyes, I see his soul as he struggles to hold on to life. Helpless and terrified, he heaves and quivers. After two minutes, he is still. His eyes are now closed. What becomes of his soul? Some say animals are put on the planet to feed and sustain us. If this is true, why aren't they respected and showered with our gratitude? If they sacrifice themselves for us, why do we so brutally slit their throats and subject them to unimaginable trauma at the time of their last breath? And one last question: This little animal will give four small bags of meat. Is it really worth shedding even a single drop of his blood for it?

Once back in the house, my morning continues with more raucousness. I have an argument with a team member over a bucket of water. Here's what happened: Relative to the local population that lives just outside our compound in deplorable conditions without food, water, shelter, or even toilets, we live like royals. Our private compound is gated and garlanded with a flowering garden that is meticulously pruned and manicured by a private gardener. Our house is spacious and comfortably furnished. There is a family room, a kitchen, and four private bedrooms, one for each expat. There is even a bathroom with a flush toilet. We also have an excellent house staff that cook, clean and care for us. Whatever we want, they are here to provide and please. We are beyond blessed and fortunate. Our only inconvenience is a lack of water. The house does have proper plumbing, but there is presently no water service. In this time of war, if we want water, we have to buy it from a water truck that comes from time to time. Unfortunately, the water truck isn't always available. Luckily, we still have a few gallons of this precious lifeline to sustain ourselves until another water truck comes, but we must use them sparingly.

Our water situation is now so dire that we have to ration the precious liquid, which has become more valuable than gold. We are each allotted one gallon of water daily to shower. How do you take a shower with so little water? Well, in tough times, you become very resourceful and find that one gallon of water is more than enough for a refreshing shower. Let me share how it is done. First, you remove your clothes and step into a little red plastic basin just big enough to place your left foot and half of your right foot inside. Next, you pour two mugs of water on your body, which is just enough to wet your skin; larger people may need a couple more mugs. Once wet, you soap yourself up. Finally, you rinse the soap off with the remaining water. If you run out of water, as is often the case, and you are still covered with soap, as is often the case, you can reuse the runoff water that is collected in the little red bucket below. There is a science to this method, and somehow, at the end of it, you feel fresh and rejuvenated.

We only have a few gallons of water left in our holding tank for drinking and cooking. One of our teammates wants to use a gallon to shower. I tell her we don't have enough water for showers today. She actually gets angry with me and goes for my jugular. Living together with people is surprisingly the greatest impediment to our peace here, not the war.

8 September 1994
Thursday

My Dearest,

The hospital's daily routine would be incomplete without someone dying. Death is such a common and habitual event that we have come to expect it each and every day. Strangely enough, if a day were to pass without a death on the ward, we would wonder what went wrong. Today, like every other day—as expected and right on time—death took yet another good person from us. Why did today's patient die? Was it anemia, pneumonia, or perhaps heart failure? I don't know. Without a fully equipped laboratory and an X-ray machine, I'm playing "Ring Around the Rosie" and *"eeny, meeny, miny, moe"* at the same time. I wanted so much to help this man, but death had already claimed him and taken all he had. I can still see him—25 years old, stoic and struggling, majestic and brave, fighting to live. Unfortunately, no one can combat or conquer death. As I quietly mourn his loss, another patient is at death's doorstep. There is nothing more I can do for him, either. He will die soon, probably from pneumonia. His wife reads my face and body language and understands that he will die soon. I feel so emasculated when my hands are tied and I can do nothing to make any difference. I feel so insignificant, ineffective and inadequate. I can't stand not knowing what to do. I can't bear not being able to do what I know I need to do. I hate when people die.

Back at home ...

You would think that after such an emotionally trying day at work, I would return home, eat, and go to sleep. But this is not the case. There is no time to sleep. After dinner, a bit of meat is left over. I can't see putting it anywhere but in the mouths of my patients at the hospital. So again, I pack up a snack and sneak discreetly out the back door, over the wooden gate, along the dirt path, through the hospital compound, to the ward. Once again, there is the dilemma of selecting the right recipients for the feast. Choosing the right people is like those multiple-choice test questions in medical school. I could narrow down my choices relatively easily, but when it came to "all of the above" or "none of the above," I was immobilized because, more often than not, I usually got it wrong. After graduating from medical school, I never thought I would have to contend with any more multiple-choice tests. I was wrong. Shoved in my face this evening is yet another such test with many confounding questions. The one that stumps me this time is, "Who should get the food?" The choices are "all of the above" and "none of the above." Again, I am immobilized by indecision. I want to answer "all of the above," but the meat is only enough to feed one person this evening. Meat is an excellent source of iron, so it stands to reason that someone with anemia should receive it. Unfortunately, all the patients have anemia. A bedraggled 43-year-old woman who could easily pass for a centenarian clearly needs it the most. But chances are she will not make it to 44, so is she the right candidate? But when I see her caring so tenderly for her young child, it makes complete sense to feed her. After all, feeding her could save the life of her daughter, too, at least for a while.

Again, everyone wants a portion of whatever it is I have. "It is only for the worst-off," I explain. As expected, everyone claims to be the worst-off. This ignites a mini-mutiny, and everyone starts arguing and yelling at one another. I stand mortified among dozens of very angry people. The escalating tension can only go in one direction—the wrong one. When people are hungry, they lose their patience and ability to be reasonable. I realize there are too many bitter feelings among the people who hadn't received anything the previous evening. I see jealousy and anger brewing in this pot of people as they watch their neighbors eat while their own stomachs are empty and aching. The only solution is to leave immediately before any serious fighting breaks out. What is the correct answer to tonight's multiple-choice question? For the first time, I can answer this question with absolute certainty: "None of the above." I have no choice but to return home with the food and throw it away.

9 September 1994
Friday

My Dearest,

Today, I have an epiphany—a profound realization of a simple truth: *Don't try to save the people who are going to die. Focus on the ones who have a chance to live.* This is so simple and straightforward. Why do I anguish over accepting this truth? Perhaps it's because I'm incapable of walking over, around, or away from someone who has no chance but still fights to live. In this case, I'm just not able to give up. I guess that is why death has to be so brutally definitive. When I can't loosen my grip, it opens my hand.

Each day, there are too many new and mounting problems to solve. Yesterday, for example, a concerned father brought his severely dehydrated son to the hospital for treatment. The child had diarrhea, and the father withheld all fluids because he believed they would cause more diarrhea. I explained to the father in simple terms: "When no gas in engine, it no go! No fluid in body, we no go." After a lengthy explanation to Dad about his child's hydration status, I was certain he understood. Reassured, I sent him and his son back home with instructions on how to care for diarrhea.

Today, Dad returns with his son. He is significantly worse.

"Child no go!" I say to the father. "Why?" I press.

"Because after he drink, he vomit," the father says. "Bad to give fluid to son if vomit. Me no give fluid to son," he insists.

"No fluids, no go!" I sputter.

What to do? This is their way. How can I impose my way? Who am I to tell him my way good, his way bad, his way *no go*. So, in the end, child no go, no go out of hospital. Child die.

Speaking of children, the little boy with bloody diarrhea who was abandoned by his stepmom and left to die on the hospital steps sits alone in his bed, fiddling with his fingers, as all the other children around him are cuddled and coddled by family members. No one touches him. No one loves him. No one even sees him. It's as if he is invisible. There is a hospital policy that requires all patients to be accompanied by a personal caregiver who is responsible for feeding, cleaning, and taking care of all their intimate needs. No caregiver, no care. This little marasmic, abandoned boy who looks like an old, shriveled-up raisin has no caregiver, and just sits alone, unattended. What do we do? There is no time to think of him, let alone attend to his many needs. No time, no staff, no caregiver, no care. But there is something so beautiful, so still, so special about him. While the other children play, pounce, jump and enjoy, this little one sits quietly and withers, a veritable *raisin in the sun*. Unable to keep myself from caring, I take a timeout, set aside my fear of contracting dysentery, and sit beside him. Timidly, I reach out my hand. He begins to touch it, exploring it slowly—very slowly. Everything he does, in fact, is in slow motion because he's so weak and severely malnourished. I nestle up to him. He responds by looking deep into my being. I am deeply moved. I pick him up and rock him in my arms. This pleases him and me … much—very, very!

Some children on the ward are far more unfortunate than this little abandoned boy; there are four, to be exact. They are blessed to have their mothers next to them, but this doesn't matter because they are all unconscious and will soon die. The four mothers remain calm. "*Si le bon Dieu veut* [if the good God wants]," they say. One of the mothers sits quietly next to her child and watches her beloved's breath become shallower and shallower until it is also still. After the last breath, she says, "*J'ai perdu mes six enfants. Si le bon Dieu veut* [I lost my six children. If the good God wants]."

Besides all the traumatized people lying nearly lifeless on metal, mattress-less beds around me, there are the countless, horrific stories that are hard to believe, let alone comprehend. One woman recounts how she watched 11 people chase a lone Tutsi woman running up a hill, trying to escape her execution. "When they caught her, they cut her head off, and it rolled alone down the very hill she had hoped would save her."

Another woman recalls how she was fleeing from a killer during the massacre. Carrying her two babies, she ran for her life from a monster manning his machete just yards behind her. While frantically trying to squeeze through a very narrow passageway, one of her babies slipped from her hands and fell to the ground. The woman looks into my eyes, then fixes her gaze on something far beyond and says, "Man stab my baby, stomp on skull with black boot, and baby head go squish."

10 September 1994
Saturday

My Dearest,

I walk out of the compound this morning, and children come running from everywhere to greet me. Like the day before and all the days before that, the children offer me a resounding *"bonjour"* and fight among themselves to take hold of my hands to escort me to the hospital. The competition is fierce. There is only one of me and many dozens of them. When they manage to claim one of my fingers, they are more than happy. Sometimes, five children claim the five fingers on one hand, and five other children claim the five fingers on the other hand. My little entourage looks disheveled, but everyone is abounding with life. As they nearly carry me down the dirt path, they sing in almost perfect harmony, *"Donnez-moi un biscuit* [Give me a biscuit]." I shake my head from side to side, and they, in turn, jump like little beads of oil on a very hot skillet. When we reach the hospital, the children scatter in all directions, and my workday begins.

The ward has basins filled with a solution of chlorine in front of each doorway to curb the spread of cholera. People are requested to gently dip the bottom of their shoes in the solution to sterilize the soles when they exit any contaminated area. And what do they do? Everyone, including the staff, jumps over the basins. I implore them to comply with the guidelines for infectious disease control. And how do they comply? They comply by jumping over the basins.

A little girl, four and a half years old, refuses to take her medicine today. The little pill is her little life. Back home, we say, "An apple a day keeps the doctor away." Here in Africa, a pill a day keeps death away. The little darling thrashes about and defiantly refuses to take the little white pill, which she throws on the floor. I value these pills like I value my life. When the pill falls to the ground, I fall to pieces. We don't have enough of this particular medication for every patient, so we established a protocol to reserve the few pills we have for the wee ones under five and the elderly over 65. What a sight! *Monsieur le docteur* crawling on all fours under and around the beds, looking for a single little white pill. Dozens of others wait at the hospital gate, praying for one of these little white pills. This particular medicine truly saves lives.

The cholera ward is filled to capacity with what appears to be corpses. How could anyone with cholera be anything else, as all their bodily fluids pour out of them faster than Niagara Falls falls? Liters go in, and gallons gush out. Managing the ins takes care and skill. Managing the outs takes logistical genius. With people too weak and withered to get out of bed and make their way to the bathroom, a cholera "crib" was created. These specially designed adult cribs are brilliantly constructed and simple to use. Basically, a metal bed frame is fitted with a wire mesh that serves as a mattress. In the center of the wire mattress is a cleverly crafted poop hole. For easy cleaning, this ensemble is covered with plastic, except for the hole. Under this hole is a removable plastic bucket that is perfectly poised and positioned for multiple, spontaneous deposits. In effect, this cholera crib is a horizontal, makeshift porta-potty. All the patient needs to do is lie comfortably on the plastic-covered wire mesh and make a mess, literally, by letting it *run its course*. And run it does. Cholera is relentless. It stops at nothing short of death itself, which in all cases indefinitely quiets the situation. The patients are so weak and exhausted that they welcome the quiet and accept their fate submissively with the words, *"Quel que soit* ce que *le bon Dieu veut* [whatever the good God wants]."

11 September 1994
Sunday

My Dearest,

Another morning, another briefing. Briefings are informal daily updates that we get to keep us abreast of the political and social turmoil in the country. Today's update leaves me feeling less hopeful and more fearful. With each harrowing account of Rwanda's brutal massacre, the more critical I become of man and his ugly ways. The endless images of hatred have created a collage of chaos that forces me off course into some faraway place, leaving me numb, contracted and careful to care. People being chopped up alive while others watch and celebrate is too much for the heart to hold. All I can do is listen. The only way to get through this nightmare is to make believe it isn't real.

Back at the hospital, there is breaking news. Every story needs a protagonist and an antagonist. In this way, good and bad are kept in check, and the storyline is certain to capture the audience's attention and affection. As long as a story has a happy ending where the bad is engulfed by the good and hope prevails, it is worth telling. Unfortunately, today's story is an exception: two displaced women have been hospitalized for weeks. Their overall condition has somewhat improved, but they remain bedridden. I would venture to say they both suffer from severe post-traumatic stress disorder (PTSD). They may want to return home, but the ever-present emotional trauma they have from the genocide paralyzes them. I wonder if they even have homes to return to, or if they were erased along with their families. These women fled their native places during the extermination sprees months ago and have not been back since. What remains of their families? Is anyone left alive? How many were killed? And how many dead members of their families are stacked in a pile in their foyers? What have these women seen? What has been done to them? Were they raped?

Our story continues with our villain, a French maiden who is a nurse and the head of our project. I don't know anything about her personal history or the baggage she carries. I don't know what chips she schleps on her shoulders or what she hides behind her rough exterior, but I can say she is mean—really mean. The only other nurse I know like her is Nurse Ratched from the tale *One Flew Over the Cuckoo's Nest*. It is, therefore, fitting to refer to our story's antagonist as "Nurse Ratshit."

Today, Nurse Ratshit orders me to discharge the displaced women. What right does she have ordering me to discharge my patients? She doesn't. She has no right, but she is the head of the project, and as I said, she is mean. And you don't cross *mean*. While these two women have admittedly improved, I am not comfortable discharging them yet. They are physically stronger, but they are emotionally traumatized and need more time on the ward to muster the courage to recover.

"I don't think these women are ready for discharge just yet," I dare to counter our villain. Like a commandant in a nazi concentration camp, she looks at me, snaps her fingers, stomps her heels, and pierces me with her wretched, razor-sharp glare.

"Don't cross me. Do as you're told!" she snaps.

Like a compliant puppy, I run for cover and write the order to discharge the women. Someone is going to be discharged, and I don't want it to be me. The local ward nurse is surprised to see my order. She hesitates and looks into my eyes, her gaze penetrating them, pleading with me to give these two women more time to recover. She knows they don't have the physical or emotional strength to take the next step to return to the real world and reintegrate themselves into life outside the hospital compound. There is a momentary yet long pause—a poignant silence between us. When I don't change my order, the nurse does what good, obedient nurses do: she complies even though it is against her best medical judgment. I want to tell her that I completely agree with her assessment of the women and that she is right. I want to encourage her to follow her heart and refuse to act on my order, but I am helpless, stripped of my power, and overpowered by Nurse Ratshit.

Like a coward, I comply with my superior's order, which was unquestionably against my best medical judgment. I feel deep down that discharging these two women at this time is premature and will ultimately lead to unimaginable pain and suffering, if not death itself. Unable to contradict the head of our project, I cross my fingers tightly as I leave the ward for the evening, hoping that when I return tomorrow morning, the women will be gone, thus putting an end to this unfortunate and quite embarrassing situation. Before I leave, I give each woman a care package, which includes soap, food, blankets, and more food for their journey home. It is the least … no, it is all I can do. I don't dare ask if they have a home to return to. Anything short of "yes" will push me over the brink.

The two displaced women can barely walk; how can they possibly go anywhere? Even if they can physically leave the compound, where will they find the strength for the long and arduous journey through hostile territories where mean men wait in dark places to claim their next prey? How could I be so cruel to order them back to that? I pretend to be in charge of the hospital, making decisions and judgments based on sound medical principles and compassion, but the reality is that I am a puppet to protocols and a Gestapo head nurse whose pink-painted lips pucker like a plunger as she orchestrates and then ordains what appears to be her plan to destroy me. I can override protocols, orders and her, but only once. Failing to obey her would give her ample justification to remove me from the project. Until I cross that line of dissent, she has to wait like a spider in her web. So far, I've managed to skirt her pestilence. But it is just a matter of time. She will continue taunting me with her pitchfork until I strike. And when I do, she will wrap me up as if I were an insect in her web and rapidly devour me.

Back home at the compound...

I now have the time to sit quietly and talk to myself. Did I do the right thing by writing the order to *dispose* of the two women? Did I do my best? Where will they go? To be honest, I never even spoke with them. I never asked them about their stories. They appeared so fragile and vulnerable that asking them to revisit what happened during the killing spree seemed cruel and insensitive. So I gave them space to be anonymous.

Most people, out of necessity, bury the past and carry on by taking their lives into their own hands. These two women were different. They no longer had the will to do that. They wanted me to take their lives into my own hands. But I have only two hands. And these hands must fight for people who are actively fighting for their lives. Yet if this is truly the case, then why do I sit alone now, berating myself for releasing my grasp on these innocent, helpless, traumatized women and letting them fall through my fingers? I wonder where they are tonight. Did the nurse discharge them, or did she make her own executive decision and decide that without the will to live, the women had no chance on the street? Maybe she went against doctor's orders. It should only be. My Dearest, make the nurse disobey me this time and every time I do something cowardly and downright wrong. Give her the strength to write a new and improved order to keep the women in the safety and care of the hospital. I will co-sign it. I promise.

12 September 1994
Monday

My Dearest,

Last night, I slept poorly, thinking of the two women I had ordered out of the hospital compound. They insisted they were displaced people and begged me to let them stay in the safe confines of the hospital. The local ward nurse had reservations about sending them away, but she has to do what she is told to do. I also have to do what I am told to do. But if following orders is the right thing to do, then why was I up all night worrying about them and their whereabouts?

As soon as I wake up this morning, I run to the hospital to check on the women. I hope to find them all cozy in their hospital beds, protected and looked after. As I near the front gate, my gait involuntarily slows. I can't believe what I see. What have I done? The two women are lying on the ground in front of the hospital gate, covered in their urine. Apparently, the women refused to leave the medical ward when they were discharged, so the staff literally pushed, pulled, and dragged them outside the hospital gate, dumping them like bags of garbage. They have been lying in their urine on the wet, cold concrete stairs in front of the hospital gate since last night. They haven't eaten since yesterday. What have I done? Who ordered the women out of the hospital? I did. Can I blame the nurse? She didn't write the order. Who did? I did.

I furiously try to find transport for the women to return to their villages. There are no trucks, buses, or cars anywhere. When I return to the hospital, the women are still on the steps. I can't help but notice a young girl crying near them. She must be the daughter of one of the women. My heart breaks in two. Being stripped of all control on the ward leaves me powerless. I am nothing more than a marionette in the hands of a ruthless despot who yanks and toys with my strings. I could demand more authority, but this would only fuel an already incendiary situation in our team. What should I do? What can I do?

The interpersonal problems we have in our small expatriate team seem insurmountable at this point. I'm so confused. The expatriates with the most field experience are the ones who are most callous and withdrawn from the very people they presumably came to help. They appear to have lost the luster of love and have become warriors themselves. A few days ago, I asked Nurse Ratshit what to do with patients who are simply too weak to leave the hospital. She responded, *"Prend le* bâton [Beat them with a stick]*!"* She was serious!

The little girl's tears tear me apart, and I do an about-face and march into the ward like a soldier with a bayonet in hand. I courageously take a piece of paper and write another order:

"Hospitalize these women for weakness." Signing this order is a declaration of independence as well as a declaration of war. Weakness is not an acceptable reason to hospitalize people and does not meet the hospital's criteria for admission, but I have to live with myself. When I go to sleep at night, I have to sleep with myself, and when I wake up in the morning, I have to look at myself. These women's suffering becomes my own suffering, and I will not multiply their misery by succumbing to scum and wretchedness from people in positions of power. So, for this story's happy ending, these women in grave need will remain here. Let this order be my personal declaration of independence, and if war comes of it, then let it come.

Back at home ...

There are leftovers again tonight. Protocol forbids us from sharing our food with the locals, but how can we wine and dine while our neighbors wander the fields looking for a bean or two to feed their families? And besides, who writes these protocols? We do! *We* write them, and *we* can rewrite them. We can ignore them, defy them, or conveniently forget them if we want. In keeping with my traditional night dance, I once again eagerly offer to clean up after dinner. Everyone is predictably delighted with my enthusiastic offer. I am equally delighted with my night duty. We don't have leftovers very often, so I spring into action at every opportunity to share. Instead of throwing the food into the trash, I put it into a container next to the garbage can. This way, anyone entering the kitchen will not notice that something isn't quite right.

When everyone is asleep, I do the snake thing and slither out back with the goods underarm in search of the most needy. Because of the brawl that occurred on the ward during my last mobile food pantry visit, I don't dare to return to the hospital. Instead, I walk through town looking for a tummy or two to fill. Everyone is fast asleep under God's roof—the sky. There is stillness, and nothing moves. I scan the open field like an eagle stalks the skies with a keen eye on something that looks delicious below. In my case, I look for those destined for a little deliciousness—a treat from above. I look for someone who is distressingly destitute. Everyone appears downtrodden, yet in a curious way, they seem to be at peace. Maybe they dream of the past before it all went wrong. Or maybe they dream of a better tomorrow. I imagine they are grateful to be alive. Somehow they made it, while many others didn't.

After some time, I find some needy people and nudge them apologetically. When they see the food, they go into a brief state of shock. For a moment, there is no time or space, just a quiescent state of oneness with their beloved Almighty up in heaven. When they smell and touch the actual food, they are reassured it is real and return to Earth to give me gratitude. One man looks at me and says, "God bless you." Another person asks me to feed her children from my magical pot. I try to explain to the poor woman that my cup doesn't runneth over, despite the lavish-appearing lifestyle we privileged pale people have in Rwanda. But there is no way to convince her. Any explanation would be in vain. After all, I am doling out leftover food—proof of our opulence.

With nothing left to give, I turn to go home. Unexpectedly, I find myself immobilized by the sight of a woman leaning against a post, looking nowhere, surrounded by her children, looking nowhere. The woman is wondering where she will find some food to feed her children. The look of hunger is an uncomfortable one to face, even in the dark. It says nothing, and nothing says everything. When I see that look, I have to look away. It is too confronting. It is too raw. As she stands leaning against the post, I stand defeated, with an empty pot under my arm. We don't talk, but she knows I am in pain because I can't feed her; there is not a speck of food left in the pot. She smiles and says without words, "Your care is enough to hold our tummies until it is God's will." With her silent understanding, I am able to move again, away from the woman in the blackness of the night, back to a house where in daytime flowers are tended by our gardener, multiple-course meals are prepared by our personal cook, and everything else is done by our nanny.

13 September 1994
Tuesday

My Dearest,

Each morning, I visit my patients and get briefed by the staff on the events of the previous evening. The first two questions I ask them are always: How many people died, and did they suffer as they went upstairs? If people must die, are we at least able to give them comfort and dignity in the last moments of their lives?

I often ask myself if I am doing anything that makes a difference here in Rwanda. Well, today I may actually have had a sign that I have made a difference, at least in the life of a little boy. The abandoned boy we found on the steps of the hospital a few days ago smiled at me. I have been visiting him daily, sometimes every hour on the hour. Until today, he was all "dis": disagreeable, disengaged, disinterested and distant. When children are severely malnourished, they often disconnect completely from the world around them. Nothing pleases them; nothing penetrates them; nothing matters to them. I wonder why they behave this way. Do they not yet have the words to describe what they are feeling, or are they too weak and consumed by hunger to have the strength to put words together in any meaningful way? In any case, the little abandoned boy, whose name I've come to know is Joseph, smiled at me. A smile may not seem like a big difference, but it is. Where he was a week ago and where he is today is an enormous difference. And it feels so good.

For several days, I have been trying to feed Joseph. It has been a battle of wills—his will and my will. When people suffer from starvation, they lose their appetite. I suppose this makes sense. If there is no food, the body takes the appetite away to help people handle the hunger. This is certainly the case with Joseph. Getting anything into him has been a labor of love. Most foods he flat-out rejects. With some prodding, however, he will eat avocado mush, baby bananas, and protein-enriched biscuits, which are specifically formulated to nourish

101

starving children. Unfortunately, it is difficult for him to eat because he doesn't yet have the strength to chew. Every bite, chomp and swallow is in slow motion, and I am held hostage, waiting to see if he will make it … or not. It's sad that no one comes to visit him except me. At two years old, he weighs barely 12 pounds. He can't walk because he has never been taught. And how can he smile when he's never been loved?

Joseph's smile deeply moves me. I could easily adopt him and be his father. I could feed him and make him laugh, and then I could teach him how to walk and do all the things dads do with their little boys. And he would be happy and smile. And I would be happy and smile too.

14 September 1994
Wednesday

My Dearest,

My favorite time is the morning. The sun rises so softly and warms everyone equally. It doesn't see Hutus or Tutsis, Black or White, tall or short, rich or poor. It just sees people. It doesn't see roses or daffodils. It just sees flowers. It doesn't see banana plantations or coconut trees. It just sees Mother Earth. In the quiet of the morning, everything is peaceful. It's as if a piece of peace itself comes to hold us affectionately for a moment. Then slowly and steadily, the peace is punctured, the silence is silenced, and the day decays.

From quiet and calm comes chaos when a child arrives to the hospital with a high fever. She has an advanced case of malaria that has already reached her brain. In addition, she has severe anemia—a lack of red blood cells, which are needed to carry oxygen throughout the body. The malarial parasite uses a person's red blood cells as its uterus to produce its offspring. In the process, it rips through, ruptures, and destroys the cells. Children are particularly vulnerable to this bloodthirsty killing machine that frequently goes to their brains and kills them in a matter of hours. This little person before me now has a very high fever and is in a coma. Since the parasite has already gone to her brain, if she is to have any chance of surviving, she will need intravenous quinine STAT (STAT is a medical term that means with extreme urgency). Unfortunately, she has no venous access, which means we cannot find a blood vessel to get the medicine into her. What do we do? We must act within minutes, or we will lose her. We have quinine in pill form, but this oral preparation does not cross the blood-brain barrier fast enough to get to the child's brain in time. With our hands tied, my staff and I stand by her bedside, forming a sort of human shield to keep death away, begging to believe that together we could prevent it from swooping up yet another one of our precious little children. Helpless, our minds and hearts go in every direction, trying to find a way to win this battle. Then there is a miracle. Laurent, my medical assistant, looks in his personal medicine chest and finds a single dose of intramuscular (IM) quinine that can be injected directly into the child's muscle. He offers it to save the child's life. Beyond grateful, I immediately write the order to administer it.

Wouldn't you know it, as soon as I write the order, who should appear? Life has a way of being cruelly predictable. Must every story have a protagonist and an antagonist? Can't life be a bit more original? Our very own Nurse Ratshit struts haughtily into the ward as if she were queen of the universe, this time decorated with violaceous lips that are perfectly puckered to accentuate her favorite facial feature. With her front side intentionally and unreservedly beckoned forward—an imposing posture that would make even Rambo run for cover—she examines the order I just wrote.

"No! You are not authorized to prescribe intramuscular quinine," she arrogantly asserts. "It can lead to abscesses and is against MSF's protocol," she fervently recites, like some hatemonger on a soapbox at City Hall, pummeling the public.

Time Out ...

Perhaps I should digress for a moment and share why this woman became my staunch enemy. When I first arrived to Mabanza just two weeks ago, I joined a team of four French women. They were living a monastic life in a remote area without prospects or possibilities. I was the new one on the block—the only man, the missing piece in their home away from home somewhere in Africa. Companionship, affection, and intimacy are so often needed and craved in these adverse times of war. With the disproportionate ratio of women to men at 4:1, a ferocious feud took place among the maidens. It was subtle, but a very real *war of the roses*. With smiles on faces and knives in hands behind backs, it was a veritable free-for-all *à la française*. In a resource-poor area, one can easily find oneself in survival mode. In this state, survival-of-the-fittest instincts take the lead, and the stalker with the stealthiest gait gets her prey—in this case, me. Let me be more specific with a few more details.

During our first supper together, each of the four suitors attended to me as a queen serves her king. Firsts and seconds were served to me on a platter; goblets were filled well before my final sip, and dessert was the perfect finishing touch. They were attentive and inquisitive, each decorated with their best bonnet. Nurse Ratshit positioned herself skillfully next to me at the dinner table. She was working hard, and just before the end of the meal, she surreptitiously placed her hand gently on my *inner* thigh and quietly whispered, "*Si tu veux passer la nuit*...[if you want to spend the night...]," cautious enough so that the others would miss the advance. She didn't finish her sentence, but her eyes certainly did, as they penetrated me with passion. And then, for the finishing touch, her fingers did the walking and punctuated her proposition with a subtle squeeze near the jewels, again with the utmost discretion.

After dinner and the usual banter that accompanies the final crumbs, we all went to our respective rooms. I did not RSVP. Instead, I retired to my own bed and slept soundly ... alone.

In the morning, a vastly different woman emerged from her room. It was metamorphosis in reverse. Unlike a caterpillar that becomes a beautiful butterfly, she went from goddess to Godzilla, with poison so venomous that the mere sight of her sent me running.

Now back to the ward ...

"And as head of project, I cannot permit it," she continues, cocking her neck to the left while gazing upward to the right with an eyebrow raised on only one side.

I stand my ground and justify why I wrote the order. "This child has cerebral malaria and has already lapsed into a coma. Oral medication given through a nasogastric tube will not cross the blood-brain barrier, and she is far too dehydrated to gain intravenous access. If, in the unlikely event, she develops an abscess, then we will treat it," I say confidently. "Without the injection, she will die. We have no choice but to break protocol and offer her one last fighting chance to survive."

"Malaria is not our mission!" she sternly counters. "We are a cholera-dysentery hospital. We don't authorize injections of quinine. It's against the organization's mandate," she decrees authoritatively, leaving absolutely no room for negotiation.

The staff and patients are all too familiar with this woman's heart, or lack of one, and keep their eyes glued to the ground to avoid engaging with her. After all, it was this kind of heart that orchestrated the very genocide that got everyone here in the first place. I have come to understand that she is willing to sacrifice this patient to avenge me for failing to RSVP and accept her invitation to sleep with her. Since then, she wants me gone and uses every opportunity and provocation to get me to break protocol. If she can get me to break just a single rule, she can prove I am a liability to the project and justify removing me from the team and sending me back to Europe.

In times of strife, I try to follow the wisdom outlined in the *I Ching*, an ancient Chinese oracle that gives insights into how to live a happy and satisfying life. "Be meek," it says, "and appear non-threatening to the adversarial forces who will pass you by." To date, I have cordially accepted the role of a cowardly lion to comply with the oracle's sacred wisdom, but somehow, this child will not die because of my meekness in the face of this wretch's revenge. Compassion, kindness, logic and reason were not enough to impress upon her the need for quick and decisive action to save this little girl's life. Nurse Ratchit made her decision. And so, I make mine: From now on, I will step forward with the honor and the authority afforded to me as a licensed physician to care for my patients. *My* orders will serve as a testament to my commitment and conviction to protect my patients' right to life and dignity. My job description as medical director gives me the authority to make the final medical decisions for all patients. Up to now, I have hesitated to assert myself and push my position because I believed in the possibility of something far better, something more cordial and amicable between us. But her willingness to sacrifice this child to avenge me unveils a profound character flaw that is malignant and reprehensible. I decide to take the risk of being thrown out of the project and accordingly declare to her directly, "*I* am the medical director of this facility, and *my* order has been clearly written." My tone is authoritative and non-negotiable. There is no room for any compromise, misunderstanding or discussion. Giving the child the IM dose of quinine may save her life. Nurse Ratshit stands in front of me as I stand in front of her. The staff stand around us. Her wickedness has finally been tamed and contained within the confines of *my* ward. I now wait for her next attack.

Back at home...

Dinner is curiously calm and cordial, given today's hospital row. Something is brewing, but I wish to believe that this lull after the storm is a permanent truce for the good of all.

Speaking of good, it seems to be a good idea to celebrate today's success with the people living outside in the field, under the sky, over a lovely pot of leftovers. And believe it or not, tonight's remaining food from dinner, I swear, seems to be calling loudly at me again, saying, "Share me! Share me!" Disguised as an obedient or disobedient child, depending on one's perspective, I quickly tidy up the kitchen and wait for the last light to dim. When it does, I do a "Dr. Cary" and slip unseen into the night to stake out the field. The journey this evening to the homeless people could be especially dangerous given today's hospital fireworks. If I am caught distributing food to the people past curfew, the antagonist in our story could finally catch her precious prey and devour me. Breaking the imposed curfew is a serious security violation that justifies and guarantees the swiftest and most definitive action—immediate dismissal from the project and the organization. That would be disastrous. What to do? I have no choice but to feed the people.

There may be legitimate reasons not to give out food, but I really don't want to know what they are. Food is life. Life is good. Those people just over yonder are hungry. What more is there to question and consider? With pots under both armpits, I go slowly from person to person. As I scoop out the pots and transfer the contents into the hands, mouths, and pots of those around me, life stands still. It almost feels like reattaching the umbilical cord and giving birth to a new life. The people see God in the mashed potatoes—a gift from heaven that answers their prayers. It must be horrible to be hungry. It must be devastating not knowing where the next meal will come from or if the next meal will even come.

15 September 1994
Thursday

My Dearest,

I can't wait to start my night job and continue where I left off last evening. Once again, when everyone is fast asleep, I raid the kitchen and mix a meal together. Concealing it in a brown paper bag, I make myself the color of wind and slide in and out of the night's folds. To my surprise, the backdoor gate has been blocked by a large rock. I manage to push it away. The night guard sleeps, but he is awakened by the scraping of the rock on the ground as I carefully move the gate forward. He sees me but says nothing. He won't ever tell. Fortunately for me, my white skin is still a master key that opens every door, everywhere, every time in Africa. How much longer *White* can maintain its sovereign status is under discussion.

My night program is consistent and predictable. You might call it an obsession. I call it "the right thing." Last night, and the many nights before, I prowled about looking for just the "right" people—the ones with the least, the weakest with the greatest needs. Tonight, it's more of the same.

This evening, it is unusually dark, cold, and muddy from the rain. I struggle to see. Wandering about, I fail to find any people, but I know there has to be someone somewhere who meets my criteria for a home-cooked meal. My heart beats audibly because, frankly, I am scared. Being outside after the military-imposed curfew is a serious offense in Rwanda. In addition, Hutu rebels prey like wild animals at night, and ambushes are still common. Military men shoot to kill. I just hope whoever holds a gun tonight has exceptional night vision and knows his colors, specifically my particular shade of white. Even with good night vision, however, I understand all too well that the white of my skin can protect me only so far. How far? Let's not go there now. Instead, let the illusion of the white knight fairy tale be the heroine worth believing.

In the distance, someone coughs. I do a 180 and go toward the sound. Seconds away, there is a woman trembling, lying on the ground, nestled among her six young children under a carport. It is damp and terribly cold. I near the woman. She is blinded by my flashlight, which I turn off to prevent people from seeing us. The woman trembles not from the cold but from mortal fear of me hurting her. She is actually terrified of me, not because I am a big man and she is a little woman, but because she just endured three months of grueling human slaughter during which time more than two hundred thousand women were raped. Was she one of them? How can I reassure her that I have come as a friend and mean her no harm? To calm her, I shine my flashlight onto my aluminum pots. She is stunned and, at first, has no reaction. Her mind struggles to unravel itself from its fear. After a few seconds, she composes herself and then gives me that look—that Oh-God-thank-you-thank-you look. Untangling herself gently from her children, who are all cuddled up alongside her like newborn suckling puppies tucked inside the tucks and folds of her tummy, she hurries through the darkness and returns seconds later with an empty pot. Our pots make love that moment, coming together as one as the life force is transferred from one to the other. Once I feel I have done a thorough job transferring the food, I pull my pot away. The woman is not convinced that I have transferred every morsel from the pot and gently takes her spoon and more thoroughly scrapes its walls, making sure every last bit is retrieved. The scraping of her spoon on the inside of the pot sends shivers down my spine, and I go into a hyper-aroused state, acutely aware of the grave danger around me. Not only is the military something to reckon with, but the scraping of the spoon wakes others nearby who share the same living space. There is not enough for everyone present, and I fear a full-fledged feud like what occurred at the hospital. It is no longer safe for me to be here or anywhere outside my house. I need to go, and go now. Fortuitously, raindrops tap the earth and drown out the sound of our pots. As I ready to bolt back home, I notice the woman trembling. Is it the bitter cold or her gratitude this time? After all, she has just witnessed a miracle. Surely, at some time in the past, she prayed for help, for a meal, for a sign. And tonight, she is reminded that all you need to do is ask.

Before bolting, I give the woman two more dishes of food. When she sees the fresh tomato and onion salad, she reacts as if she has just found a golden treasure. The woman timidly says, "*Murakoze* [thank you]" from the deepest place. I nod my head in a way that begs her to forgive me, for this is all I have to offer. If I could, I would invite everyone present to my house for a real feast of firsts, not seconds or leftovers.

I quickly leave, making sure that there is nothing of myself left behind. For all practical purposes, I was never here, there, or anywhere except in my bed this evening. In the cold, damp, and danger of the night, I dart back through the darkness in reverse: away from the field, over the stone, through the gate, in the backdoor, into my room, and onto my bed. Everyone is asleep; all is quiet; the guard will say nothing, neither will I.

16 September 1994
Friday

My Dearest,

It's more of the same—a rerun of a popular television soap opera. War rages around us; poverty prevails and prospers; hungry people poke around looking for a bean or two, and Nurse Ratshit reigns over the ward once again, like a murderer with a machete aiming to macerate.

A child too weak to feed herself needs to be fed through a nasogastric tube. I write a standing order in the patient's chart to leave the tube in place for continual feedings. Our villain again inappropriately starts evaluating patients on the ward and antagonistically contradicts my orders. "Pull the tube," she writes in the patient's dossier. She has no right to write orders. She has no right to see or treat patients. The local medical staff, however, will never challenge a foreigner, and though her decision to pull the tube makes little sense to them, they have to yield to her authority. This passive-aggressive behavior undermines our team's professionalism and puts the entire staff in an awkward position. They have had enough discord among their own people; they don't need additional battles on their doorsteps. Why starve an already starving child just to irk and undermine me? Why sacrifice yet another person? We came to save lives, not starve them! She taunts me, hoping I will break ranks and defect. But I won't abandon these people, no matter how brutal and oppressive her reign becomes. She has no right to be on the ward. She has no right to interfere with patient care. I am the doctor here. It is *my* ward. These are *my* patients, and I am ultimately responsible for them. Yet I have no right to counter her. It is hard for me to cope with this woman's unadulterated disdain for me. I have been here just two weeks, and I am beginning to weaken from the constant barrage of abuse from her. She walks a different path from my own, and I cannot find an opening in her heart to resolve our differences. What will happen in the next act of this vile performance? Do I have to wait until the next act or after the intermission to find out?

17 September 1994
Saturday

My Dearest,

Once again, late at night, I make contact with the people outside the hospital compound. There are only sounds of birds and frogs and steps of soldiers. I shake. It is too dangerous to do what I am doing, but my pots are fuller than usual, so I can justify one more drop-off. I promise to make this the last time.

Tonight, I choose an alternative path, hoping to find other people in need. The darkness camouflages even the biggest and boldest beasts. In the dark, I can see no more than a few feet in front of me. This calms my nerves and gives me an illusory sense of security. What I can't see doesn't exist. Oops! There are suddenly three soldiers walking toward me. My instinct is to turn and run toward the house, but what if they shoot me? If I am not guilty of something, why would I be running away from them? It is unlikely that they would shoot an expatriate, but how good is their night vision? Does white skin look different from black skin in the night? I don't know. I can't tell by looking at myself. The weight of just a single pot and pan becomes unbearable as I fail to find my footing. Standing still, I can't imagine what is about to happen. I am breaking curfew. No one dares to disobey military orders by trespassing the night. I know no soldiers, and none of them know me. Cary is not prepared for this. The infamous, highly esteemed *Médecins Sans Frontières* T-shirt that is supposed to afford me full diplomatic protection is hanging on the clothes-line; my stethoscope is in the hospital, and my identification papers are on a ledge in my bedroom. For the life of me, I am unable to move as the soldiers walk in my direction with assault weapons swaggering on their shoulders. I involuntarily start to hyperventilate. What else is there to do?

At first, the only audible sound I hear is the thumping of my heart. Then there is my breath. Then there is the sound of boots trudging through mud and over gravel. That sound gets louder the closer the soldiers come to me. It is now midnight.

111

The evening curfew started five and a half hours ago, at 6:30 PM to be exact. I stand still with porridge dribbling from my pot onto my bare forearms. Men in military garb approach me nearly nose-to-nose. This is my first encounter with the Rwandan military. Because we are an apolitical and neutral aid organization, any contact with them could compromise our status and damage our operations in the country. Usually, in such situations, looking directly into someone's eyes could be seen as a provocation, a hostile act, or an invitation to engage. Trembling, I have to do something and do it quickly. I must humble myself, acknowledge their greatness, and put them graciously in the power position by raising an imaginary white flag to indicate submission. But without identification, papers, or even a flag, I do the only thing I can do in this situation—I hold up my pots of potatoes, cabbage and chicken porridge. They are my white flag—my sign of surrender, my peaceful proclamation that I am unarmed, mean no harm, and come without malice. Not a single word is exchanged between us, yet an entire dialogue takes place, rich and full, articulate and sincere. To my surprise and delight, the soldiers are kind. They are not the enemy and give me their full support and respect, all in silence. Such heart talk is something exquisite and novel to me. Having tacitly given me their blessings and permission to continue with my illicit night program, I feel reassured and more confident to carry on. Initially, I saunter a bit, and then pick up the pace, scurrying on my merry way to some other place, like a mouse near a tiger.

A bit disjointed by what just happened, I stumble about mindlessly in the darkness. Still stunned, I fail to pay attention to details of the terrain around me and go astray from the usual path. I am farther than I want to be from the compound where I am supposed to be. Just down the road, there appears to be a camp for displaced people. I never visited the area before. I didn't even know it existed. Maybe I can find some needy people there. With hopes high, I near the camp which is protected by a bamboo picket fence. Inside the enclosure are hundreds of igloo-shaped huts made of leaves, straw and twigs covered with aquamarine-colored plastic sheeting. Hundreds of people live in this camp, yet it is remarkably quiet; there is not a single sound, snore or sneeze. I look through the bamboo barrier for anyone who might want my sacred and delicious food that has increased in value tenfold after the ordeal I had with the military. Unfortunately, there are no people around. Everyone is bundled up inside, incarcerated by the curfew.

As I leave the camp, I notice a man exiting his igloo to relieve himself. Elated to finally find a person, I run toward him as quietly as possible, not wanting to attract any attention. The man sees me. I raise my pot and pan in the air as a gesture of goodness. The closer I come to him, the farther away he goes from me. Before anything more can be done, he runs into his igloo, shutting the thatched door quickly behind him. Why? I stand down, defeated, motionless and numb. All the running leaves me covered with cabbage and mashed potatoes that run down my arms like lava expulsed from an unhappy volcano. Without a mouth to feed, I head home.

The almost full moon in its grand splendor does little to light my way back through the mud and muck, past the military men who have been observing me silently. We nod to one another, affirming our mutual respect for each other's positions. I can't imagine what they are thinking as they watch *White* me sneak about in the night, past curfew, covered in cabbage and mashed potatoes, carrying chicken porridge.

I would be happy to feed other families in need, but in a country where guns, machetes and soldiers are more numerous than grains of rice and beans, I understand why few would trust a stranger or wait attentively for me to unveil potatoes and porridge from a pot at midnight. With no other option, I return to the family I fed last night. Heading back in that direction, I am amazed to see in the distance the woman from the night before standing quietly with a large pot in her hands. She is waiting for me—hoping I would come again! The magical moment is a repeat of the previous night. Once again, I watch her tremble as she scoops the contents from the pot.

And then, with a big smile, she says, "*Murakoze!*"

I return home with a smile on my face and a happy heart. Mission accomplished. Back in bed, under my mosquito net, I feel safe and snug. Sneaking out to deliver dinners is just too dangerous. I have no choice but to stop. The consequences of being caught would be disastrous: I would be sent home, the hospital would have no doctor, and then what misery would come to the sick? Giving a few people some porridge and vegetables gives them a fighting chance, but is it worth the potential fallout?

I wonder if I perform this "night duty" to ease the guilt I have living in luxury while, just meters behind my bedroom window, people suffer more than anything I have ever seen. The squalor broadcast on TV in professionally produced and exquisitely edited reportages is nothing compared to the reality I see in front of, next to, over, under and around me day after day. Just over there, near our garden, is a cesspool of human carnage that is still alive… barely. The people use each other as blankets to get by… barely. Maybe they ate today, maybe not. Maybe tomorrow they will eat ... or not. And once again, I ask the same question: Does the risk of giving food to these people outweigh the consequences that I would face if caught? And once again, I answer with another question: How can I *not* risk being expelled?

18 September 1994
Sunday

My Dearest,

My mind is all over the place today, jumping from politics to paranoia to an unshakable sense of guilt.

On the political front, things are deteriorating, and I find myself increasingly agitated, paranoid and incapacitated. How can I not be? On the social front, things are no better. I hear that the patients we are treating are the very people who massacred the Tutsis. Who can I trust among them? Everyone is suspect.

A mother and her baby come to the hospital for help today. Baby is eight months old, weighs five and a half pounds, and looks skeletal. The mother has no milk or food to give to her baby, so Baby starves. We have an abundance of milk, in a powder, in a package. Just add water, mix and drink. It is like a magical potion, especially for hungry, skeletal babies. Give babies a bottle of it, and they go immediately from a wail to a coo. I give Baby a bottle of my magic and she magically settles. It is good for her, good for mom, and good for me. What is not good for me is having more than others. In fact, the hardest thing of all is having more and then some, while others have none—and then some more *none*.

19 September 1994
Monday

My Dearest,

I find the people's stories so outlandish, so outrageous, and incomprehensible that even the most gifted storytellers would be stumped to repeat them. In the people's own words:

"A person with mixed ethnicity takes the identity of the father. So, a child with a Tutsi father and a Hutu mother is Tutsi. And they are killed along with the entire family."

"They would come in groups of about 100, 200, or even 300 people, and kill all the Tutsis."

"A head was completely severed from the body right before my eyes."

"I saw a hundred people killed. One man had his head nearly all cut off, and they left him thinking he was dead, but I managed to sew him together, and he is still alive today."

"A single word on our identity cards determined our destiny. If the word on the card said 'Hutu,' we lived. If the word on the card said 'Tutsi,' we died."

"Those who were rich were killed quickly; they could pay for their quick departure, while the poorer people got chopped up slowly, alive and alone."

20 September 1994
Tuesday

My Dearest,

I go with Joseph on a walk today. Well, actually, he can't walk; his legs are still too weak to support his body, and his belly is still too distended to balance properly, so I walk for him. As I carry my boy, he clings to me like a sloth clings to its mother, arms and legs barely reaching halfway around me. He now smiles and starts to feel comfortable with his new friend—me. I am very touched because until recently, he has been quite guarded and reserved. Gradually, he seems to be giving me a chance, daring to open his heart one more time. He begins to have feelings for me as I begin to have feelings for him. I'm going to miss Joseph so much when I eventually leave. What has this little one seen in his first two years of life? What happened to his mother? How was she killed, and how did it feel to watch a dad walk away? No one knows anything about him or the circumstances that led up to him coming to the hospital. What we do know is that his father was a Hutu and his mother was a Tutsi. We also know she was exterminated because she was labeled an unwanted cockroach.

Seeing Joseph grow is delightful. He came to the hospital as a malnourished piece of listless flesh, exsanguinating from bloody diarrhea, and now he is completely cured. His appetite is ravenous; he is growing like a weed, and he begins to trust. I'm looking for someone to adopt him because he is now an orphan. His mother is dead, his father deserted him, and his stepmother is indifferent. But who will take him? No one has the strength or money to raise someone else's child during this tragic time. Laurent is sensitive and compassionate and would be the best for the position, but his mother is dead, his father is old, and there are already eight children to look after in his family.

Another candidate is Lilliose, one of our medical assistants. She is 23 years old, kind, pretty, married, and already a mom. Before the genocide, she was rich and privileged; her clothes attest to that. Now, she is poor but pretends to be what she isn't, behind a fortified façade of fancy. Lilliose could step in as mom, but I see her wearing clothes that were donated to the displaced people who have no clothes. I am not sure she is the right person to care for my Joseph. He needs a doting mother, not a princess. He needs stability, a good education, and lots of love. Yes, he needs lots of love. Where am I going to find a suitable home for him? What is suitable? Going with me to America, where racism is the rule, does not seem better than his options here in Rwanda. While the villagers may not have much, they have their land, culture, traditions, pride and dignity. Rwanda is their home, their cradle, their birthright.

In school, I was told Abraham Lincoln abolished slavery, and Rosa Parks defiantly sparked a revolution that brought American apartheid down. I mean no disrespect to them, but this could not be further from the truth. Today in America, Black people remain enslaved in a covert climate of racism. Today's slavery is not flaunted in public squares with shackles around muscular necks as beads of sweat drip down black flesh with White bidders clamoring to possess a piece of them. No. Today's racism is not mentioned in public places or hanging from tree branches with a noose around necks. KKK white robes with pointy head coverings aren't there either. But when it is safe and no people of color are around, slavery and racism are still very much alive and well.

Joseph is king in his nation and pauper in mine. As much as I have come to love this little boy and would like to take him with me when I leave, Joseph must remain in Africa with his people. I must find a home with a family who will love him. I can support him financially so he won't be a burden to the people who agree to adopt him, but finding such a family is the problem. I have asked dozens of people to take him, but either they are not in a position to do so at this time, or they ask for an exorbitant amount of money for their childcare services. Seeing little Joseph as a prime opportunity to secure foreign funds to gain a financial advantage won't happen on my watch. I wonder how it would feel to be his dad.

21 September 1994
Wednesday

My Dearest,

Joseph and I again spend some quality time together. After bathing him, I feed him his usual: avocado, baby bananas and protein biscuits. We then go on our daily walk. I hold him ever so close to me, pretending to be mother, father and friend all wrapped up in one. Whoever he needs me to be, I will be. We cannot speak to one another with words, but we can speak *heart*, a language so few know in this world of ours today. Somehow, I know he loves me. This is what keeps me going. I never imagined a little abandoned boy left on the front steps of a makeshift hospital somewhere in Africa could give me such an experience of unconditional love and make my world turn around so fast that I am dizzy.

After our walk, I return to the ward and try to give Joseph to one of the ward nurses. He refuses to release my finger. His grip is surprisingly tenacious, and letting go is not negotiable. It is like withdrawing a mother's nipple from a suckling child who is still starving. Hmm! I stand there a bit awkward. The nurses chuckle and do not miss the opportunity to tease me: "*Monsieur docteur, hier, Joseph a crié 'Papa' quand vous l'avez quitté* [Doctor, yesterday, Joseph cried out "Papa" when you left him]!" He thinks I am Papa—his Papa. The allure of fathering him is a common mind game I play with myself. I could "papa" him and give him a chance at a better life. But how? I know nothing of fatherhood. But then, does any father know what to do the first time around? And how could I leave my path to serve the poor, become domesticated, and assume the responsibilities of a householder? Having a child at this point would turn my life upside down and inside out. Logic says I should stick to my path of service because I can help a lot more people as a doctor than as a father and householder. But what about love? Love is never logical and certainly never the shortest distance between two points. It is also not known for its efficiency when going from A to B. So what should I do with my little Joseph?

22 September 1994
Thursday

My Dearest,

Today, the military makes a surprise visit to a nearby camp that houses hundreds of displaced people and forces them out. The people are told to return to their homes. Indifferent to the plight of their fellow countrymen, the men in uniforms burn the people's huts and destroy whatever infrastructure they so painstakingly created. The military's action sets the people in motion once again. Without shoes, they walk or limp barefoot to anywhere on unpaved roads, carrying the few possessions they have on their heads. They are given no leeway or extra time for extenuating circumstances. The military is adamant about closing this chapter and shoos everyone away, as if they were animals. Mother Nature also jumps on the military's bandwagon as she opens her sky and spits randomly on the people, drenching their worn-out rags with cold rain. The fabric clings to their skin as if alive, clutching to life, begging not to be left behind. People shiver. Legs tremble. Dampness penetrates. Streams of displaced people follow other displaced people in single file as they all march mechanically in other directions, perhaps to the hills, maybe to their villages, and possibly to nowhere. No one knows what or who awaits them back in their respective homes. Most are still too traumatized to return and find out. I thought the fleeing had stopped. I was wrong. The displacement continues.

As the people walk through the mud, their toes grip the gravel to prevent themselves from slipping and losing their footing. Mothers strap their babies to their backs with a piece of fabric, and their hands clutch a pot or two. An available arm cradles another one of their children as they balance a basin or a sack of something on their heads. And the cold and the rain and the mud make it all so brutally unfair.

The international community organizes transport trucks to take the people back home into the interior of the country, but nearly no one goes. Incentives are offered to those willing to risk returning home—food and non-food items are part of the package. But the people will not leave the UN peacekeepers, who they wishfully believe will protect them from rebels and government forces. Apparently, the people don't know that the UN mandate prohibits the peacekeepers from using weapons. They are here as a …. They are here to …. I am not sure why they are here. I'm not sure anyone knows why they are here. To be honest, I am not sure the UN peacekeepers know why they are here. I suppose their presence gives the people a sense of security, even though it is a false one.

23 September 1994
Friday

My Dearest,

With people on the move, we go out to assess population shifts and get updated on the current military pressures. As we drive around the area, people on the roads look at us in our brand-new four-wheel-drive, high-tech, luxury Land Cruiser. I feel terribly uncomfortable with this lavish pageantry, and I turn my head away from them, feeling ashamed. The reality of the divide between them and us, poor and rich, is too real and too close to home. I find it unbearably difficult to drive past people without offering them a ride. They carry their lives on their heads and shoulders and their families on their backs as they hobble and hug the side of the road. We have space in the vehicle to carry one, two, three, or even more of them, but for insurance and security reasons, this is not allowed. In this current unstable political climate, transporting locals could be misconstrued by opposing factions as helping the enemy, which could put our work and lives in jeopardy.

As we pass people walking on the road, mud spits from the vehicle's rear wheels and soils them. They don't seem to mind. As they walk in perfect single-file lines, our vehicle deranges their line formations. Again, the people don't seem to mind. They just smile and generously wave at us.

With displaced people constantly on the move, we search for the temporary settlements where they gather. It is safer in numbers, so people prefer each other's company. Eventually, we find a large group of displaced people camped out near the UN peacekeepers, stationed on the top of a steep hill. It is windy and cold up there, but this is where the people have built their huts. They clearly feel safer near the peacekeepers.

We make our way up the hill to see how the people are doing. After quite a hike, we arrive. Everyone is elated to see us and becomes very animated. They feel protected when we are nearby, less exposed and vulnerable. Hundreds of people gather around and listen attentively to our questions and to each other's responses. It is moving how polite and respectful they are to us and each other. Despite there being hundreds of people, it is quiet—so quiet you can hear the sound of silence.

"Do you get all of your food rations? How much do you receive? Does the plastic sheeting protect you from the rain? Do you have blankets? Do the soldiers harass you? Did they take your boys away to join ranks with their troops?"

We continue bombarding the people with more and more questions in order to assess their overall physical, emotional and mental well-being. They answer candidly yet humbly, and always with gratitude—lots of gratitude.

These site visits allow us to keep our finger on the people's pulse. Knowing their daily challenges helps us respond more promptly and effectively to meet their changing needs in this unstable and highly volatile environment. In this way, we hope to minimize further suffering, morbidity and mortality.

The information we gather is firsthand surveillance that we use in our reports and share with international agencies both in Rwanda and abroad. Unfortunately, these reports are far too intrusive and revealing for the government, which does not appreciate international attention or public scrutiny of its people or its conduct. As a consequence of our reports, the government accuses us of meddling in their internal affairs.

24 September 1994
Saturday

My Dearest,

I am not sure if I am in charge of the hospital or if the hospital is in charge of me. It becomes clearer by the day that my hopes, wishes, and aspirations to help and heal people are mere mirages.

One of the orphans we are treating is eight years old. She lost both her mother and father in the conflict, but luckily, she still has her *older* sister, who is eleven years old. By default, this older sister is now her baby sister's guardian and guardian angel. She cares for her as a mother would care for her own baby. Today, sadly, baby sister died. Now this guardian angel has no mother, father, sister, baby, or anyone else left to guard.

Another child who is being treated with the strongest drug we have for Shigella continues to exsanguinate from a very bloody diarrhea. Just eighteen months young, she bleeds to death. As her mother watches the slow ooze of her daughter's life, she sobs, making it especially hard for me. Usually, the people silently bear the pain of a loved one passing. They are stoic in my company, so I see and hear nothing. They seem to be protecting me from their pain. Silence makes it easier for me to cope with the crass reality that I am essentially impotent when death comes to stake its claim.

Speaking of silence, the extermination of the Tutsis was a silent genocide. People tell me that while the Tutsis were being slaughtered, they had to remain silent to prevent their loved ones from coming to their rescue and meeting the same fate. Survivors of the genocide were also silent. Oftentimes, they would conceal themselves in ceilings, under floors, or behind doors when visited by their friendly neighbors holding machetes. They heard and witnessed their parents and children being killed and had no other choice but to be silent or risk ending up a collection of unrecognizable bits and pieces in a pile by the front door. The killers who hacked people to death were silent, too. They wanted their crimes and identities to go unnoticed. Hopefully, in the aftermath of the genocide, silence will be silenced. Survivors of the slaughter can no longer be silent. Their stories must be told if reconciliation and enduring peace stand a chance.

Mom's tears tell her story powerfully as her baby bleeds to death. I have done everything possible. There is nothing more I can do except join Mom and watch her baby die. Her tears quietly come. They silently roll down her cheeks. It is hard for me—very hard for me. The sense of inadequacy I feel in this situation is unbearable. The emotions stirred when someone is dying affect me more than death itself. Unable to alleviate Mom's pain or do anything to save her daughter, I put together a care package of clothes, blankets, soap, oil, sugar, food, and more food, partially for Mom but mostly to lessen my own pain. I would give her the world if it were mine to give—anything to stop these rip-my-heart-out tears.

25 September 1994
Sunday

My Dearest,

Again, I had a good time with little Joseph today. He has gained some weight since we started caring for him, and his demeanor is more alive and engaging. He is starting to look more like a little boy and less like a crotchety, cranky old man in skin and bones. When he first arrived, he paid no attention to me. Now, when I come into his room, he gets animated and effervescent, similar to the fizz in champagne. Over the past few days, he has started lifting his arms in the air as I near his bed. This gesture means "lift me up" in *Joseph*, a new personal language he is experimenting with. I do as he wishes and lift him high in the sky. Then I squeeze his little bony body and hold him close to me. He responds by resting his head on my chest. And both of us are happy.

Joseph still does not know how to walk. He can stand in place, but taking his first step is still a skill he has yet to learn. With support, he can do the foxtrot, but without a hand to hold, he falls to the ground. I've been trying to teach him how to walk. Standing just a few feet in front of him, I lean forward and say, "Come, Joseph, come." I extend my arms toward him, and he extends his arms toward me, trying desperately to make his way into them. "Come, Joseph, come," I say again. Standing bent over with both of his forearms resting on his legs for stability, he arches his back, stretches his neck upward, and looks into my eyes. He hesitates to take his first step. I move nearer to him, so close I can feel his breath. "Come, Joseph, come." He wants to walk. He wants to show me he can do it, so with all his might, he hobbles, shuffles, and shifts until he eventually manages to take a couple of steps forward alone.

Completely overjoyed, I lovingly scoop him into my arms and whisk him up, up, and away on Aladdin's amazing carpet, far into the fields of green and around the ravines outside the hospital compound. I witnessed Joseph take his first steps, a proud moment for both of us. As I walk, I hold my boy tight and talk with him as though he can understand me. It is what I imagine a real father-to-son talk should, could, and would be. The wind is tender, the sun is warm, and the greens are as diverse as the shades of brown skin worn proudly by the people here. No cares, no worries, nothing but the two of us—leaves in the wind on a fall afternoon that leave no footprints. I *coochy-coochy coo* him and then tickle his tummy with my stubble and kiss his hairless head. He isn't a giggler, but his eyes get really big and show much excitement when he is happy. We enjoy. Little white cotton-ball clouds pass coyly overhead. And if I'm not mistaken, they enjoy, too. It is a superb day.

As we go deeper into what appears to be endless fields of rolling hills, I start my heart-to-heart with Joseph. He can't understand me, but I have to have this monologue to convince myself that putting him in an orphanage is the right thing to do. Actually, with the project soon closing and my imminent departure nearing, it is the only choice I have; at least, this is what I convince myself to believe. What a shame that, in spite of all my interviewing and searching, I could not find him a foster family to adopt him. To be honest, no one wanted him.

Joseph listens intently to my incomprehensible gibberish while resting his head on my chest. Engrossed in my own monologue, I accidentally stray from the footpath into unfamiliar fields. The thought of stepping on a landmine crosses my mind. Landmines are as common in Rwanda as bananas on a bush. During the genocide, landmines were indiscriminately placed around the country. For our safety, we were given strict instructions never to stray from the main footpath. I slow my stride and look more carefully at the terrain for black boxes— clandestine killers that don't require any human resources to detonate. They prey on the nonchalance of the nonchalant and target the innocent, unsuspecting pedestrians on the path. I am suddenly seized by terror. What a terrible way to go—a click, crackle and pop! This is not how I want either of us to go.

I try my best to make my way out of this labyrinth of death, but fear gets the better of me, and I completely lose my way. I no longer see the hospital. All I see is a hostile landscape that no longer seems to be a friend but an impediment in our path to peace and freedom. Stumbling about, I do my best to trace my steps in reverse. The heart-to-heart with Joseph regarding our unavoidable separation will need no further clarification or justification if I step on a mine.

Back, forth, left, right, I cautiously slide my feet along an unfamiliar dirt path, likely laden with landmines. My nervous system is in overdrive. Meters down the path, I quickly realize I am not alone. Shocked but not surprised, to my left is a skull; to my right is a femur; in front of me are more skulls, and behind me are a number of African headdresses. Actually, they are carrying rings made of dried grass in the shape of a bagel that women typically wear on their heads to carry heavy sacks of potatoes, yams, rice, and other goods to the market. Many of these carrying rings are among the bones scattered about. This place was a killing field. The Tutsis were chased up these hills from all directions, only to meet their shortcut to heaven. Wild dogs consumed their flesh but left their bones and headgear. How can I pretend that these killing fields don't exist when I am standing in the middle of one? How can I deny that people hacked Tutsis to death when there are dozens of them decapitated and dismembered all around me?

I go into a state of shock and instinctively know to cover Joseph's eyes. Whatever he has seen of the genocide is more than he ever should have seen. He doesn't need to see what is in front, under, and all around us now. I quicken my pace in an attempt to rescue him from this defiled place. Whenever I near something terrifying, I put my hand over his face and eyes, and pretend to play peek-a-boo with him. With so many disturbing displays of death scattered about like driftwood on a beach after a storm, it takes considerable dexterity to distract him. I need to process everything quickly and force myself not to linger in my thoughts. We have to leave this site immediately; Joseph's mother could be one of the pieces.

26 September 1994
Monday

My Dearest,

Only preventive healthcare measures can tame the ruthless and unrelenting diseases that are decimating the people here. Health education in schools would be ideal, but there are no schools. Educating people about washing their hands before eating and after going to the bathroom would be helpful, but no one has soap, clean water, toilet paper, or even toilets, for that matter. Encouraging people to drink boiled water would reduce the disease burden, but most can't afford gas, and firewood is in short supply. Often, people have to walk for hours to find any. Those who manage to find some would certainly not use the priceless commodity to boil water. They would use it to cook their food—that is, if they had any food to cook. Given the poverty and deprivation here, the most effective way to prevent disease is, without question, vaccines.

Vaccination campaigns are quick, simple and effective. To orchestrate them successfully, vaccines are prepackaged in Europe and expeditiously flown to a location somewhere in the world. Meticulous management of vaccines is essential to ensure that the cold chain remains unbroken. This means the vaccine must be continuously refrigerated without interruption at a specific temperature from the day it was produced in a laboratory to the moment it is injected into the arm or buttocks of a person. Given the logistical challenges in areas with no roads, transport, electricity, or even water, sustaining the cold chain is nothing short of a miracle. We like miracles. Because of vaccinations, polio, mumps, measles, tetanus, and other childhood illnesses are nearly nonexistent today. As a result, infant mortality has been significantly reduced.

We have set up a free vaccination clinic today and expect thousands of eager recipients to come. Logistically, we are prepared and ready for the onslaught. Everyone is in place manning a table, and everything we need to get the job done is on hand and ready to go. Now we just sit and wait patiently.

To our amazement, attendance is pitiful. Only a few people come. Did we fail to announce our arrival? Did people forget or confuse the location? Everything is free, so why wouldn't people come running? Is it ignorance or arrogance on our part that we assumed everyone would rush the lines to protect themselves from the deadliness of diseases that dominate their frail lives? Why wouldn't the people want this security in a country where the only sure and secure thing is suffering, suffering, and more suffering? How senseless it would be to survive the genocide and then succumb to an infinitesimal virus. I ask some people nearby why they don't come for our free vaccinations. They say we are working with their enemies and using needles to infect villagers with disease. I can't believe that anyone would think we would hurt them in any way. But then, does the word "trust" even remain in their vocabularies after what they witnessed and endured? Did the White man not gift smallpox-infested blankets to the Native Americans to rid them from their land? Did the White man not bring an equally devastating genocide of sorts to the people of Africa through colonization and cull their population through a notorious slave trade? Can the people here ever trust White people after what we did to them?

27 September 1994
Tuesday

My Dearest,

Mother Nature accompanies me on my jog today. Her hills show off their bountiful beauty. They seem to say, "If you've got it, flaunt it." They are rambunctiously alive and strut their stuff for everyone to go gaga. I, too, go gaga and find myself in awe. Mother is unabashedly resplendent and in her element here. If she could talk, I wonder what she would say to me right about now.

Four scintillating rainbows wrap the sky above Lake Kivu. Their colors rival a peacock's plumes and take my breath away. But no need to worry; I'm in Mother's hands and heart. Nothing can harm me, not while she's around. Mother can't talk with words, but she can move my spirit and make me feel many sensations in the fullness of her presence. She can also cook. Her *soul food* is pure deliciousness. My soul, as a result, is well nourished and satisfied right about now.

Rwanda is often called *Mille Collines* [one thousand hills] because the terrain is so hilly. From the sky, the contours of the land resemble the curves of a voluptuous goddess idolized in those esteemed Renaissance paintings—divine and sublime. Prior to the genocide, Rwanda was con-sidered to be the pearl of Africa.

As I jog, people bless me with radiant smiles, while dozens of children jog alongside me, trying to get a touch of my hairy arms and legs. They have seen something that looks like me in the wild, something hairy that walks on all fours—a gorilla. Yes, some children actually think I am a gorilla. They stare at me with innocent curiosity, like when they saw fire for the first time. It's fun. They like the attention and affection I give them, and I like the attention and affection they give me.

The children beg for biscuits. *"Donnez-moi un biscuit* [Give me a biscuit]," they shout. Back home in the States, we have the muffin man. Here, they have me—the biscuit boy.

28 September 1994
Wednesday

My Dearest,

What a terrible, terrible day. Little Joseph was taken from his hospital home and placed in an orphanage in a neighboring district, Kibuye. No one told me of today's plans to transfer him, so I was shocked and shaken when I looked for him and found he was gone. To add salt to my wound, the nurses tell me Joseph started crying when they took him away. They say he cried because the man who took him away wasn't me. Maybe or maybe not, but one thing is certain—we loved each other. He smiled when he saw me; he didn't smile for anyone else. And he would crawl into my arms and rest his head on me. He didn't do that with anyone else either. Gosh, I truly believed I was his "Papa." What a gift it would have been to father him. What a privilege it would have been to give him a better life. But would life in America have been better? On paper, it's supposed to be. Just look at our revered American Declaration of Independence: "We hold these truths to be self-evident, that *all men are created equal*, that they are endowed by their Creator with certain unalienable Rights, that among these are Life, Liberty and the pursuit of Happiness." How ironic that Thomas Jefferson, a co-author of this coveted declaration, owned 200 Black slaves, and that 41 out of the 56 signatories endorsing the declaration owned slaves too— Black African slaves. Could it be that our highly esteemed Founding Fathers who authored the Declaration of Independence forgot to include people of color in their magnificent prose? The only thing that is colorful or color-friendly about their declaration is the parchment paper it was written on. In reality, life in America is hard, if not hellacious, for people of any color. Joseph has had enough hostility and adversity in his short life to last a lifetime. He doesn't need any more.

I want to see my little Joseph. I want to go to the orphanage and spend more time with him, get my fix of his love, feel needed, and be wanted. It's been less than a day since he left the hospital, and I'm already missing him too much.

129

29 September 1994
Thursday

My Dearest,

Mabanza has changed. It was once a bustling little outpost town with displaced people camping out in and on every imaginable habitable place. Now it is a deserted ghost town. Since the displaced people's camp was burned down and the residents were forced to leave, our hospital has only a few patients. Soon there will be no need for us here. The hospital will be dismantled, our makeshift clinics disassembled, the staff relieved of their posts, and I will not be playing hide-and-seek anymore—looking for the poorest of the poor to feed the hungriest of the hungry late in the evenings. This means no more burning myself with mashed potatoes or fearing for my life when encountering military patrols enforcing the evening curfew. No more cerebral malaria, bloody diarrhea, doubt, disdain or death. I can't believe it. Can it really be so?

30 September 1994
Friday

My Dearest,

The hospital cooks—a few teenage girls—stand like witches around a cauldron, boiling potatoes for the inpatients' dinners. The girls meticulously peel potatoes, careful not to waste any of the precious potato pulp. They were given strict instructions to safeguard the food, which is by far the most valuable life-sustaining resource we have at our disposal during this time of war. The food we provide is limited and reserved exclusively for the hospitalized patients.

I happen to be passing by our makeshift kitchen when I notice a frail sliver of a woman shuffling toward the boiling cauldron. Her gait quivers. She is weak; she is worn; she is worried. She looks to be about 80 years old, an age not often reached in the rigors of this country. I stand off to the side and watch her. The old woman approaches the young girls ever so timidly and asks them for a potato. They are young enough to be her great-grandchildren. She is old enough to be their great-grandmother. But that doesn't matter. The full wrath of these young girls is unleashed on this aged, speck of a soul, and she is verbally flogged, then sent away. After all, they have been given strict instructions to reserve the rations for patients only.

The old woman retreats and sits on a tree trunk near the sizzling cauldron. I remain out of sight, off to the side, still and silent, but inside I am deeply disturbed to see how this grandma is being treated. If she were my own grandmother, would I let her go hungry? Would I leave her brokenhearted on a tree trunk in an open field? Absolutely not! Truly speaking, what harm is there in giving a single potato to a frail grandmother who is near the end of her life? Why can't we bend the rules just this once? Would it confuse the staff? Could this simple act of kindness send mixed messages to them about following our policies and adhering to our rules?

I look at this woman all hunched over, hungry and destitute, hopeless and helpless, wanting a single potato. It is insane that I am standing here tormented over a potato! How distressingly indecisive I have become—unable to distinguish right from wrong, or wrong from right. What is the right thing to do? The frail elder has nearly a century under her belt. She has defied all odds—warding off illness, beating the war, and surviving life to carry her ancestors forward. She is regal. She is noble—an African queen in her own right, who now cowers over a tree trunk, stick in hand for balance, looking at a potato in a cauldron.

I discourage handouts because they only disable people, but really, what is a potato? It's just one potato. I could discreetly give her one. Nobody needs to know. A single potato would feed more than her body—it would feed her spirit. It would give a little nutrition and a lot of hope. A single potato would give this woman another day, perhaps another week.

Unable to bear this any longer, I pull out a 1,000 Rwandan Franc bill, which is about 25 U.S. dollars. I fully understand the potential fallout of giving money to people here, but I have to make an exception for this grandma. This money is enough to buy food for two months in these warring times. It is the equivalent of 50 hours of hard labor in times of peace. In times of war, 1,000 Rwandan Francs becomes the equivalent of a lifetime. I fold the note ever so discreetly into a small square, which I hide in the palm of my hand. I then look to the left and then to the right, making sure the coast is clear before heading in Grandma's direction. Pretending not to notice her sitting on the fallen tree trunk, I casually take her hand. She is surprised, but takes hold of my hand as a reciprocal gesture of kindness. Without anyone noticing, I press the folded bill into the palm of her hand and squeeze her fingers tightly around it. She does not realize there is anything in my hand. As her grip loosens and she starts retracting her hand, the money stays in my hand. I quickly re-engage her hand and squeeze it around the folded bill. I hope she won't show it to the others. She still doesn't understand the small fortune she holds, so I squeeze her hand with both of my hands and look intensely into her eyes. She somehow is able to read my mind and comes to understand. I then walk away as though I had never been there. Once I am a safe distance away from her, I turn and see her discover all of creation in the palm of her hand. I can feel her rapture. I could drown in her tears.

1 October 1994
Friday

My Dearest,

With the dismantling of the hospital and everything we so painstakingly planned and produced, our creative talents end in nothingness. Whatever we humans create in this fine world is eventually destroyed and recycled. And we are once again reminded of our powerlessness and ephemeral position on the planet. Everything is temporary. From makeshift hospitals to huts and camps constructed from leaves, everything is just a moment in time. Nothing stands still, and nothing is intended to remain standing for very long. Rocks are reduced to sand, mountains are eroded by wind, steel rusts, and water washes away shorelines. Nothing lasts longer than a moment.

We humans praise ourselves generously for the good work we do. We celebrate our accomplishments with applause and accolades. Bronze, silver, and gold medals, platinum plaques, and tinseled trophies are among the toys we get when we do exceptionally well to show and tell about our achievements for years to come. And world records are recorded in halls of fame and written up for posterity in believe-it-or-not series on bookshelves. But everything is only temporary, and in time, someone new will come along and outdo us. We are inevitably forgotten and replaced, as are all things. Regardless of our strength and purported greatness, the hills over there in the background are stronger and greater than we will ever be.

Sometimes, I wonder what we are doing here. If everything is just temporary, what are we really accomplishing?

2 October 1994
Sunday

My Dearest,

With the camp in ashes, the project closing, and my time here nearing its final hours, I make my way to the orphanage to see Joseph. I am like a child going to an amusement park. I can't contain my excitement knowing I will soon see my little boy again.

After about an hour's drive, I finally arrive. The orphanage is simple and clean, with about 60 orphaned children running here and there. When the children see me, they think Santa Claus has descended from the sky to bring them heaven. They are beaming like fluorescent lights and fizzing like ice cream phosphates. Unlike children in the West, who expect goodies in socks hanging from a fireplace and gifts wrapped up in big boxes under an exquisitely decorated Christmas tree, these kids are different. They don't want any gifts. They want a loving mother and father and a home to call their own. The children have seen foreigners come from time to time and leave with one or even two children who become part of a family somewhere over a rainbow. No one ever knows whose endearing little fingers will touch the heartstrings of one of the visitors, who may very well adopt them and take them to a place far away—a place beyond the clouds and behind the stars, somewhere over a rainbow.

When the children see me, they jump up and down and wrestle to get hold of my hand. The competition among the young players is fierce, and they quickly understand it is more realistic to simply settle for a finger. And the winners are ten children, each claiming their conquest—a single finger. There is absolute euphoria in this place, something rare in Rwanda nowadays. The children, now shielded by walls and protected in a permanent structure, seem to have forgotten what they had seen, heard, smelled, felt and tasted only a few months ago as their parents were permanently taken away from them.

Anchored by ten little ones desperately holding onto my fingers, I wade through the crowd, looking for Joseph. He is not among them. I can't see him being able to compete with such joyousness. He is a solemn child, serious, focused and loyal. He would not have been distracted by the play of the children around him. And besides, he still can't walk. In the hospital, he never interacted very much with other people; it wasn't in his nature to be social. He was just an old soul in a child's costume.

I continue looking for Joseph amid the commotion and as the children jostle with one another to get hold of an already claimed finger. I can only hope he is here somewhere. What if someone has already adopted him? I would be so devastated, though I suppose adoption would be the best for him. As I inch around the corner to the sleeping quarters, I enter a room filled with tidy beds and folded linens. Each bed is vacant, except one. In this bed sits my sweet Joseph, quietly twiddling his little fingers. I gently untangle my hands from the children clinging to me, still hoping for a miracle. They understand I have not come for them and quickly scurry away like mice being chased by a broom.

Joseph is not distracted by all the noise and continues to explore his fingers, as if discovering them for the first time in his short-lived life. I stand near the doorway and watch him quietly for a bit. He doesn't know I have come. At one point, he looks up from his captivating fingers and sees me. A glow of love and light illuminates his face. He sparkles with a smile so bright that light itself is humbled. As has been the case so many times before, he raises his arms, extends them toward me, and says without saying, "Hold me, Papa." I approach his bed, and as I did so many times before, I extend my arms toward him and say without saying, "Hold me, child." He does. And then he tumbles into my arms.

Oh, this little boy knows how to rub me right in the heart. I hold him, and he holds me. Though his arms aren't big enough to wrap around my body, he tries really hard. And in this way, we are together.

Joseph and I take a stroll around the compound. We enjoy. It is like old times. Time stands still. Words don't matter. The twilight doesn't dull his light. We are at peace this way.

After roaming together for almost an hour, sadly, the driver reminds me that the evening curfew is rapidly approaching. With the sun nearly gone from the sky, I reluctantly return to the orphanage and enter Joseph's bedroom. This is when a very bad thing happens. When I start to unwrap my boy's arms from around me to return him to his bed, I notice his light is gone. He looks directly into my eyes, but he doesn't see me; he sees through me. There is this moment of truth. Joseph realizes I have not come to take him home with me. He realizes that I am joining ranks with all the others who have abandoned him in his life. The flame that had been kindled so tenderly between us has now been definitively extinguished. He finally understands that I have come only to say goodbye. Unable to bear the pain of being abandoned again, Joseph seals his soul and casts out the one and only remaining key. He will never allow himself to be hurt again. I am now the color of invisible to him as I walk away.

3 October 1994
Monday

My Dearest,

Weeks ago, I wrote an order to administer intramuscular quinine to a child dying of malaria. It was our only hope left to save her life. Nurse Ratshit saw my order and forbade me to use it because it was against the organization's protocol; IM quinine can, in rare cases, cause abscesses. Given the gravity of the child's condition and her poor prognosis, I felt breaking protocol was the appropriate medical action to take. After all, are we not here to save lives? And besides, if this child should develop an abscess, we could treat it.

Nurse Ratshit has surprisingly not returned to the medical ward since I asserted my authority and disobeyed her order. I thought perhaps her absence was a truce, or maybe even an apology for her conduct. I was so wrong. Today, I discover she has been preparing for my expulsion from the project. She wants me fired. How do I know this? Because my teammates secretly met with me this evening and told me so. They also told me that she has come to the end of her contract and is leaving tomorrow, and taking me along with her to Kigali to present her case against me to the administration. Since no teammates will be accompanying me, I will have no support and no way to defend myself against her allegations. As head of the project, her judgment, critique, and recommendation to the administration will carry the greatest weight.

Somehow, having me thrown out of the organization will bring her untold satisfaction—her final retribution for the time I declined her offer to be sexually intimate with her. Huh.

"Whatever you do, do not get into the car tomorrow," my teammates warn.

Later in the evening, the antagonist in our drama springs the news. "You will be leaving the project tomorrow." I was already prepared for this directive. "Pack your bags and be ready when the driver comes," she arrogantly announces.

4 October 1994
Tuesday

My Dearest,

A car pulls up to the driveway. The entire house staff and my teammates gather to bid us farewell. Nurse Ratshit has her luggage loaded into the trunk and already sits in the passenger compartment. I stand with my backpack outside the car.

"Get in the car," she commands in a supercilious tone with a disingenuous smile plastered on her face as she is now in full view of the entire staff and team.

"You know, I was thinking, since the project is still open and the other staff members will be here, I think I'll stay a few more days," I say, knowing full well that I can't get in the car.

"No, Dr. Cary. You need to get in the car so we can go to Kigali together," she counters, still with a smile plastered on her face, as she does not want the staff to see her malice and vindictiveness. She works very hard to keep her smile.

We all know what going to Kigali means. It will be an unprecedented lynching and a public humiliation for me.

"No, I think I'll stay a few more days and come later with the others," I repeat.

"You will get into the car now," she insists, still working hard to sustain her pretend smile for those standing nearby.

"No, I think I'll stay a few more days and come later with the others," I repeat again like a broken record.

And then it happens. It does. She loses it. She completely loses all self-control and shouts at the top of her lungs, "You will get in the car immediately. Get in the car!" she roars. "Do as you are told. I command you to get in the car!"

The woman's face is bright red. Her jugulars are engorged and protrude from her neck. Sweat beads up on her forehead, and her pinkened lips are distorted beyond recognition. The staff stiffen and look blankly ahead. They have all witnessed

137

this woman's wickedness numerous times before, but such a display of hatred catches them off guard, and they don't know what to make of it. All they can do is watch this woman self-destruct from her own hate and vengeance.

I stand at attention along with the others and just stare at the ground. I do not budge, nor do I say another word. She's trapped, beaten and powerless, like a caged, rabid animal driven mad by her own rage. Her plot is foiled. Without any alternative, she has no choice but to leave alone.

5 October 1994
Wednesday

My Dearest,

The head of our mission unexpectedly calls and asks me to come to his office. I know that he has already met with Nurse Ratshit, and I expect he will chastise me, then throw me out of the country. If this should happen, I will be heartbroken. I spent so much of my life studying to be a doctor for this organization—to be a doctor without borders.

Hours later, I find myself at the door of the man in charge, cowering like a soon-to-be scolded puppy. I have never met this man before, and I have no idea what to expect. How can I possibly defend myself? What proof do I have? I have nothing but words to make my case. Where are my patients and staff to defend and vouch for me? As I wait in the reception area, I bombard myself with unending questions and work myself into a frenzy. A guillotine is about to seal my fate.

The head honcho's door finally opens, and I am invited inside. At this point, I am on the verge of hyperventilating. To my surprise, a kind, gracious, and gentle-spirited man warmly welcomes me. I am immediately put at ease and finally able to relax enough to exhale. Then something miraculous happens.

"Dr. Cary, your teammates have bravely come forward and shared with me what you have endured since coming to the project. I had no idea, and I am so sorry for failing to protect you. The head of project assigned to your mission did not act responsibly, nor did she respect or uphold the organization's fundamental principles to support patients. Please forgive me."

I sit still and stare at this stranger in front of me. I don't know what just happened. I don't know what to say. I don't know what to do. Weeks of grief and anguish have been cleared from the slate, and I've been exonerated and hailed at the same time. I assumed my teammates' silence and failure to defend me against the head nurse's brutality all these weeks was a vote of confidence for her and a condemnation of me. But I had it all wrong. My teammates' silence was the only way they could protect themselves from getting trapped in the same cycle of abuse and brutality from this wicked, vindictive woman who was also their boss. When they finally realized to what extent she would go to destroy me, they put themselves at risk and went of their own accord, behind her back, to the head of the organization to defend me. I am speechless.

"Please accept my sincere apologies," he continues. "Our project has been terminated, but if you want to stay here I would be more than happy to help you find another project."

"Yes, that would be great. Thank you," I say hesitantly and somewhat cautiously, as I find it hard to fully believe him. "Thank you so much," I repeat, a bit shaken. It is difficult for me to grasp what just happened.

A tale I heard many times as a child comes to mind. I have personally experienced such footprints in my own life, so I can attest to this tale's authenticity. Once upon a time, a pious man dies and goes to heaven. He says to the *One* in charge, "God, throughout my life, You and I walked together, and there were two pairs of footprints in the sand—Yours and mine. I don't understand why every time I had hard times, I couldn't help but notice that there was only one pair of footprints in the sand. Where were you when I needed you most? Why did you abandon me in my greatest times of need?" And God replied, "I never abandoned you. Those were my footprints—I was carrying you."

6 October 1994
Thursday

My Dearest,

Last month, I boarded a plane for Africa after seeing some disturbing images on a television screen at a bed and breakfast in a small rural town in Wisconsin. Blindly following my heart, I dropped everything and embarked on a journey to a very dark place on the other side of a very big ocean. It might not have been rational at the time, but is love ever rational?

I was in love with humanity and believed I could make a difference. One month later, I can say with certainty that I have not made much of a difference. Sure, I did my best, and while some might argue that my best was not good enough, I did try. A few people got a potato or two, others got some respect, and a few ended up with a bit more hope. Perhaps some people will miss me. I certainly will miss them. I will also miss my innocence. I came a boy, and now, with death under my belt, I have quickly reached manhood here. Being a man is not all that different from being a boy. The only difference between the two is that a man can't go home to mom and cry anymore.

With the project officially closed, we close our suitcases, then our rooms and the house, load the car and look around. The hospital is empty, the camp is burned, the workers are gone, and the landscape swallows every trace of us. The birds now claim what was once our garden, and the abounding banana bushes scattered around the grounds, like sprinkles on a cupcake, wave in the wind as if bidding us farewell. There is no one left to tell our story. There is no trace that we were ever here. And we are humbled.

Arms wrap tightly around our Rwandan mom and dads. We will never see them again, but we will take them with us wherever and whenever, for they are a part of us. Then, slowly, we drive out of the driveway, through the town, up and down the hills, and along a much-neglected dirt road back to Kigali, where, unlike a month ago, signs of life begin to try again.

7 October 1994
Friday

My Dearest,

With the closure of our project, our team is disbanded and will return to Europe. Amid such dire need, I cannot accept leaving, so I look for another assignment. After numerous calls, I find an opportunity just over the border in Uganda.

MSF arranges transport, and off I go to visit the project. Once over the border, I cannot believe my eyes. I was under the impression that Rwanda had a monopoly on the world's beauty, but I am quickly corrected. Uganda has the patent on exquisiteness. Dense forests look like cauliflower from above, and cotton-ball clouds voluptuously envelop volcanic gorges. Bamboo jungles teem with baboons that jump from branch to branch, and patchwork-quilted terraces studded with crops grow on intimidating inclines. There are volcanoes in every corner as far as the eye can see, and eagles claim the sky with unwavering confidence. But the most beautiful of all are the people. They are so stunningly warmhearted. Everyone I pass welcomes me and waves from their fields with faces decorated with humongous smiles. What a phenomenal place!

The rapture of this beauty overcomes me, and I find myself unexpectedly reflective. There is still so much to see and do in this life. How could I ever have been so irresponsible with my own health and safety by taking risks and living dangerously? Before coming to Africa, my life seemed to have had little value or purpose. Life was something I took for granted— something I assumed was my birthright and nothing special to respect or protect. Taking risks beyond logic and good sense made sense. After all, what did I have to lose? But now, I am beginning to feel a fervor for life. There is so much yet to live, do, see, learn, give, receive, understand and love. Life is the ultimate gift, our greatest asset, the most beautiful blessing. Oh, I think I am falling in love with it.

Back to the road, the driver enters a dense patch of jungle. I ask him to stop for a moment so I can listen to its sounds and

141

feel its wetness. He stops. I exit the vehicle, walk a few meters down the road, and stand quietly. The cicadas are deafening, but they do bow back a bit for the crickets to harmonize with them. Birds, somewhere in the thick brush of bamboo, make music too. And then there is the humidity that joins in and douses me with beads of sweat, while a kaleidoscope of fluorescent greens from this garden dazzles me with dew. Being in a jungle is a surreal maze of miracles. Look at me in the cradle of man, where mankind took its first breath! Look at me, breathless from everything's sheer breathtakingness. I can do nothing but stand silently with the utmost reverence.

Suddenly, the awe-inspiring moment abruptly ends when a massive monster thing springs from the dense foliage and lands inches in front of me. I never prepared myself to be in the face of a wild whatever it is. It is my height and clearly stronger than I am, if it chooses to be. Monsters this big are only supposed to be in those pretend King Kong movies. I was wrongly misled and misinformed, as one is in the flesh right here, right now. The monster is so big, so hairy, so dark, so wild and unexpected that I stand paralyzed with terror. Is it a baboon, orangutan, gorilla, or chimpanzee with acromegaly? It stands directly in front of me, looking into my eyes with the same terror and surprise. Neither one of us moves. I know gorillas and monkeys are vegetarians, and since I am not a vegetable, I should be safe, but baboons and orangutans are carnivores, and I gather Dr. Cary is grade A, B, and C beef to them. Tenderloin or filet, I have no time to compose myself or my thoughts. Hopefully, this animal can see that I am quite thin and have little on my bones to satisfy his or her palate. Being such a sparse specimen, it would be a shame to eat me.

I see my life flash in front of me. I never imagined being devoured by a small, medium, or large-sized primate in a Ugandan jungle. How could this be my life's end? Without hesitation, both of us turn back-to-back and flee for our lives in opposite directions. The big, black, hairy thing runs back into the jungle as I run back to the truck. I have never been so frightened in my entire life. The driver is hysterical.

8 October 1994
Saturday

My Dearest,

The project in Uganda is admirable, and the team running it is kind and committed to providing preventive healthcare to the indigent population, namely mothers and children. I am very happy to join them. With my knowledge of obstetrics, I could help the people. Uganda is currently enjoying peace. I would appreciate a piece of peace for a while. It's hard to imagine what a restful evening would feel like without war outside. But I have to admit, part of me struggles. Leaving Rwanda at this time seems selfish. There is such tremendous need there now that it feels irresponsible to walk out on them.

I return to Kigali to complete the necessary papers to join the Ugandan team. They are keen to have me, so their organization has fast-tracked my application. Minutes before the official signing of the contract, however, I am approached by a representative from Doctors Without Borders—Holland. Apparently, one of their doctors had an emergency and can't come to Rwanda. Without a doctor, the hospital they manage can't function. They desperately need a doctor. I am happy to be of service and agree to visit their medical facility.

I leave immediately for Ruhengeri, a city in the northwest corner of the country. I'm told this locale is the most beautiful part of Rwanda. Apparently, this place is internationally well known because of Dian Fossey, a Western woman renowned for protecting the mountain gorillas in the area. She was unfortunately brutally butchered to death for caring. The price of a gorilla made into an ashtray or something stuffed was more valuable to the poachers than her life, so she was erased.

Driving across the country and through the hills toward our destination, I can say with certainty that the area deserves its reputation. It is stunningly beautiful, exquisitely manicured, and downright regal in its own right. Green has never been greener, lush has never been lusher, and sensational has never been so sensational.

After a few hours on the road, I arrive. My first impression of Ruhengeri is a good one. I am told this place was once more bustling than Mabanza, but the genocide culled a large segment of the population, leaving behind a more reserved persona, something resembling a timid tortoise cautiously sneaking a peek after a rainstorm.

My tour begins at the local hospital. Proudly plastered on the front gate is a sign that says, "Arms are prohibited on the premises." The word "arms" triggers an unsettling flashback of the notorious arm I saw in the field in Kigali. Go away!

The layout of the hospital compound is simple. At the west end is the laboratory. In the northwest corner is the pediatric ward, which is next to a kitchen, a multipurpose room, and a few on-call suites. The intensive care unit and surgical ward are in the northeast corner, and at the south end are outpatient examination rooms attached to the internal medicine ward. If I accept the assignment, this ward will be my new home.

After the hospital tour, I am taken to the expatriate living quarters, which people call "Base Camp." All operations for the organization's projects are carried out in this residential compound. Base Camp is completely surrounded by a secure brick wall. Before the war, this place was the residence of a family with obvious means—Tutsi, no doubt. No one knows their current whereabouts, and no one wants to find out either.

I am warmly welcomed by everyone and made to feel right at home. One of the members of the team, Anne, a nurse from Holland, invites me to have a seat and serves me a bowl of soup. Welcoming a guest in this way is the norm in our culture, but after having been so tormented by that wretched, loathsome nurse in Mabanza, this simple act of kindness is truly something extraordinary. It feels stupendously good.

After lunch, I mingle with the team and find everyone very enthusiastic about the project. The people seem to genuinely enjoy each other's company, and I feel I have come home. I have no choice but to sign the contract and join this team.

RUHENGERI

UGANDA
ZAIRE
[CONGO]
Ruhengeri
TANZANIA
Kigali
Mbanza
BURUNDI

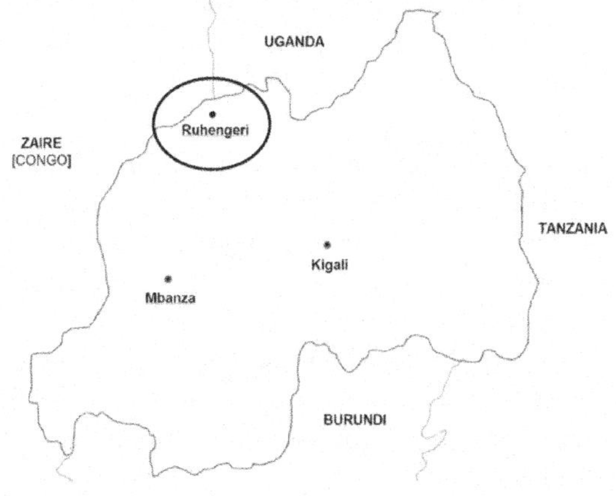

9 October 1994
Sunday

My Dearest,

My first day…

I am eager to begin work at the hospital. The staff are also eager to begin after being without supervision for too long. They have had a number of other doctors cover the service before me and are used to the frequent turnover of expatriates. Working with foreigners, they have learned that we each have our own individual styles, personalities, and quirks. Mixing cultures and expectations can be trying, but the staff and I are guardedly optimistic that we will work well together.

I share with the staff that my primary objective is to teach them everything I know so they can take care of their own people independently of me. In this way, I will make myself redundant, and they will be the true leaders and caregivers of their community. They smile. I then invite them to see a new beginning for Rwanda, a beginning based on the oneness of all people. I gently invite them to consider forgiving those who lost their way during the genocide. I know this is a larger-than-life request to put on their plates for them to swallow at this time, but perhaps when tomorrow's tomorrows come to be, they will find it in their hearts to love thy neighbor in spite of what he or she did. Everyone listens politely without giving too much of themselves away.

Later in the day, as we start our rounds and see patients together, I offer the staff some teaching. Everyone inhales it. They are noticeably hungry for knowledge and have ravenous appetites to learn. Whatever I know, I share. Whatever I am thinking, I share. Whatever I do to make a diagnosis and construct a treatment plan, I share. They listen intently and soak it all up. After seeing numerous patients, Odette, the head nurse, unexpectedly gathers the staff around me, then takes my hand. and says, *"Le Seigneur nous vous a donné* [God gave you to us]*."* What a heartwarming moment! What an encouraging beginning!

After a full day, I return home. I allow myself the luxury of lying down for some quiet and much-needed pause. A candle burns. A mosquito net protects me, and a feather quilt wraps itself snugly around my body to keep me warm. French music serenades me over mini speakers attached to a Walkman, my portable audio life-support system. It is a poor man's version of a high-end sound system and works well to induce deep reflection. I am at peace.

As I think about the Rwandan people, I try to imagine what their lives were like before the genocide. Life must have been hard. From what I see, it still is. They till their fields without regard to the sun that brutally beats them from top to bottom. And they pay no attention to it. They carry buckets of water for miles and miles to irrigate their fields, which are often hours from their huts. And they pay no attention to it. As they try to work the land, the earth defiantly resists every plunge of their makeshift plows made from wood and stone. But they plow, push and pull—not with machine or beast—but with their own hands. And their hands dig into a parched planet that looks like useless moonscape without a lot to show for their labor when the harvest comes. And they pay no attention to it.

The people wrap the sum total of their life possessions in cloth rags that they place in tree branches woven into baskets that rest regally on head mounts. When all is properly in place, they set off for the market. Their calloused and cracked bare feet know the way, straddling the irregular ruts in the road gracefully. They march in the sun, in the rain, in the heat, in the dust, without water, food or safety, sometimes for 12 hours with 100 pounds of potatoes on their heads. Dust from dirt roads billowing up behind passing trucks is so thick people can't see their children holding their hands. And they pay no attention to it. They ask for nothing more than something to feed their families that they may live yet another day or two. Sometimes, soldiers passing on the same road brazenly invite themselves to partake in the people's bounty by stealing their precious goods. *And they pay no attention to it.*

10 October 1994
Monday

My Dearest,

I wake up and can't wait to go to work. Many ideas flood my mind as an inner passion calls me to plow fields and move immovable mountains. The people I work with are kind and dedicated. I sense a deep bond with them as I discover how similar we are to one another. Their history has been a rocky one, as has been mine. We have been violated and abandoned, lost loved ones, and are haunted by things better forgotten. We also share the privilege to make amends, forgive, and let go of the past. Besides living through tough times, we share another important binding commonality—optimism. We believe in the possibility of change and something better. We believe we can individually and collectively change the world. I was under the impression that I came to Rwanda to help heal the people. To my surprise, I find the one being healed the most is me.

Before starting rounds on the ward, I share my vision of our work together: "Basically, I believe we are all equal," I begin. "Just because I am a doctor doesn't mean I outrank you or that I am more important than you. We are all important. Everyone is necessary. When we work as a team, we can give our best to the patients," I tell my attentive audience. "You are frontline healthcare workers. This is your country. These are your patients. These are your people. I am only here to remind you of these things. My hope is that you all regain your confidence and rebuild your communities so that compassion and forgiveness overflow." Truly speaking, I wonder if this can really be achieved. Most of the people working at the hospital are barely educated and have little to no knowledge of math and science, let alone medicine. To be honest, they have not been employed to work in the hospital because of their clinical skills or their grade point averages. They have been engaged because they care. And in this time when it all went wrong, who is better than these caregivers to make it all right? I am honored to be part of this country's history. Helping people help others is a wonderful life.

My Dearest,

There is growing public concern that the government is going to be attacked by the Interahamwe sometime between now and mid-December. Since we are just a few miles from the Zairian border, where the militia has concentrated, locals are worried that we will be the first to be attacked and caught in the crossfire. Candidly speaking, I don't want to die.

When I write home, I sugarcoat my letters with layers of multicolored fabrications and frank lies. I write that there are no security incidents whatsoever and that the war has ended with peace prevailing. To distract from the reality here, I write of little luscious fruits dangling from every bush in the brush and tell of the elegant eagles circling the skies.

My letters paint a pretty picture of perfection in this pearl of Africa. The painting I create includes bananas, butterflies, and bushels of bunnies, along with children who gather on all sides of the Pied Piper—me—who happily outpaces them on my way to work. I expunge the submachine guns and the men holding them. I convert the gunshots I hear into imaginary ribbits from frogs on lilies in make-believe ponds, and the landmines into handmade soccer balls made from stuffed stray socks. If I were back in school, my letters would surely earn a distinction in creative writing and the art of war. My pretty pictures are painted by an untamed imagination that runs wild when, in reality, I run for cover. I have no choice but to hide from my fear, which would otherwise paralyze me and people who care for me. Fooling myself and others helps me believe that at the end of the tunnel, there is something brighter, or at least something less dark than this darkness.

There is a volcano on the border that separates the killers from us. It is said that they wait there impatiently while they prepare for their next attack. "I look over yonder and what do I see comin' for to carry me home?" Don't let them carry me home.

A Letter to Friends

My Dear Friends,

My dream is coming true. Finally, after years of medical training, I hold a medicine bag filled with valuable tools to do something meaningful.

From the beginning...

After residency, I took a year off and traveled around the world, far from responsibilities, pagers and patients. After a year, I missed being useful and decided it was time to be part of the world again. So, I returned to the States, got a job, and started practicing medicine as a full-fledged physician. All was on schedule, and I envisioned a fruitful career. Being needed was invigorating and satisfying. I had indeed found my path.

One evening, I saw a report about the Rwandan genocide, with its trails of people walking to nowhere, shivering from cold and listless from hunger. The images left me tearful. I knew what I needed to do. The following day, I called Doctors Without Borders and asked if I could join their team. A few weeks later, I found myself in charge of their Shigella and cholera wards in a remote town in southwestern Rwanda. One month later, the cholera epidemic was over, and the army demanded that all displaced people from the genocide return to their homes to cultivate their fields. Without people, our mission was terminated, and our medical team returned to Europe. Knowing there was still much work to be done in the area, I looked for another assignment. Gratefully, I found a position with Doctors Without Borders—Holland, and was shuttled off to a hospital in Ruhengeri, a city in the northwest part of the country. Ruhengeri is renowned for its indigenous gorillas, whose plight with poachers was well documented in Dian Fossey's acclaimed account "Gorillas in the Mist."

I am now in charge of the internal medicine ward. I know I vowed after residency never to do hospital work again, but the patients were desperate and so deserving of care. I couldn't refuse the assignment. And besides, this isn't really a hospital. The only thing our facility has that resembles a hospital is a sign hanging at the entrance that reads, "Hôpital [hospital]." We do have oxygen, though. The only problem is that the tool to open the gauge is gone, and no one can find the tubing that connects the cylinder to someone who's in respiratory distress.

The hospital also limps in the personnel department. Many of our medical staff are barely literate. But it's not an issue. With a bit of this and that and some creativity, all is possible, starting with a new and improved medical delivery system that I devised to make sure patients get their medicine. The system uses numbers instead of words, so there is less of a chance for errors when administering pills. Built into the design is also a foolproof way to monitor that the patients are actually getting their medications. I was so proud of myself for the ingenious system I implemented, but my self-praise was short-lived. To my great surprise, I discovered that members of my staff were far more ingenious than me; they were systematically stealing the medicines and selling them at the market. So much for my foolproof monitoring system, which did nothing more than offer proof that I was the fool. I suppose I shouldn't complain because at least my staff don't kill our inpatient babies like in other parts of the country. Apparently, a Hutu nurse working at another medical facility somewhere in the country was found to be killing Tutsi children on his night shift.

Speaking of killing, by the time I arrived in Rwanda, the fallout of hate, along with its many dead bodies, had been cleaned up. Some stray body parts remain in fields, but these are well camouflaged and out of sight. It is hard to believe such an enormous loss of life occurred, but I guess it accounts for why there are so few people around. Most of the country's Tutsis are dead, and many of the country's Hutus have fled to Zaire. This country used to be the most densely populated in Africa. Today it is the most densely populated graveyard—one without gravestones, one without names.

You are in my thoughts and in my heart ... always. -- Cary

12 October 1994
Wednesday

My Dearest,

Anne, our expatriate outreach nurse, brings in a young man from the field today. She notices him at an outlying clinic and brings him to the hospital because she is concerned about him.

"Cary, this patient has an unremitting fever of about 104°F (40°C), she reports.

"I bet it's malaria," I speculate. After all, this is what most people with high fevers have here. Anne has no history about him other than some vague, sketchy, unconfirmed report that the patient's 11-year-old brother passed away in the morning. Our new patient does appear feverish. His vitals are taken, and everything is normal except for a fever of 104°F. In spite of this, he remains coherent, well-hydrated and stable. At least we have the luxury of time on our side.

I examine the patient in the outside corridor of the internal medicine ward. Many people are busy doing their business. The day is hot, but not too hot, and the sun is bright, but perhaps too bright. When I look into the patient's pupils with my ophthalmoscope, he squints. Everyone squints when a light is directed at their retina. Everyone also squints when they look directly at the sun or any bright light. I don't think there's anything abnormal about his squinting, so I dismiss it. I continue examining him, trying to confirm my diagnosis of malaria. The young man's lungs are clear to auscultation, and he has no rhonchi, rales or wheezes, which makes pneumonia or some other respiratory infection unlikely as a source of his high fever. His abdominal exam is also unremarkable. The abdomen is soft, nontender, nondistended, and has normal bowel sounds. These findings rule out an acute abdomen, cholecystitis, appendicitis and peritonitis. Neurologically, he appears normal. He walks without difficulty, speaks clearly, and is cognitively intact. His neck is soft and supple, and he has no vomiting, which is important to rule out meningitis. I inquire more about his younger brother's passing, but all I can discern from the translator is that the boy had some difficulty breathing. His brother may have had asthma or pneumonia. I dismiss any connection between the two boys. These guessing games are like playing charades. My translator is good, but I can't get clear enough details to make a definitive diagnosis. It's frustrating to be in the dark or pushed into a corner with a timer attached to a potentially lethal ticking bomb. I have no choice but to fill in the blanks with what feels good, rings true, and intuitively makes some semblance of sense.

"Do you think he has meningitis?" Anne asks. Anne is a highly qualified nurse with extensive experience. I adore her. She is motherly and compassionate, and could have rightfully been Mother Teresa's teacher and inspiration. Anne was the one who greeted me with an enormously open heart the day I arrived in Ruhengeri and served me a nice bowl of soup. After the emotional beatings I endured in Mabanza, I will never forget her unsolicited act of kindness.

"Meningitis?" I ask myself. "No, I don't think so. There's no evidence from the patient's history or physical exam to support the diagnosis. I'm pretty sure the boy has malaria," I say with near certainty. Acutely aware of malaria's penchant to kill and kill quickly, I immediately start him on intravenous quinine, the treatment of choice for advanced cerebral malaria.

The ward is already inundated with patients suffering from malaria, so the staff know well what to do. The patient is taken to a bed and started on our standard antimalarial protocol.

It's cerebral malaria that personally paralyzes me every waking hour while incarcerating me under a mosquito net at night. Supposedly, it only takes one bite from one mosquito to vegetablize the strongest and most robust forever. People who come from places where there is no malaria are much more vulnerable to the disease because their immune systems have never been exposed to it. As a result, they are completely ill-equipped to defend themselves against the parasitic infestation and often succumb to it within hours.

After everyone is comfortably tucked in for the evening, I head home. Before leaving the hospital for the night, I give the night nurse explicit instructions to contact me if there is any change with our mystery patient.

At home, I spend the rest of the evening thinking about the young man with malaria and his brother, who had died just hours earlier. My mind spins in circles as it tries to figure out what else could be wrong with him if, for some reason, the antimalarial medication doesn't work.

13 October 1994
Thursday

My Dearest,

As soon as I get to the hospital today, I inquire about the condition of the patient with malaria. The head nurse says, "*Il est mort* [He died]."

"*Ce n'est pas possible* [It's not possible]," I chuckle out loud, then roll my eyes. "Don't be ridiculous! You are mixing him up with someone else," I counter. "The guy who came in yesterday, the 22-year-old with the fever! We started him on IV quinine for malaria. Remember?"

"*Oui, il est mort. Ce garçon est mort* [Yes, he died. That boy died]," she repeats.

"*Ce n'est pas possible, pas possible* [It\s not possible, not possible]*!*" I protest. "I left last evening and he was fine. I left at 10 PM, and he was resting comfortably. It is now early morning; only eight hours have passed. Not possible, not possible," I repeat like a frustrated parrot that can't get himself understood. The nurse just stands there without anything more to add to the conversation. She's telling me what she knows, and I'm telling her she is mixing up the patients.

Then, from deep inside, I hear Anne's words: "Do you think he has meningitis?" I stop abruptly. Changing my tone, my interrogation shifts. "By any chance, did the guy have any neck stiffness?" I dare to ask but manage to get the words out.

The nurse reports matter-of-factly, "Yes, he got a stiff neck and became delirious at about 2:00 AM."

"Ughhhh," involuntarily bellows from deep in my belly, as if someone has just sledgehammered me in my stomach. The night nurse doesn't know what this means, nor does she know why I unexpectedly bend forward, grabbing my gut.

"Uhhhhh," again, Anne's words—"Do you think he has meningitis?"—come forth like projectile vomit, along with that all-too-familiar vile bile taste. My brain goes mad. "Do you think he has meningitis?" I hear Anne's words over and over again. Nuchal rigidity is a cardinal sign of meningitis. But neck stiffness can also be seen in cerebral malaria. This young man could also have had photophobia (sensitivity to light), another cardinal sign of meningitis. I recall he squinted when I shined light into his eyes with my ophthalmoscope during my examination. But squinting is a normal response when shining light into the eyes or looking directly at the sun. Was his squinting an early neurological sign of meningitis or a normal response to light?

I cannot deny the real possibility that this young man may very well have had meningitis, as Anne suggested. His brother could have had it, too. Both of the boys lived in close quarters, most likely a mud hut without windows or ventilation. Why wouldn't they have meningitis? But then, malaria often affects people living in close quarters without windows or ventilation. If only I had treated him with an additional drug to cover this serial killer that causes meningitis, he might have survived. But even with treatment, he might not have survived. Also, if the source of the meningitis was viral, the drug wouldn't have worked because there is no treatment for viral meningitis. But then, it wouldn't have hurt to have tried an antibacterial. Why didn't I just piggyback an antibiotic against meningitis along with his antimalarial? We had the drug. We had the personnel. In fact, we had everything to possibly save this young man's life. The only thing missing was the order to give it.

My Western training is often a liability here. Many of the fundamental medical protocols I learned and used in my practice back home are simply not appropriate here. For example, we don't blindly treat patients with unnecessary medications. We are taught to narrow our diagnoses as much as possible and use only essential medications to avoid drug interactions. As a result, we go to Herculean lengths to find and identify infectious agents. Once a pathogen is identified, we tailor our treatment to eradicate it. Here, on the other hand, without a lab, it is impossible to isolate and identify an offending organism. As a result, we are forced to use broad-spectrum antibiotics. As the name implies, these drugs are effective against a wide range of infectious agents. These powerful, all-encompassing drugs are especially useful when a definitive diagnosis cannot be made. They are like bombs that treat almost everything. The problem with these nonspecific medications is that they have more side effects and can also cause drug-resistant bacteria that could be difficult, if not impossible, to treat in the future. Because of these issues, I do not typically reach for these powerful pills and infusions.

I realize now that if a medicine can possibly save a life, it is worth risking any side effects, drug interactions, or future resistance problems. I must confess, this treatment option was not first and foremost on my mind as I treated our patient for cerebral malaria.

They say every doctor has a cemetery; to date, mine hasn't had any occupants. Is my cemetery now home to an innocent and unassuming 22-year-old young man who died silently in the night, unprotected, without his mother holding him? Was there no one to shed a tear as he passed? I slept comfortably in my bed last night, tucked safe and sound under my mosquito net, shielded from possible danger, protected by guards and an elaborate security system, which includes satellite phones, fax machines, walkie-talkies, and detailed emergency evacuation plans that can be activated at a split second's notice to ensure my safety. Everything is in place to protect me from the advent of an external attack, while this defenseless young man lay isolated and unprotected on a mattress-less hospital bed, most likely attacked mercilessly by millions of meningococci that hide like cowards in his meninges, waiting to murder him.

I hit my head against the wall for possibly missing it. Missing what? It. What is "it"? Meningitis ... maybe; I still don't know. We don't have the technology to test for it, so I'll never know why he died. What I do know is that I either lost the chance or never had the chance from the beginning to make a profound difference in the life of this young man, who will never have the chance to be an adult this time around. He lost his mother and father in the genocide. He lost his brother to some disease yesterday. And today he loses his life. This young man came to me to protect him. He trusted me and believed I would save him with my magical medicine. He had faith in me because I am White—a White doctor. He was under the false impression that White was better than Black. He was mistaken. I am not White; I am human. He is not Black; he is human. We are one and the same, equal in every way. Oh, My Dearest, give me strength. Give me peace. Give me any reason to hold on. Mr. young man, I'm so sorry. I failed to protect you. I failed to save you. I am so, so sorry.

14 October 1994
Friday

My Dearest,

In addition to the young man who died last night, another four people died the same day. This means five people on the ward are gone. We had a total of 25 people. That is one-fifth of the ward ... dead. Malaria, in particular, is indiscriminately obliterating people's brains regardless of their age, though the malarial parasite prefers to attack and kill children. In wealthy countries, people have strokes in their senior years, often from hard living. Here they have strokes in the single digits, which gives them hardly a chance to live. Shigella is also rampantly killing people here. It bleeds them to death.

Five wonderful mothers and fathers, sisters, brothers, sons, daughters and friends are dead. Meningitis, Shigella, malaria,

HIV, and simple dehydration from diarrhea decimate people here. I can't help but wonder if I could have done anything more to have made a difference in their lives. In my world before Rwanda, when a severely ill patient came in for care, I would refer them to tertiary care centers generously endowed with fully equipped laboratories, modern high-tech machines, and the very best specialists in every field. I don't have any of these medical marvels here. There is no CAT scan, MRI, ultrasound, X-ray, proper laboratory, or specialist to confer with when I need a second opinion. It's just me and my judgment, my prejudice and bias, experience, and lack of it too. I also don't have properly trained nurses or a qualified translator to get a reliable history from patients to help me make an accurate diagnosis. I still don't even have a reference book. Five people died in one day, and I wonder if I could have or should have done something other than what I did or didn't do.

Going forward and putting the past aside is the only way for me to survive here. Brooding on my failures does no one any good. There is no time for it. Celebrating my successes also occupies time. There is no time for it, either.

Speaking of time, it seems to pass faster than the speed of sound. I wonder if the clocks here have had their minute and hour hands broken or amputated, leaving in place only their second hands to mark the time. Imagine time passing at the speed of a clock's second hand. There are only split seconds available to dwell on the past, be in the present, and consider the future. Maybe time is intentionally in short supply here so I can't fixate on things that I can't change, like the flashbacks and the daily deaths, which appear and disappear and appear again. Today's disasters and deaths have again come.

A man with probable peritonitis, an inflammation of the covering over the intestines, died today. As he was dying, he looked into my eyes. He seemed to be pleading with me to let him live. I wish I had the power to answer his plea. When someone is on the verge of death, there is little we can do except, perhaps, hold their hand or place a cold compress on their forehead. It comforts us to comfort them, but all we can really do is step aside and watch death do its duty. When people are dying, they don't moan or groan, or thrash about. They just accept. But when I truly look deep inside, I see that, while they may accept their fate, they are not ready to let go, even when they have nothing left to let go of.

An 18-year-old girl stepped on a landmine today and had both her legs blown off. Nothing more needs to be said. I should honor her by asking her name, in case someone in the years to come wishes to acknowledge her. But it is not possible. I am suddenly deaf, mute, and blind as my eyes lock onto her *limblessness*.

Landmines immortalize no one. They are not fair and do not negotiate. Their sole purpose is to maim or, if you are lucky, kill you. These small black boxes of explosives are made abroad, mostly in Western countries. They are offensive weapons that hide themselves and play by their own rules, against all terms of engagement. These benevolent-appearing little black boxes have an insatiable desire to disfigure and an obsessive penchant to murder young and old, rich and poor, Blacks and Whites. They don't differentiate or discriminate. Anyone is fair prey for their sport. They are serial killers and enjoy their lot in life, which is to destroy life, as they wait patiently, often for years, for that unassuming, perfect step to activate their fury. Landmines may be small, but they never, ever lose. Who sent these little black boxes to Rwanda? Who made them? And how do their makers sleep at night?

Speaking of night, I am on call this evening. This means I have a sleepover alone at the hospital. The call room terrorizes me. With iron bars on each window, it looks and feels like a prison. A touch of yellow paint that someone kindly used to beautify the bars does make them a tad less imposing, but I'm still uneasy here. The room is attached to a kitchen that has a pot, a stove with a single burner, a canister of Nescafé, and a can of powdered milk. I feel isolated and insecure when I am alone in this room all night. It is in the darkness of the night when things frequently go wrong. And things do go wrong— sometimes very wrong. I am certain Mr. Murphy would agree with me. Murphy's Law states that if something can go wrong, it will. I think in a previous life my name was Murphy.

15 October 1994
Saturday

My Dearest,

The day started splendidly, but then suddenly everything went terribly wrong. It is 6:41 AM. I am deep in meditation, grounded and at peace. The stillness and calm are especially nourishing for me this fine morning. Wouldn't it be nice to stay in this serene state for infinity? Infinity, unfortunately, is abruptly retired when I am interrupted by static receptions crackling over a walkie-talkie that stands at attention on a table next to my bed. For security purposes, we are required to leave the radio on at all times. Until now, the mobile device has been nothing more than a nuisance because the channel designated for security issues is constantly being misused by people all over Rwanda for their personal entertainment.

"Hannah for Cary. Over."

Still in a semi-meditative state, I'm a bit disoriented. I grab hold of the walkie-talkie. "Yes, Hannah, Cary here. Over."

"Hannah for Cary. Over," she repeats.

"Yes, Hannah, this is Cary. Over."

"Cary, there is *some security problem*. I repeat, a security problem. Please stay at the hospital. Stay at the hospital! Stand by! Over."

Hannah's voice sounds contrived and bated.

"Okay, Hannah. Over."

So much for the calm. I set the handset back in its holder and wait. "Some security problem?" What does that mean? Just over the hill behind the hospital, the Interahamwe hide.

We anticipate being attacked by them, but according to people in the know, not until December, if at all. "Security problem?" Hannah was tremulous and uncertain, guarded and noticeably bewildered. What is going on?

I have been on call since last night at the hospital, which is about one mile from Base Camp, where most of the rest of the team resides. Suzanne, an expatriate nurse, is also on call and sleeps in an adjacent call room. I quickly get out of bed and go next door to inform her of the news. My intention is not to alarm her, so I knock gently on her door and casually say in a demure voice, "Rise and shine, Suzanne. Can you come to the kitchen? We have a *little* security problem." According to our security guidelines, if there is any security problem, we are required to assemble in a predetermined secure area. In the hospital, the kitchen was chosen to be our secure space.

Minutes later, Suzanne enters the kitchen. She is calm; I am not. Naturally, she wants more information, but all I can offer her is, *"Some security problem."* Her mind takes off like a llama in the hills of Patagonia being chased by a mountain lion. The two of us just sit, staring at the small black plastic handheld radio device, waiting, wondering.

Over the radio, we hear, "Can we help you, Bungalow?" ("Bungalow" is a term we use for Base Camp.)

Someone else interjects, "Stay out of the yard!"

What is that supposed to mean? We then hear a foreign language with some African music playing in the background. Someone wearing their walkie-talkie may be secretly pressing their handset button to broadcast the incident live, in real time, to alert everyone present on the public radio channel. Or perhaps a militiaman has shot someone, taken their walkie-talkie, and unknowingly activated it. My mind goes into overdrive, then into major pandemonium mode. I worry some catastrophic event is occurring at the Bungalow.

The snippets of information in the background that are being broadcast, unbeknownst to the probable attackers, give pieces of a terrifying puzzle that is still too fragmented to figure out. It sounds like some troops attacked someone in the yard. Was anyone killed? What do we do if they come for us at the hospital? Where do we run? Where do we hide? If they were truly after us, we would not be easily camouflaged; our white skin sees to that.

Humanitarian organizations are under the protection of the United Nations. Unfortunately, the militia does not subscribe to the Geneva Convention or follow the standard international laws for the humane treatment of prisoners. I wonder if they can even read and write. Have we somehow implicated the militia or the military in any wrongdoing? Have we strayed too far from our mandate of neutrality by favoring a particular side in the conflict, thus losing our diplomatic immunity? Is anyone with any power angry with us now, and do they have any intention to eliminate us? Are we assets or enemies to them?

Until now, the authorities have needed our medical facility and expertise to treat injured comrades. For this reason and this reason alone, they have tolerated our presence. But in all fairness to them, the organization has been monitoring and reporting what they see daily in the field. Bearing witness to and publicizing political *faux pas* is in no one's best interest, except perhaps the international community's. The industry of killing does not reflect well on those currently in power. It can be argued that the organization might have gone way beyond the call of duty by transmitting the country's dirty laundry to the outside world. Do the people in power here know this, and are they now angry with us?

"Some security problem." What can this mean? It would have been better to keep the radio silent. Suzanne and I sit in this kitchen with bars barring the windows like in a prison. We are already incarcerated. If they—whoever *they* are—come to know we are here, will we be victims of their extermination campaign? I fear we will. They did it with the Tutsis, so why not with us? Where do we run? Actually, there is a way to escape into the field outside the hospital compound. We could go through the back door of the kitchen to the fence just a few feet away. I once noticed a small opening in that fence, which could now be the perfect escape route into the area outside the hospital wall. I mention my idea to Suzanne. She does not approve of it at all. She reminds me of the security guidelines and our obligation to stay in one central place so we can easily be rescued. If we breach the guidelines and stray away from this assigned area, our rescuers will have to waste precious time looking for us. This would not only delay our evacuation but put others at risk as well. We have no choice but to stay put and wait for the next order. In the meantime, I pace back and forth in this cramped enclosure, examining the adjoining call room for perhaps a safe place under the bed or in the closet. The radio has been quiet for what seems like an eternity and then some. Why aren't we receiving any more information? We sit here like helpless chickens in a coop, waiting with angst for our inevitable slaughter.

A three-ring binder with the organization's protocol for emergency evacuations is on a shelf. It was proactively placed there for all of us to read, but who really took the time to brief themselves on the ABCs of a quick and coordinated escape? I never looked at it before. For me, it was nothing more than a library reference book that sat unread on a shelf behind a counter, like the ones attended by librarians who tenaciously guarded them from theft and protected them from overuse and plagiarism at the public library. It never was something any-one would actually read, and apparently, no one did. It is now in our hands as we try to decipher it. Supposedly well written and clear, it is nothing more than a garble of incoherent, nondescript words, as well as irrelevant information that offers no solution to our current situation.

In defense of the security document, it does have some valuable information, like the *code*. The code is an essential part of our emergency evacuation protocol. Because all NGOs in Rwanda share one public radio channel to communicate, the organization has devised a way to exchange sensitive and confidential information by way of a secret code. For security concerns, I cannot divulge this sensitive formula, but what I can say with absolute certainty is that if there is ever an evacuation, people will confound the details of the code.

The document states that in the event of an emergency evacuation, we should wear our *Médecins Sans Frontières* T-shirts. This simple garment serves as an identification banner to call attention to the fact that we are verified humanitarian aid workers providing free medical care to all Rwandan citizens equally, regardless of race, religion, color, personal activities, historical engagements, political convictions, or associations. We are also instructed to take our passports, flashlights, local currency, and any hard cash we have in U.S. dollars for safe passage. Money pays for favors and payoffs to those who might consider it profitable to have us in hand. In other words, pay whatever ransom is demanded before we are kidnapped and our personal worth is inflated. Naturally, I have nothing in hand now. The passport? It's at Base Camp. The T-shirt? It's in the laundry. The money is in the safe; no one ever told me the combination. The only person who knows it is the logistician, and who knows where he is now? But all is not lost. I do have a flashlight!

It is utterly irresponsible that we didn't plan ahead and suss out some hole somewhere to hide ourselves in the event of an attack. We could have prepared a secret hiding place under the floor or above the ceiling to protect ourselves. Instead, we are like cows locked in an abattoir, waiting to be decapitated. The field in the back of the kitchen looks more and more inviting.

As the minutes pass and no further instruction comes over the walkie-talkie, I scan the surroundings for our next plan of action. Suzanne is notably agitated, yet she controls herself well. She is compliant and sees no reason for an alternate plan as she waits for the next command from central control. I pace the premises. Ingo, our logistician, joins us in the kitchen.

"Are we just going to sit in this room and wait for the killers to come and massacre us?" I rhetorically ask the others.

I can't decide if we are the Three Musketeers, the Three Stooges, or the Three Little Pigs, waiting for the big bad wolf to come and blow the door down. I look through the back window for that hole in the fence and a patch of grass to hide in.

"Why don't we run up the hill and hide until they rescue us?" I suggest with gumption.

Suzanne and Ingo are both as silent as the radio, paying absolutely no attention to me.

Physically, I've lost so much weight since I came here. My arms are the size of tiny twigs, and I barely have enough strength to hold a flailing infant. My courage is equally twig-like, and holding a gun, soldier, or any other warring thing would be comical. I would be of no use in any armed conflict.

The walkie-talkie might as well take a walk because it's certainly not "talkie." It's not even doing that static stuff. It's just broadcasting silence at the moment—absolutely nothing more: no news, no chit, no chat, no chatter—just a lot of nothing. Suzanne is getting more nervous and agitated, and I do nothing but incite her more. Ingo is calm and shows little emotion: no flinch, no twitch, no squirm. He just sits in a chair, seemingly looking comfortable and composed as he reads the paper. He pays no attention to Suzanne or me, which makes me look ridiculous, running around like a hen without a head. His calm irks and agitates me. There is something incongruous about it. There is something inauthentic about his posture. Is he posing, praying, or pleading internally for something other than this? He reads an old newspaper that was lying on the table. Does he realize it's upside down? I won't expose him. He is scared, as is Suzanne, as is Cary. It is at times like this that we are forced to go inside and silently evaluate our lives, our commitments, and our need to matter. Had we known this mission would have been so dangerous, would we still have agreed to sign on? As crazy as it sounds, especially now, not knowing if we are going to be butchered to death, I would have to admit I would.

The hospital compound is located on a heavily trafficked street that passes through Ruhengeri. The street is about 150 meters from our kitchen door. From our window, I can see people outside moving about. Nothing is out of the ordinary. From a distance, it appears to be just another normal day. This is reassuring. But then again, Rwandans live with a constant military presence, so *not* seeing them would be more unusual and alarming to them.

A military truck rushes in front of the hospital compound. I am convinced it has come for us, but it passes the front gate and disappears. Why didn't I suss out a hiding place before? I am completely unprepared. Why don't I have my passport with me? I can't get over the border without it. And why don't I have any pocket money to exchange for favors—like a little more time on the planet? What if they butcher us? Waiting to know our fate is the hardest exercise of all.

Fortunately, after nearly an hour, the silence is broken. The handset speaks. "Come to Base Camp!" We are also told to leave the hospital compound quietly without letting anyone know that anything is wrong. I quickly run to the bedroom, grab a pillowcase, and stuff it with all my possessions. I'm the first one out the door as I dart through the hospital compound. Running at first, I slow my gait and head toward the medical ward to tell the staff that I would not be seeing patients today. I offer no explanation. Feigning normalcy, I try hard to remain calm and collected. Informing anyone of our situation would not be in our best interest. Drawing attention to ourselves could create pandemonium and jeopardize our chances of getting to the Ugandan border. Regrettably, we cannot bring locals with us because this would compromise our neutrality and put our lives in danger. Is my life worth more than theirs? Absolutely not, but while abandoning them breaks my heart, this is an unfortunate reality of war. If something tragic should happen to them, I will carry the shame for the rest of my life.

As I inform the staff of the change in today's plans, my demeanor is aloof, my movements are shaky, and my speech is rushed and incomprehensible. To avoid suspicion, I make my message brief and plaster a smile on my face: "We have a little problem and need to have a little meeting. I'll be back in a little while." The way I repeat the word "little" may rouse suspicion. But who cares? I can think of nothing that makes more sense than a quick exit. I like everyone in my staff very much, but Cary likes his life more. I have to go.

Off to the house ...

Instead of walking back to Base Camp, we are transported in our intimidating Land Cruiser that intentionally displays all of its daunting, heavy-duty security hardware, along with its famed and commanding *Médecins Sans Frontières* official logo. The whole package says, "Don't mess with me." And until now, no one has.

People on the streets are calm. What has happened? What has gone wrong? What will we find as we make our approach to Base Camp? If the militia has launched an attack, then why is there such calm around the city?

To get from the hospital to Base Camp, we pass a military patrol post. In the past, whenever the soldiers saw our vehicle, they raised the road barrier and allowed us to pass without interfering with our activities. A courteous nod of the head, a smile, or a casual wave of the hand was all that was necessary to maintain our good relations. This time, however, the gate is not raised, and we are forced to come to a complete stop. The soldiers are not impressed by our courteous nods and look intensely at our vehicle and then at us. It is policy never to engage or converse with any soldiers because any familiarity with them could be a provocation to the Hutu militia. Any such misunderstanding could bring our neutrality into question and jeopardize our work here. Now at a standstill, the silence is quite distressing. The soldiers, with weapons draped over their shoulders, look around our vehicle and at us. After they are satisfied with their inspection, they retreat from the vehicle and saunter to the barricade that blocks the road. Hesitating for a split second, they open it for us to pass.

The soldiers have never hesitated before. This hesitation is the most overt sign of aggression that I have experienced since coming to Rwanda. There was not a single word exchanged between us, but their monologue was indisputably threatening and provocatively aggressive. In this lone split second was an oration, a declaration of dominance made loud, bold and clear. In this split second was the truth of a genocide that erased the lives of more than a million innocent people. More disruptive than the human bones and grass bagel-shaped carrying rings strewn about in the killing fields, this split second affirms the military's resolve and what they are willing, able, and ready to do to assert their dominance. The gun is their word, and the life they take is only the resolve of their word. The demise of a generation, the erasure of a child's silhouette, the death of a man's dreams, and the loss of a mother's love are never even considered. Their hesitation asserts who is king in this jungle. This split second reminds us that we are guests if we fulfill their needs and comply with *their* rules and regulations. It is an ominous reminder that when our invitation to be here expires, we have overstayed our welcome and should leave well before needing to be asked to leave.

With the barricade raised, we are free to proceed. Relieved to have passed that hurdle, we arrive home. That single mile took its time and toll. Inside the compound, nothing looks disturbed—except the team. There is a lot of purposeless pacing. People are silent, stunned, withdrawn, and disengaged from each other. Something bad has happened. Rachel, the project coordinator, is picking at her cuticles and perusing her palms as if looking for something that has gone missing. It is clear that she is troubled and caught off guard. Papa Junior is chain-smoking. Denis, the logistician, is also smoking. He is not a smoker. The others sit quietly. They appear comatose. Everyone waits for a security briefing.

Rachel begins by describing the events of the previous hour: "Twenty soldiers armed with submachine guns stormed the compound by scaling the brick wall. Once on the property, they raided the house and turned every room upside down.

People's possessions were scrutinized, and their diaries and personal letters were read. Closets, cupboards, suitcases, and chests were opened, and all their contents were dumped on the floor. People's privacy was breached, and their trust, hearts, and hopes were violated. Fortunately, no one was hurt."

I can't grasp the terror of aid workers being confronted by soldiers with submachine guns. Thank goodness I was away on call in the kitchen at the hospital, out of the way, and spared this sparring. I can't imagine how I would have fared during such an assault. The project coordinator believes that the military wanted to exert some subtle authority over us, force us into submission, and confirm who is ultimately in command. It could be argued that, as a significant donor to the rehabilitation of the country, the organization has acquired too much power and influence for the military's comfort.

Doctors Without Borders has gained heavyweight status in the humanitarian arena and will not succumb to political or military intimidation. The organization knows that what it brings to Rwanda is invaluable and essential for the country to function. It will not be mistreated, bullied or threatened. So, in response to today's inexcusable events, it swiftly issues an ultimatum to the head of the Rwandan government: "Either we are granted complete immunity from military activity, or we will immediately close the mission. If the organization is to continue its humanitarian activities, there will be absolutely no guns in our compounds, and all aid workers must be given full protection as mandated under the United Nations code of conduct." The organization's position is clear and binding. There is nothing negotiable about it.

Later in the day, an emergency gathering of all leading humanitarian partners in the country is called to discuss the incident. Together, they unanimously draft a united code of conduct, along with a unified response from all contributing parties. Now the military's might is in a standoff with the might and will of the world's humanitarian community. Who will surrender and hold the white flag in the end?

The expatriate community is increasingly fearful about the rapidly changing security situation. The deployment of troops and military convoys suggests there may be an armed conflict somewhere in the country. The Rwandans are also alarmed and share our angst. Many have started fleeing the city.

As the security situation around the country deteriorates, the organization continues to monitor the military's actions and report its findings to international audiences. The current Rwandan government does not like us witnessing or reporting its activities. To intimidate us, they falsely accuse us of hiding weapons and militiamen in our compound. This is nonsense, and they knew it when their commander in chief ordered the raid today. They were not surprised when they found nothing but private letters, along with terrified aid workers cowering on the floor, when their troops ransacked the compound.

Papa Junior, a French expatriate in our team, is terrified because the French allegedly played a particularly potent and poisonous role in the politics that led to and facilitated the Rwandan genocide. As a result, French nationals are at greater risk of reprisals. Given France's role in the genocide, it is understandable that Papa Junior is concerned for his safety. Fearing for his life, he acts and reacts somewhere between anxiety and hysteria, which sets off waves of panic in the entire team. We are all affected. His argument for everyone to immediately evacuate from the country is compelling and persuasive. Given the current state of affairs and the reality of our vulnerability, some members of the team are strongly considering leaving. Meanwhile, to reassure us, the project leaders have temporarily closed our mission and barred us from returning to the hospital until the military agrees to give us diplomatic immunity and ensures our personal safety. Once again, we sit and wait for the next radio message, but this time, we hope it will be on our terms.

16 October 1994
Sunday

My Dearest,

It's 4:00 AM. I'm exhausted, but I'm unable to settle. I want to sleep. I need to sleep. I have to sleep. But here I lie, wide awake and panic-stricken, paralyzed by fear, terrorized, and distressed by a hysterical mind in overdrive. My mind, which has always been my friend, is now out of its mind and takes on a life of its own, divorced from central control.

Yesterday's drama rebirths itself throughout the night. The military's reckless behavior haunts me. I was spared the raid, the guns, and the close encounter with death, but could it soon be my turn? Why was I spared? Why was I left unharmed? I can't imagine how I would have reacted had I been at the house while it was being attacked. Being confronted by men in military uniforms with machine guns on their shoulders and hatred in their hearts is too traumatic to bear. I can't fathom armed men invading my personal space and tearing through my possessions like clochards ripping through alley trash bins looking for something of value.

There are 24 expatriates in this team. Sixteen live at Base Camp, four in a house on the main road, and four in another house tucked deep in the bush. Who lives in the house tucked deep in the bush? Well, wouldn't you know it, *I* live in the house tucked deep in the bush. Why haven't those men of ugly come to harass us in this house? They know we are here, and if they indeed wish to assert their dominance and exercise their authority, wouldn't we be the best ones to harass and dominate? Our house is ideal for them. Off the beaten path and totally covered in jungle, their covert operatives would go unnoticed. It would be just another unwitnessed crime against humanity. When are they going to strike next? When are they going to mobilize and storm our house under false pretenses of arms smuggling, drug laundering, harboring Hutus, or any other fabrication? And if they don't make their attack tonight, then what about tomorrow or the next day?

171

Last night, Ingo, Suzanne, and I found ourselves trapped in a room with bars on every wall and window waiting to be slaughtered, like pigs in a pigsty destined to be made into bacon. After our release, we felt not only lucky to be alive and unharmed, but grateful to have been out of harm's way. The others at Base Camp were not as lucky as us. Or were they? Just look at us now. We are again imprisoned, this time by our own minds.

Prior to this latest attack, our worst enemy and impediment to our freedom was the unknown. Now, as my brain goes berserk and tortures me with its incessant chatter, it is unclear if it is the unknown or my own brain that is the real villain.

It is early morning, and the moon still claims the sky. The sun is nowhere to be seen. The passing of the baton between them is still in the waiting. Usually the handover is flawless, as is everything else in nature. I listen intently to the sounds of life outside. These little treasures are so ingratiating and realigning. They reaffirm the magical gift of life and remind me of the privilege I have to be alive. But is this privilege afforded to me soon to expire? I consider my personal safety. Am I safe? Tucking myself under a mosquito net gives me no protection at all. My room has a security lock on it, but what good is it? There is a guard at the front gate, but he is not allowed to bear arms, so how is he supposed to guard us? If there is ever an armed confrontation, what does he have to protect us? The answer is nothing! Admittedly, his uniform does make him look official, but the man is small and meek. He is also very kind and gentle, two attributes that don't necessarily instill confidence in his capacity to protect us.

I think of the 20 militiamen from yesterday's raid climbing over our fence, storming our living quarters, ripping through our belongings, and throwing everything on the floor. I see them with their submachine guns, taunting and intimidating us. What will they do? And when will they do it?

We come as volunteers, risking our lives, living in lack, and dancing with death. Those in power abuse their power and manipulate us like marionettes as they act out their fanatical fancies and proceed with their political agendas. They exploit the international community's goodwill by parasitizing us. Rents for expatriates are a hundred times more than locals pay, and administrative fees, visas, and other required services are astronomical because we have money, and they want it. The international community pays because our mandate is to serve at any cost. Millions of dollars are doled out with no strings attached for permission to remain in the country. In the end, we are allowed to stay here on the condition that all our material resources, like vehicles, communication devices, and office suites, are surrendered to them at the end of our service. I am not bitter, not sweet, not savory, but acidic.

We are being attacked not only by people with political power but by rebels as well. Three landmines were placed in front of our clinic in the outlying border town of Gisenyi. Was our clinic intentionally targeted, or was there a mistake? Were those landmines intended to sever our limbs? Or were they a warning not to challenge the authority of the Interahamwe, the Hutu militia responsible for orchestrating and fomenting the massacre? These Hutu rogues are beyond infuriated because they were shamefully defeated by the very Tutsis they had intended to exterminate. Their failure to annihilate the entire Tutsi population will inevitably cost them dearly, as they are certain to be avenged sometime in the future by tomorrow's Tutsis, whose successors may very well carry on the hate.

The Interahamwe are presently hiding somewhere in the bush. They make their moves at night under the cover of darkness and engage in a sort of guerrilla warfare intended to terrorize the population and destabilize the current Tutsi-led government. They also terrorize us, humanitarian aid workers, because we add stability, credibility, and viability to their arch-enemy—the government—by providing financial assistance, medical services and infrastructural support. As a result, they do not want us here. To be honest, I do not want to be here either. I am no good dead.

17 October 1994
Monday

My Dearest,

People procure pills under the table and sell them on the black or open market. The vendors have no medical training and know nothing about drug interactions, contraindications, or dosing. They sell to the poor, who are too poor to afford medical care and too illiterate to understand the difference between the little purple pill, the triangular yellow one, or the sky-blue rectangular variety. The rampant, indiscriminate, and inappropriate use of drugs has emboldened pathogens, which are now resistant to many medications currently on the global market. The mosquito that causes malaria and the bacterium that causes tuberculosis, for example, are now resistant to our treatments worldwide.

People around the world may feel immune to what happens on the African continent, but in a world where international travel is so easy, no one is safe. Tourists and business travelers are perfect vectors for all infectious agents, which they carry unknowingly from place to place, across borders, over oceans, through cities, and even into people's bedrooms. We are all connected. We are all interconnected.

18 October 1994
Tuesday

My Dearest,

Days ago, the head of our mission called for a countrywide suspension of all humanitarian activities until the government apologized for its military aggression against us and gave its assurance that it would not happen again. This morning, the government finally met our demands, and we are once again allowed to return to our posts at the hospital. This is a very good development because the suspension of our medical services only punished the people needing medical attention. The in-house patients, unfortunately, suffered the most. The military and government officials were not moved, disturbed, or inconvenienced in any way.

The staff are ecstatic to have us back with them. They give us hugs and smile big smiles when they see us, then shower us with more hugs. This affection is precisely what I need right now—a real sense of *divisionlessness*. When we are connected, unified, and care for each other, a better world is possible.

A bit later in the day ...

The elation from our morning reunion at the hospital lasts just a tad over a moment. It all goes from great to good to bad to really bad in the span of a blink. While evaluating the patients for the first time in two days, I discover the medical service has been completely neglected. The patient's charts were not done, discharges were not made, medications were not given, and many of our pharmaceuticals have mysteriously disappeared. The ward is unrecognizable—a veritable ruin. I spend hours trying to put the pieces together again to where the ward looks somewhat recognizable.

One step forward and ten steps back seems to be the local dance here. Little is sustainable, workmanship is shoddy, and indifference is the rule. I lose hope. I lose patience. And I lose my focus. I should practice patience, but patience is a virtue I don't have in abundance, especially when I see patients paying the price for the staff's poor performance.

One of my nurses publicly denounced me for scolding him in front of the patients. He is correct. I did. And I was wrong. I apologized, but that doesn't give back his face that I took from him in front of the patients. In my defense, I have absolutely zero tolerance for any of my Tutsi staff neglecting, taunting, or abusing our Hutu patients. When I see them reversing the discrimination by hating or hurting a Hutu, I go ballistic. They cannot bring their war onto the ward. While there are no guns permitted in the hospital, the staff are armed with a plethora of weapons at their disposal to dispose of their enemies: drugs, needles, and HIV-infected blood to name just a few. Does anyone really believe this war is over or that the genocide has ended? Round one may be over, but round two has just begun. The game is the same. The players are the same. In this second round, however, the Tutsis have taken the lead and are literally and figuratively beating the Hutus. I seem to have become the referee now, calling the shots and fouls and fining the players when they step out of line or go too far.

I am so out of balance. My expectations are unrealistic, my pursuit of excellence is impractical, and my tolerance level is teetering. Life here is starting to wear on me. The lack of order, the lack of security, the lack of comfort, and the lack of hope are breaking my spirit. Again, I wonder what I'm doing here at all. Maybe tomorrow I'll find my answer.

19 October 1994
Wednesday

My Dearest,

There are babies in front, back, next to, and all around me. They are all critically ill. We have the resources to try to save only one of them. But which one? Which baby deserves to live longer than the others? I am tasked with making the decision.

Four of our babies need surgery. In *Lands of Lots*, there is no discussion, debate or negotiation. When it comes to saving a life, all is clear: the sky's the limit, full speed ahead, all hands on deck—anything and everything to save a life. In a place that has no food, however, saving a child's life is not so clear. There are numerous sensitive issues to consider. For example, the worth of a single infant is, by necessity, weighed like a pound of potatoes. Sadly, the value of a child goes down exponentially when food is in short supply. When food is scarce, a child becomes one more mouth to feed. One more mouth becomes a burden. In the case of illness, when a child is unable to contribute to the household, one more mouth to feed becomes a major liability.

To save this baby, or not to save this baby ... that is the question. What makes this place unique from other places is the stark reality that I am the judge, the jury, the prosecutor, and the plaintiff. I'm the deliberator, police force, insurer, and the insurance policy. I'm the guardian. I'm the janitor. I wipe up messes afterward, both physically and emotionally. This is too much responsibility in the hands of a single person. Who am I to play God? Who am I to decide whether or not to save a baby? Yes, this baby deserves a chance to live, but what about all the other babies? Which baby has the greatest chance of surviving? How do I know? And how am I going to face the parents who watch, wait, and wish their precious one is the one we choose to treat? There are not enough resources for everyone. So, do I do another *eeny, meeny, miny, moe*? Do I make a random decision or postpone making the decision until a baby's condition degrades enough for the decision to be made by default?

After three hours of intense deliberation, I am exhausted. No number of hours deliberating can make this decision right. Four children need surgery. We can only help one of them. I choose to save baby number four. The other children—baby number one, baby number two, and baby number three—are tragically abandoned, knowing full well that death will feast on them. I make my decision with considerable consternation of the *One* upstairs who is making mess after mess with my patients. We are due for an angel to come and offer us a ram. Abraham in the Bible was said to have been given a break, and I think we should get one too. Please, no more tests of our faith. Let the children live. Let the mothers and fathers live too. The Rwandan people have been slain enough. I wonder if I should put some blood above each door of every child so death passes over them. Or should I offer an olive branch?

20 October 1994
Thursday

My Dearest,

Yesterday, I played God at the pearly gates and made the agonizing executive decision to save a particular baby. While it was grueling deciding who to save and who to surrender, I eventually found solace in my decision. Baby number four was going to live because of us. Eventually, I started feeling proud that I had the power to block this little girl's trip to heaven by offering her surgery. It is always uncomfortable for me to play the role of Mr. Big Wig, deciding people's fates, but this time it felt gratifying. Admittedly, Ego made a surprise visit and insisted on participating. We all want our moment of grandeur from time to time, no? Well, apparently, it wasn't the time. It wasn't the time for any of us. Heaven had a change of heart and took not only baby number one, two, and three but baby number four as well, despite all of our heroic efforts. I was abruptly checkmated and put in my place, shoved horizontally like a pawn pummeled by the king. I am once again reminded that I am not in charge.

21 October 1994
Friday

My Dearest,

Death won yesterday, wins today, and will win tomorrow. I am no match for it. Daily deaths are so commonplace that when there are none, I think something is wrong. Death has beaten me to a pulp, and there is nothing left but pulp. At this point, I don't battle the battle anymore. I just surrender.

A young woman comes in quite ill today. She looks old and "graggled." Graggled isn't a real word but describes her very real debilitated state. What is the differential diagnosis for graggle? She could have tuberculosis, malaria, psychosis or even AIDS. People infected with tuberculosis have a typical pathetic appearance, a characteristic way of breathing, and a particular rhythmic, hacking cough. They are often wasted, apathetic and lethargic. Malaria also comes with its own brazen barbarism: very high fevers, rigors, stupor, coma and death. It is ruthless, merciless, uncompromising, incorrigible, and immensely powerful—king of the jungle. Malaria could cause anyone to look older than they are and graggled. It could also cause psychosis, which is so mind-deforming and debilitating that anyone with it would be blessed to die. The same could be said of HIV, the Human Immunodeficiency Virus—the king of kings and dukes—the demon of all diseases. It is nuclear. It is arrogant. It is fanatical enough to commit suicide bombings that kill its host and itself. Nothing is its match. Everyone is prey to it, and no one survives it.

People with AIDS have a distinct look. The young woman I speak of has the distinct look. How can I describe it? It doesn't need description. It doesn't deserve the time and place to acknowledge its miserable, wretched ways.

Africa is believed to be the birthplace of HIV. In fact, some researchers suggest that the virus originated in this very region. As a result, the percentage of people infected with this killer virus is one of the highest in the world. At any given time, 30–40% of the hospital beds are occupied by people who have AIDS. It is just a matter of time before 100% of the beds will be occupied by people suffering from the same. Tragically, I can do nothing to help these people other than send them home with a bar of soap and worthless blessings.

AIDS is ruthlessly cruel because it starts, in most cases, by first taking the man of the house and then inevitably taking the woman of the house, who goes through all the suffering twice: first with her husband and then with herself. As she cares for her husband, she does not yet realize that, in due time, she will also fall ill and depend on the kindness of loved ones—if she has any still living, of course. The woman's ordeal only gets worse. After her death, her children will have to fend for themselves and be their own guardians and advocates because there are not enough orphanages in the country to welcome them. Unfortunately, children who have no adult supervision or family support often end up on the street, where they beg and borrow and do what is *necessary* to satisfy passersby who ask for *kindnesses* in the dark of the night in exchange for a pittance that will barely fill their bellies for the evening. Regrettably, the men who toy with these children do not practice safe sex and too often fill their conquests with HIV-infected ejaculate. The children know nothing about HIV. They come to know about it and their status when they are too far gone and find themselves on their deathbed in a hospital, if they are lucky. The worst part of this tragedy is that the men violating these children know they carry the virus and intentionally seek out virgins to infect them. Why? There is a prevailing myth here that claims when an HIV-positive person has sex with a virgin, the virus leaves their body and enters instead into their sexual partner. In other words, these men premeditate the murder of the little people in the hope of curing themselves. The catch? For this *cure* to work, it has to be a virgin to make the transfer complete; hence the condom-less deposits dumped into the unsuspecting, innocent, young hosts. Having sex here is like playing Duck, Duck Good or Hot Potato. The one who ends up with the virus is out—plain and simple. In this particular romp, sorry to say, everyone is out.

Later in the day, I review the patients' lab work. The young, graggled woman I tested for HIV is positive. As her physician, it is my responsibility to give her the information. How do you tell someone they are going to die soon when they have come to you for help? It is said that medicine is an art. Well, I am quite hard-pressed to find anything artistic in the medicine we practice here at this hospital.

In college, I flunked Art 101. The professor told me my art was primitive. I told him Picasso's art was primitive too. My painting this evening to my patient is not even primitive. It is brutally honest and inappropriately accurate. I tell the young woman that she has AIDS. It is a death sentence, and she knows it. When she hears her diagnosis, she has no reaction. Is this bravery or shock, denial or indifference, or maybe even relief? Her husband has already died of AIDS. Did he know he carried the virus? Did he intentionally inject her with it to save his life? If so, why is she being punished for a crime her husband committed? She suffered through his death, and now she is being punished again by going through her own death. Is this not a case of double jeopardy? She has already endured enough. Why again?

The woman's mother asks me for my advice. I say a simple thing: "I think your daughter should go home and be with her family." I tell her that I am not God and cannot predict what will happen tomorrow, but it is likely that her daughter will die within a year. The woman responds by not responding. Why did I spell out her daughter's future? Why did I set her dear daughter's death date? How did my words help her make it through another day? My artwork deserves no more than a flunking grade. It is not even primitive; it is barbaric.

22 October 1994
Saturday

My Dearest,

The young woman who came in yesterday with AIDS is in isolation room four. It will be her private suite, a refuge from the real world, a place where she can feel safe and supported as she adjusts to her diagnosis of death. Regardless of this hospitality, death hovers at her door, ready to snag her if she dares to peek out. As I pass her room, I cringe at giving her a limited warranty that is due to expire at the end of the year. Why did I spell out the terms of her contract with life?

I don't approve of some of the responsibilities outlined in my job description as a doctor. Why are doctors expected to explain the contractual agreements as well as the fine print of people's non-negotiable life insurance policies? It is unfair that some people are cheated by being given policies that don't pay off or out, or shoddy ones that expire prematurely. It is cruel and inhumane to bring someone to life's playing field only to have them kicked off the team before they have a chance to play. I understand we were never promised 80-plus years to play on the planet. I also understand that it is our responsibility to make the most of the game in the time we are given. But for some, life is just not fair.

Why did I disclose this woman's termination date? I only wanted her to have a realistic picture of her future so she could plan and prepare, forgive and forget, and spend quality time with people she loves. How does anyone prepare to die in Rwanda? There are no life insurance policies to procure, no pensions to pass on, and no wills to write.

181

I go to room four to care not only for the patient but for the patient's mother, who has been exquisitely attentive to her daughter. Last night, she was up the entire evening, silently and selflessly attending to her child's every need. Mom does not want to miss a minute of togetherness since the minutes they have together are so abbreviated. I bring them food, blankets, and provisions to make life a little easier. Taking care of both of them makes me feel good. Being able to help people when they most need a heart to feel and a hand to hold is a real privilege.

23 October 1994
Sunday

My Dearest,

Am I drunk? I don't drink. What is wrong with me? My body feels as if it has been run over repeatedly by a semi. I can barely move. I am completely exhausted and can't get up from my bed. Is this malaria? A single bite from a mosquito could do this. I mourn the impending premature loss of a woman with AIDS, while I may very well depart before her.

There are four distinct species of *Plasmodium*, the parasite that causes malaria. Three of them cause just mild, flu-like symptoms. The fourth species, *Plasmodium falciparum*, kills. Different species affect different regions of the world. The one we have here in Rwanda is—that's right—*falciparum,* the one that kills. Most expats elect to take malaria prophylaxis, just in case. I don't do "just in case," so I'm not on any prophylaxis, which might have come in handy right about now.

Death seems to have won me over. My body is surprisingly unable to cope with whatever I have. Could I have cerebral malaria? Cerebral malaria occurs when the malarial parasite reaches the brain and blocks its blood vessels. If blood cannot flow through these obstructed vessels, the brain does not get enough oxygen to function and essentially suffocates to death. The part of the brain affected determines whether a person will live, die, or be permanently disabled. Some people fully recover, but others end up with paralysis of the face or limbs, aphasia, or cognitive impairment. Some can remain in a coma for years, while others die within hours of being infected. Many people in Rwanda, regardless of their age, have had strokes from such brain blockages. Their distorted faces, life-altering paralyses, and cognitive impairment attest to cerebral malaria's crippling consequences. I don't want to be crippled. I don't want any facial distortions. If I get cerebral malaria, let it take me and all my pathetic parts.

24 October 1994
Monday

My Dearest,

I'm feeling so much better. Thank You. Now, out of mortal danger, I can breathe again. Curiously, while this should be cause for celebration, I find myself surprisingly withdrawn, overcome by an awkward, melancholic nostalgia. I was doing well until I started writing to friends back home and realized there was nothing to say. What I am experiencing in Rwanda cannot be conveyed in any meaningful way to people on the outside. Our world here is out of this world, and trying to bridge it with the West is senseless and almost unkind. For some reason, it seems inappropriate to share details of our personal trauma with people on the outside. It's not that we are a secret, sacred, or special society, but this hell we are living is a sort of private matter to be kept within the family. Parading our sorrow for everyone to see is akin to putting us on display at a freak show for all to gawk at and pity. I use the collective pronoun "our" because patients and aid workers are in this thing together. Together, we are the ink that writes this page of history in this indelible nightmare.

Next subject: Three more people are diagnosed with HIV today. After much reflection, I have decided not to tell patients anything more than nothing. HIV is a death sentence in Africa. Villagers don't know anything about this wicked disease, but they do know that everyone who has it eventually dies prematurely. In other words, saying "You have HIV," means "You are going to die." So I will say nothing when they

183

test positive. And I will say nothing about their prognosis. Unlike pregnancy, where you give patients a due date, I will not set an expiration date on anyone's life. I think it is best to gently say, "Ma'am, you have a small virus in your blood, so small that you can't see it with your eyes. It is making you feel unwell. Soon you will have no more pain or suffering." This will be my new and improved artwork—something more picturesque.

The weight of loss is too heavy for me just now. It feels like I'm running a race with an enormous weight on my shoulders. Sometimes I need a hug or something special to make it to and through the finish line. Coincidentally, I did get something special today: a few patients said, "thank you." Patients rarely acknowledge our efforts, so when they do, it is truly special. This is exactly what I needed because I'm constantly berating myself when things go wrong with patients.

Regardless of the circumstances, I take every death on the ward to heart and blame myself for everything that goes wrong. I call this the "Could Have, Should Have, Would Have Syndrome." If only I had… I should have … Why didn't I … become broken records that play and replay again until I feel I have been punished enough for the losses of life. But enough is never enough. Even when people live and leave the hospital cured, I can't celebrate these successes because they can't unearth, resurrect, and reanimate the corpses in the coffins just six feet under in my own private cemetery.

Appreciation from patients does go a long way to soothe the sores and self-deprecation. A simple "thank you" makes a world of difference. When such words come my way, my heart is hugged and spins wildly on its own axis. Gratitude is wonderfully healing. A simple smile massages my spirit and rejuvenates it. Sometimes patients extend a hand or wrap their arms around me as a way of blessing me. These too make my heart beat boldly. Such gestures of gratitude are reminders that, despite all the things I could've, should've, or would've done, I have also done some good.

My Dearest,

"How many children do you have?" I ask.

"Three," she answers.

Next to the woman are six children. "Whose children are these?" I inquire.

"Mine," she says.

"How many children do you have?" I ask again.

"Three," she repeats.

Women here do not include their children who are under five years old in the family census. Infant mortality is so high that children are only counted once they reach the age of five. If they make it to five years old, chances are they will survive, barring genocide, of course. I wonder if this counting custom isn't practiced to protect parents from the pain and suffering that comes with the death of a child. It just hurts too much to bury child after child. So, don't consider them yours until they reach the more viable age of five; it hurts less.

One reason children die in Africa is measles. This disease of childhood didn't stir much commotion back home in my youth. For children, it is actually kind of cool to get it. As compensation for a few inconveniences like a fever, cough, and some red skin marks, you don't have to go to school for a few days, and you get extra television time, ice cream, kisses, and lots of cuddles from mom, too. What could be better?

In places where immunizations are plentiful and routinely administered to children, measles is essentially obsolete today. In fact, in my entire medical career, I have never encountered a single case. In Africa, however, the medical texts warn of an alarming 35% mortality rate when unvaccinated children are infected with it. I am not good with statistics, but if I'm not mistaken, this means that out of 100 people with measles, 35 will die. But when did the theory in medical texts ever reflect the reality in the field? Statistics are meaningless. I have to see things with my own eyes to believe them.

Measles has just come to Ruhengeri. With this virulence in our backyard, *Médecins Sans Frontières* takes the lead and immediately mobilizes an immunization campaign around the country. The overall vaccine coverage among children in Rwanda has historically been abysmally low, so MSF acts swiftly to head off disaster. Our team goes early to the field and sets up camp to vaccinate as many people as possible. Villagers flock to our health posts, hoping our supply will last long enough for them to get vaccinated. What a difference from our previous vaccination campaign, when no one showed up. Judging from today's frantic turnout, it appears the people already understand the implications of a widespread measles epidemic. Have they gone through this before, and if so, are there any survivors left to tell what they saw?

After a grueling day vaccinating hundreds of children, we return to the hospital. Everyone is exhausted. On our arrival, there is a man waiting for us in the outpatient department. He brought his two sons to us for a consultation. I examine them. They both have measles. Luckily, the boys are only slightly feverish and do not appear to be ill. They tolerate solids and liquids, have no diarrhea or vomiting, and remain active. The virus is in its early stages, so I tell Dad to return home and give the boys plenty of fluids and acetaminophen for fever. I also advise him to follow up with us for further medical care if his children's conditions worsen. This is the usual banter for benign viral infections: observation, fluids, fever control, and follow-up. To date, there are no medications available to treat viruses like measles, unlike bacterial infections, which are treatable with antibiotics. Therefore, the treatment for measles is only symptomatic care for now.

The father is not happy with me. He wants his children hospitalized. I consider his request, but as this is potentially the beginning of an epidemic, many other children will surely be coming in with more severe symptoms and will require hospitalization. Given our limited bed capacity, I decide to save vacant beds for them. There is also another problem to consider when bringing people with measles into the hospital. Our hospitalized patients are weak, immunocompromised, and very vulnerable to infections, especially those who have AIDS. I must minimize their exposure to the measles virus, which could have catastrophic consequences for them. My reasoning is clear, my mind is set, and I remain adamant about the father returning home with his children and following up as needed. The father continues to plead with me and begs me to reconsider. I am unbudgeable. Eventually, he reluctantly gives in and returns home with his children. It is abundantly clear that this man loves his sons. It is obvious in the way he holds them. It is also abundantly clear that he is not happy with me. It is obvious in the way he looks at me.

26 October 1994
Wednesday

My Dearest,

Part of my work here is to impart knowledge, promote public health, and help people make decisions based on what is best for the greater good. This is a monumental task because people here are living in survival mode—from hand to mouth. Waste disposal, handwashing, and education are luxuries for the rich. Most people here lack such luxuries. It isn't practical for people to go to school or think of the greater good when they're barely hanging on to life. Out of necessity, they must spend every waking hour scrounging around for their next meal, whenever that might be—tomorrow, the next day, or even the days after that. If they manage to find something to eat, they still don't have the luxury to wash their hands, read a book, or concern themselves with waste disposal. They have to collect wood to cook and fetch water to drink, both of which require transportation and time—lots of it. But they don't have transportation. What they do have are bare feet to carry them to the fields, calloused hands, backs, hips, and shoulders to toil the fields, and heads to carry their fields' generosity.

187

27 October 1994
Thursday

My Dearest,

He came back. The man I saw two days ago with his two sons came back. He came back with his two sons … dead.

Dad's skin is beaded with sweat, as if it were crying. His heart is broken; his face is terrifying; his posture is menacing.

"You killed my boys. You killed my boys. Killer! You killed my boys!" he shouts at me in the hospital corridor. In each hand is a dead son, limp and lifeless.

I stand before him feeling vulnerable and deeply wounded. I stand there shamed, disgraced and humiliated. Patients look on, trying to make sense of things and find a solution to this standoff. My nurses come quickly to my rescue and take my side unreservedly in a show of solidarity with me. I will never forget how they rallied around me, creating a buffer zone between Dad and me. Odette astutely notices that something is critically wrong with me. She senses my entire body shutting down and takes immediate action to revive me. Pushing me into a nearby supply closet, she shuts the door. There is no light. We stand in the darkness as she tries to comfort me.

"Listen, Dr. Cary, you didn't kill these children! Dr. Cary, you didn't kill these children," she says over and over, trying to reprogram the event and retrieve any remnants that may have gone into the cells of my soul. Completely in the dark in this small supply closet, I hear her words, but nothing registers. I am in a profound state of shock. I can't see Odette, but I can see the two dead, limp boys hanging from the man's hands. I am in excruciating mental pain, unsteady, trembling, and out of my mind and body. I'm elsewhere. I can't say where, but not here. "Dr. Cary, you didn't kill these children," Odette repeats. This can't be happening. This can't be real. I remain this way for a while, until I'm exhausted. "Dr. Cary, you didn't kill these children," Odette rhythmically chants in the background of an abyss I've thrown myself into.

By the time we emerge from the closet, the nurses have calmed the dad and managed to get him to leave the hospital and return home. But he'll never, ever be away from me. My cemetery is forever mine. "Killer! You killed my boys!" The boys weren't that ill to justify hospitalization. How did they deteriorate so quickly from a minor malaise to death in just two days? Why didn't Dad bring them back to the hospital for medical attention sooner? It's my fault. I didn't think. I didn't know. I didn't plan. I didn't understand. I didn't anticipate.

These boys died because of me. I shouldn't have sent them home. Their home was barely a hut—a hut without water, without windows, without light. Dad never went to school. He can't read or write. How could I have asked him to assess his children, monitor their fevers, and check their mental status? How would he know how to assess a severely ill child? How could he check his children's temperature? He didn't have a thermometer. Even if he had one, he is illiterate and probably doesn't know his numbers. He doesn't even have light in the hut to see the thermometer. How could Dad know how the children were progressing without light to see? My ignorance and stupidity killed these children! None of this would have happened had I admitted the boys to the ward and cared for them myself. They may have died of simple dehydration from a lack of fluids. Water may have been their medicine. Water could have made the difference between life and death. No one in their hut knew what to do. Had I given it more thought and truly listened to Dad's plea to hospitalize his children, they would most likely still be alive. Instead, I sent them home, or should I say, I sent them *hut*. Why didn't I go to check on the children yesterday? House calls are not permitted because of security concerns, military curfews, mines, and Interahamwe hideouts, but I'm sure I could have figured out a way. What have I done? Dad's tears will drown me for the rest of my life. These boys were over five years old. They were counted, and now their lives are discounted.

Dad goes back home alone. I go back to my graveyard with his two boys.

28 October 1994
Friday

My Dearest,

Yesterday was hard on me. The loss of those two young boys left me emotionally black and blue. My wounds are deep, my pain is severe, and my morale is beyond broken. Last night was rough. I couldn't sleep. Instead, I spent the entire evening beating myself up, hoping the beating would somehow bring them back to life. The only way I can get through this is to trust that there is something better for them after death. I also take solace in the fact that I am human and can't really take, give, or save life. I must trust that something much bigger than me is ultimately responsible for taking or leaving, starting or ending a person's timeshare on the planet.

If I'm going to stay here and be helpful, I need strength to know my limits, wisdom to know right from wrong, and faith to believe in things I cannot see, hear or touch.

When I'm down this way, I go to nature. It always gives me insights, perspective, clarity and peace. The volcanoes, for example, are my elders. They stand stoically and remind me to stand tall and be still, to pause and be patient, no matter how hard the wind blows. There are also the clouds. They poke their way to the foreground, and though just a collection of white and puff, they manage to block the sun, which is bigger, bolder, hotter, and stronger in comparison. The clouds remind me of the majestic power in the things that look meek. They epitomize the infinite potential of the underdog. The clouds also tell stories through their changing configurations and remind me of the transient nature of all things. Everything is temporary: love and hate, life and death, sickness and health. They, too, shall all pass like the clouds. Then there are the expansive forests. Resembling florets of broccoli from above, there is not a free millimeter of space between their florets to be individual. They teach me about the importance of cooperation. Consider nature's thousands of different plant species living in cramped and congested places. Yet, they all live in harmony. Nature's gardens remind me of the gift we were given to have each other. While we are all different, we are also all the same. And then there are the birds flying above. They are oblivious to the chaos that man orchestrates below. The birds sing a sweet song that touches everyone equally. They sing to every ear and every heart. They remind me that all I have to do is be like a bird—sing sweetly to everyone equally.

29 October 1994
Saturday

My Dearest,

I ask one of my nurses, Jamuel, about his personal story of the massacre. Immediately, tears well up in his eyes. He says nothing. I wish so much to be let in—to touch the hearts and see the souls of those who lived through tortured times. I want so much to comfort those who saw things they shouldn't have seen and are now destroyed because of it. It is hard to broach the subject of the genocide. Any attempt to do so feels like I am trespassing on territory that is still too raw and mined.

How will the people cope in the years to come? Can they ever forgive, forget, and move on? I still have not recovered from seeing just a single severed human arm in a field weeks ago. How could anyone ever heal after seeing a mom or baby cut into pieces while still alive? What is Jamuel's story?

30 October 1994
Sunday

My Dearest,

It's raining today. Life seems to stop when it rains. I escape to the call room to hide away from the sum total of everything. I'm physically and emotionally exhausted. My heart and mind are at odds with each other, and my confidence crumbles. What am I doing here? This question plays in my mind like a mantra that repeats itself robotically. What is our purpose, and what are we accomplishing? Everyone in the team begins to wonder if what we believe and what we are doing are misaligned.

I look at the Rwandan people struggling to put their lives back together. Where does one begin? They came to the world without a manual to maneuver themselves through this maze called life. Had there been a manual, I can say with certainty it wouldn't have included a chapter on post-genocidal recovery. The people are all so battered, so helpless and hopeless that they no longer recognize themselves—a broken people, their emotions in tatters, their spirits mangled. Many see themselves permanently disabled—too crippled to care, too handicapped to walk. Under the current circumstances, it is understandable that they use aid workers as their walkers and wheelchairs. We aid workers, in turn, feel needed and indispensable, carrying them, tending to all their needs. Much like parents, we feed, shelter, and teach them new skills to survive in the real world again. It feels good to lend a shoulder and hold a hand. It is so satisfying to care. But what if those with strong legs refuse to walk, and those with keen ears refuse to listen, and those with sharp minds refuse to learn?

I have been carrying people who could have and should have been walking. And now my back aches, my heart hurts, and my will wavers. The sense of satisfaction that I once had preparing a fledgling for flight wanes. The joy of harvest is slashed, and the stench of senselessness gets stronger.

There is a growing sense of entitlement here. The patients see the sun and it's too yellow. They see the moon and it's too bright. The food is not enough, the transportation is too slow, the medicines are their birthright, and those at their disposal are disposable. And as for gratitude, well, there's little to none as far as the eyes can see and the ears can hear.

I find that I am becoming intolerant of people's demands and expectations. "Give me" and "get me" are the new hellos and how-are-yous. The patients and caregivers make no effort to help their neighbors. They eat, spit, and even defecate on the floor, expecting the custodian to clean up after them. What was once excusable, given the times and trauma the people endured, is now intolerable.

Something has shifted for me, and I struggle to make sense of it all. Can a person love too much? As silly as it sounds, I believe this is what we aid workers have done here. We have loved too much. As a result, a once strong and resolute people have become demotivated dependents, waiting for the next handout. What have we done? How can we help them regain their power and stand on their own two feet again? How can we break the dependency we created by doling out diamonds, which in the end have only crippled the people more?

31 October 1994
Monday

My Dearest,

Security around the country is rapidly deteriorating: forty-six people were slaughtered just one hour from here; five people were *macheted* to death two days ago; one of our residences was looted; and more landmines have been placed around the country. To make matters worse, a female expat was attacked and forced to "comply" with a gun to her head. She may have survived the gun, but her "compliance" may have cost her life because of an even mightier weapon—HIV. Did the man have it, and if he did, did he infect her with it? She has to be tested to find out her fate. The woman came here with an open heart to serve the people. Little did she know that she walked into a lion's den with a much more virulent beast that would feast on her flesh from the inside out, leaving her skeletal, and then gone with the wind.

And speaking of fate, the head of the prefecture dislikes our organization because we report human rights abuses that we encounter here to the international community beyond the Rwandan borders. Our mandate is *doctors without borders*. We are supposed to be neutral, impartial and apolitical. We are threatening our good standing and putting our safety in jeopardy by observing what we are not supposed to see and reporting what we are not supposed to repeat. "Hear no evil, see no evil, speak no evil" should be our mandate. Or should it?

193

1 November 1994
Tuesday

My Dearest,

Tough day today… The a, b, c, d, and e go like this:

a) People in Kigali are attacked with guns and robbed.

b) I test ten people for HIV. Eight are positive.

c) A staff member gives patients nalidixic acid instead of aspirin. Nalidixic acid is an antibiotic used to treat Shigella, a bacterium that causes severe dysentery. Aspirin, also known as salicylic acid, is used to treat inflammation. Both salicylic and nalidixic end in "*ic*," so the staff member figured they must have similar properties. Luckily, no one was hurt.

d) A man fakes an asthmatic attack to stay in the hospital. Many other patients have their stories and lists of ailments to stay in the hospital too. Why not? We have everything they want: food, water, beds, shelter, medication and security. In addition, we have no mines, machetes or machine guns. If I could, I would go against protocol and do what I see as the only conscionable thing to do: open the hospital gates and feed, clothe, and protect everyone who comes for a helping hand. But there are so many blocks between could and should, too much distance between here and there. Also, there are many people who need a helping hand, and too few of us helpers with free hands. We just don't have the manpower, the security, or the resources to accommodate everyone's needs. Things are so critical that we are even low on food and have to count the grains of rice we ration to the patients, stingily stretching our stockpiles to feed as many people as possible.

e) And then there is Sandrine, our amazing nurse from France. She gives her blood to a 14-year-old boy during an emergency operation. Her donation saves his life. Apparently, she has done this twice before and has now become anemic herself. She tells no one of the countless times she's touched and saved lives. It is moving and inspiring to see someone with such a strong commitment and capacity to care.

2 November 1994
Wednesday

My Dearest,

There is nothing particularly unusual about the day. It starts like every other day, with the village children accompanying me along a one-mile stretch to the hospital. Like every other day, they compete to hold my hand as they parade with me down the road. By default, I have become the people's Pied Piper with my little entourage of benevolent beings. And as usual, once we reach the hospital gate, they smile, giggle and laugh, then wave goodbye and scatter in all directions.

The view from the hospital gate is like every other day too, with military convoys carrying prized and precious human cargo—soldiers—pretentiously robed in uniforms that boast a gross shade of green, like phlegm, the next best thing to ugly. Besides the display of military might, people briskly walk in all directions, barefoot, on the street, going somewhere.

Life inside the hospital gate is also "same same," as is my routine: enter the internal medicine ward and greet the staff and inpatients, review the new admissions, and then see the outpatients waiting patiently in line at the clinic entrance. The serenity inside the hospital compound remains an oasis in a quagmire of chaos that stirs irreverently just beyond its gates. This compound is a place of refuge. It is in the country of Rwanda but separate from it. What is on the outside is not permitted on the inside. Within the hospital's walls, fences and gates, life is the closest thing to normal. It may be stark with just the basics, but we are so fortunate because we have peace and safety, which, in these times, are at a premium.

Speaking of safety, because of security concerns, we are not permitted to stray too much beyond our residences or the hospital compound. This means that we are essentially under house and hospital arrest. There is one exception to this rule, however. We can walk from our residences to the hospital, which is about a mile away. The chance of being attacked or hurt along this one-mile stretch is unlikely, so the organization

195

has allowed us to walk this short distance unaccompanied and unprotected. These few feet are strikingly sensational, not only because of the lush tropical landscape, jungle vocals, and majestic volcanoes, but because we are free. Being caged in compounds day and night makes us go stir-crazy. We crave more and more of the forbidden fruit—freedom. Not having it, understandably, makes it indescribably delicious. We want to pick it. We want to savor it. We want room to roam in it. Gosh, if freedom were an edible fruit that we could grow and eat, we would be morbidly obese. But it's not. So we return to reality and tolerate the bars and barbed wire that surround and incarcerate us. Fortunately, we are so busy that we don't pay much attention to them. There is just no time to dawdle with disdain for our captivity. It is a bit contradictory. On the one hand, we don't like being caged in a compound, but on the other hand, we are too frightened to be uncaged. For now, this arrangement works. In other words, it's not broken, so don't touch it.

Today is a typical day—until 9:00 AM. Then it is far from typical. Without any warning, the peace and tranquility in the hospital compound is interrupted by a tirade of paralyzing explosions that sound as if they are coming from only meters away. Sustained bombing accompanies massive artillery fire that resounds throughout the entire hospital compound as bullets seem to ricochet in every direction. The menacing sounds resemble a high-budget wartime movie that takes the unassuming audience by complete surprise as a deluge of death is heard in stereo through a Dolby sound system. The only difference is that we beat Dolby. There is no need for contrived sound effects for effect. I've never heard anything so intensely ominous. Judging from the reactions of the other people on the hospital grounds, they haven't either. Hundreds of people from around the compound start running toward me. I am standing on the veranda of the internal medicine ward, paralyzed by fear. I can't move. I can't react. My primal fight-or-flight goes immediately to a *state of stun* as I experience the end of the world right here, right now on a veranda. The people huddle around me, believing I can protect them. Is this our moment of truth, the moment we have all been expecting and fearing? We knew it would happen sooner or later. The patients figure that if this is the siege to end all sieges, I would be in a better bargaining position than they would be. Do they really believe my life and influence matter to a man clutching a Kalashnikov?

I grab my shortwave radio and fumble with the buttons. Calling for help seems like the logical thing to do. I pace a few feet to my right and then the same number of feet to my left. All eyes are on me as the people tremble, pleading for protection. I activate the emergency call button. No reply.

"Cary to base. Cary to base. Over." Again, nothing. *Please answer me!* I beg. "Cary to base. Cary to base, over."

There is still no answer. I pace back and forth, silently repeating a new mantra: *"I'm outta here! I'm outta here!"* Losing my patience, I shout aggressively into the receiver, *"I'm outta here!"* praying someone will answer and send a convoy to rescue us. No one answers. How could I have been so irresponsible to come to Rwanda? I'm sorry for putting myself in harm's way. If I make it through this ordeal alive, I promise I will leave. Please don't take me this way, I plead.

The deafening sounds of sustained explosions and machine gun rounds continue, terrorizing everyone. Haven't the people gone through enough? How will this end? This is too much, too much, too much! I didn't come here to die.

"Cary to base. Help! Cary to base, over."

Nothing. There's still nothing—not a word, *not an any-thing*. Where can we run? Where can we hide? Congregating in the internal medicine ward offers none of us any protection. And again, if they believe I have any clout or negotiating power as a foreign national or physician to protect them, they clearly do not understand how fragile my tenuous position is here in Rwanda. The truth is the militia, guerrillas, troops, bombs could care less about us, or the rules of engagement.

We are in a secured hospital compound that is supposedly a safe haven, a refuge, a sanctuary, protected by walls, gates and fences. But no steel barriers or braided barbed wires make any difference, and we know it. Like animals behind bars in a zoo, we are trapped and the easiest targets.

Finally, the radio operator answers, "Yes, Cary, over."

"Help! I need help, help, help! Over."

The sounds of machine guns and bombs continue in the background. The operator replies with a calm one would have ordering a takeaway pizza over the phone.

"What's up? Over," he asks.

"What's up?" I shout. "Can't you hear? Bombs, bombs, and more bombs. Everywhere bombs! Everywhere machine guns going wrong. Help! Please help us! Come quickly! Rescue needed! We're being attacked! Over!"

The operator's demeanor is so composed that I become immediately incensed and then irate. I completely lose it.

"Cary, calm, calm down," the operator says patronizingly, intimating that I'm overreacting.

Before he can finish, I interrupt his transmission and holler, "Calm down? Help! We are being attacked! Help! Over."

Again, he repeats, "Calm down," then adds, "Is the military action coming from behind the hospital? Over."

"Yes, exactly, affirmative; it seems to all be coming from behind the compound. Over."

The people are shaking with each explosion as we huddle closer and closer to one another, as if this will make any difference in our last moments of life.

With the nonchalance of a fawn in a forest nibbling on some wild berries, the radio attendant responds, "Cary, that's a military practice range. Over."

I don't understand him. Perhaps he can't hear me. "We are

being attacked. Attacked! We need evacuation. Help! Over."

He then repeats, "There is a military practice range behind the hospital. A military practice range, I repeat! The military is engaging in a mock drill. Over."

"A military practice range? A what? A military practice range? Over."

"Hmm," he says flippantly.

I can't believe it. I can't believe no one ever told us about this important detail—a military practice range! I am beyond stupefied. Given the unstable security situation in this country, how is it possible that we were never informed of this?

I immediately inform the staff, patients and caregivers. They are so traumatized that they can only stand frozen in time and wait for their bodies to thaw.

After some minutes of the same, quiet again is restored. I must admit, it never occurred to me that despite the incessant bombing and thousands of rounds of bullets fired, no one fell to the ground, no direct or collateral damage was sustained, and the earth was unmoved. I feel ridiculous. Over.

3 November 1994
Thursday

My Dearest,

I have recovered from yesterday's mock madness, and with that recovery went my fervent pledge to abandon ship. The team found the incident so amusing that I was able to see the humor in it and renegotiate with my higher self for perhaps another chance to make a go of it here. Once out of harm's way, it is easier to settle into the day's routine and face the mundane with more enthusiasm.

The days pass quickly, and there is never enough time to finish all the work. It would help if the ward functioned and the staff had better attitudes, but this isn't the case. The ward, at best, limps, and the staff are disgruntled. To be honest, our relationships are strained. I am not pleased with them, and they are not pleased with me. In all fairness, things have improved somewhat. Protocols are in place. Medication theft has been reduced. The staff are far more professional, and patients are receiving better care. Admittedly, I am strict and hold everyone to a higher standard than what they were used to, but when it comes to patient care, it must be so. While it would be nice to be liked by everyone on the ward, if it means compromising care, then I prefer the tightfisted, controlling version of myself that they so much resent. It is important to mention that my allegiance is also to the staff. Every second that I spend with them is an investment in their futures. The knowledge and skills they acquire can translate into promising careers for them. I do understand, however, that they are dealing with immense loss at this time, and anything having to do with their future is the least pressing thing on their list of priorities right now.

Helping people is ecstatically gratifying. I look forward to the day the staff also experience the ecstasy that comes with simply helping people. But can it ever be? We are on opposite sides of a long continuum, and the difference between us is enormous. On one side is me, the volunteer aid worker living his dream. I live to give. On the other side are the staff— employees trying to earn a living. I have everything I need and want, and then some. They are light years away from having the same fortune My future is more than secure; theirs is not. They are so entrenched in survival mode that they can't see anything beyond just getting through the next 24 hours.

Speaking of fortune, the best part of the day is a quiet excursion at sunset to a special, secret place that overlooks a valley. This valley hosts the night's colored clouds that crouch over the banana bushes below. It is exceptionally peaceful. It is generously endowed. After work, I often walk with Anne to this private, undisclosed Shangri-La. We walk and somehow talk without talking. She knows what I feel, and I feel what she knows. All around us is such beauty, such serenity, such sublime simplicity. It is all ice cream for the soul.

4 November 1994
Friday

A letter to Friends

My Dear Friends,

Tomorrow, someone is going to Holland and will mail our letters. Since there is still no postal service in the country, we remain dependent on the kindness of strangers. I will take full advantage and get this letter in his duffel bag.

Rwanda has been an exceptional, defining moment in my life. Without a doubt, it has transformed me. How everything I have seen and done will affect me in the future remains to be seen, but I will do my best to keep a healthy perspective when I return home. Hopefully, I will be an improved version of myself and not incapacitated by all that has happened to me.

Rwanda is beautiful. You would not believe that such a magnificent place exists in the world. Volcanoes, rolling hills, jungles, sunshine, and big white puffy clouds teased by ever-gliding eagles are only a few of the country's treasures. You would think this is the Garden of Eden. Unfortunately, this garden is heavily seeded with landmines that bloom with a blast and leave people limbless, or dead if they are lucky. This Eden, unlike the one Adam and Eve enjoyed, is under constant threat of war and vicious reprisals from a militia that carried out Rwanda's genocide. Recently, a woman was shot because she screamed when they forced their way into her home. In another household, a man had his head cut in half when he resisted their entry. This Eden is also home to a military that has not been paid for months and loots to stay alive. Foreign humanitarian aid workers are increasingly disliked by them and others in influential positions, which puts our position in the garden in jeopardy.

Despite it all, there is something indescribably gratifying about being of service to the people in this country. I am formally "Monsieur le docteur [Mr. Doctor]," but I am still not quite certain if I am making any difference.

201

The Rwandan people are in shock. No one was spared the atrocities. No one sleeps without nightmares. No nightmares go unnoticed. The massive extermination campaign was very effective because a significant segment of the population was convinced to kill and fill the graves with another significant segment of the population. Babies were intentionally crushed to death, people dismembered, and families butchered simply for being Tutsis. The hatred between the people is palpable and haunting. And the worst part of all is that there could very well be a rendition of the same massive extermination at some point in the future.

Here, the incredible is the credible. Mass graves, fields of savagely amputated limbs, and churches filled wall-to-wall with carpets of corpses are discovered day after day by United Nations teams that try to uncover, recover, understand, and document this story of human hatred. This is not a story you will find in the fiction department at your local bookstore. It is a story told just down the next aisle, tucked quietly among the non-fiction books.

If you're so inclined to come and visit this area right now, it is officially off-limits to all tourists and spectators. Many Rwandans have crippling shame for what has happened here between their people. They do not want the world to sit in judgment of their complex history. They also would prefer not to expose their own people's version of Mein Kampf, which the extremist Interahamwe may very well have called "Kill the Cockroaches!—Rwanda's Final Solution."

Thanks for letting me vent.

My love, Cary

5 November 1994
Saturday

My Dearest,

I have a dilemma: I don't know right from wrong anymore. What I know to be right back home is wrong here. What I know to be wrong back home is right here. And in the end, my mind churns in endless circles trying to make sense of things.

What is today's dilemma? It has to do with the children. As I see it, children are the fruits of the human field we cultivate and eventually harvest. These beautiful beings come from us but do not belong to us. Our role is to care for them and impart life skills so they can do the same: cultivate and harvest their own fields. This is the cycle of life everywhere.

Children need the basics: a roof over their heads, water to drink, food to eat, air to breathe, and education to have a chance. These basic needs are indeed basic and available in abundance to nearly every child in developed countries. But here in Africa, this is often not the case. There is food, but no money to buy it. There is water, but it is too far to fetch. There are roofs, but they are flimsy and collapse, especially in the rain when you need them the most. And there are schools, but where are the teachers? Sometimes they come to class, and most of the time they don't. Sometimes they are paid, but mostly they aren't. And sometimes there are blackboards and desks, but usually there are none. What Africa seems to have in abundance is poverty. This is where I have my dilemma. Despite lacking the basics, people make more and more little people. In this way, the cycle of poverty perpetuates itself.

Westerners often criticize the African people for making babies when they don't have the resources to provide for them. There may be merit to the criticism that it is reckless and irresponsible to bring new life into a world where there is only abject poverty at the other end of the umbilical cord. But there is a valid African rebuttal worth noting. The people may be poor and have no money, clothes, land, food, or even utensils to eat with, but they have children—lots of them. Children are invaluable family assets. African households could not survive without them. They work the land, fetch the water, scavenge for wood, thatch the roofs, wash the clothes, cook, clean and then some. In addition to all these responsibilities, without a government-sponsored social security program, welfare, social services, or employee pension plans to provide for elders, children become their parents' pensions and caregivers by default. In this way, their cycle of life turns, twists and teeters.

Given the high infant mortality rate in Africa, people have no choice but to have many babies to increase their odds of having living offspring. It is not uncommon for parents to have ten children and end up with only two, one or none who make it to adulthood. And now there is this new kid on the block—HIV. It not only takes the infants but the adults, too.

Is the Western way better than the African way? Who is to say. Despite our vast resources and tremendous prosperity, are our lives richer, and are we happier? We have strayed so far off the beaten path that we cannot find our way home. How many of us have become lost souls looking for meaning while stumbling about in life, going nowhere? How many of us have found good times in drugs: potions pushed through needles, powders shoved up nostrils, and little potent pastel-colored pills that require copious fluids to prevent kidney failure? This has become our *ecstasy*! We have food in excess and then some, but our souls are suffering from starvation. As a result, we are spiritually malnourished and turn to alcohol to soothe ourselves, as well as antidepressants to "anti-depress" and bear our lives. Then there are our cherished elders. We are so busy that we can't be bothered to call or visit a grandmother, grandfather, or an estranged uncle. And what about our moms and dads? When was the last time Harold called his mother, or Samantha saw her father? So, I ask, what is right and what is wrong? Whose way is better, and whose way is worse?

Back to reality, I put my reflections and philosophizing to the side, adorn myself with my stethoscope—a doctor's pearl necklace—and make myself useful by going to work.

6 November 1994
Sunday

My Dearest,

Robin Hood and Santa Claus came to town today. In the world of humanitarian aid, policies, procedures, and protocols reign supreme. Well, today, I broke them all and shared the robust resources we have without looking back. Giving is the most rewarding of all gifts we have to offer. In resource-limited countries where receiving is rare, giving becomes even more priceless. It makes the heart go wild and throb audibly.

What in the world am I talking about? Let me back up a bit. An old woman, accompanied by her daughter and her daughter's daughter, comes to the clinic this morning. "My heel hurts," she mumbles barely. I follow protocol and inform her that the clinic is closed on Sundays and apologize for any inconvenience caused. I know this sounds harsh, but setting limits is the only way to survive here. Without rules, there would be chaos in the hospital. Without regulations, nothing would function properly, and a lot of people would be hurt. But how can I refuse her? She looks so frail and helpless. And who knows how far she has traveled to get here. Maybe a little exception to the rules can be made—just this once. After all, the pulse of primary care comes not from the treatment but from the joy of giving, whatever that might be: a bandage, a brace, or an embrace. Looking at her, I have no choice but to break the rules and treat her heel. The day of the week doesn't matter and shouldn't dictate who I see and when I see them.

The woman's heel is minimally swollen. The soles of her feet are parched, cracked and callused—something akin to the hooves of a horse. But there is nothing unusual, serious or disabling about them. Perhaps the problem is not with her sole but with her *soul*. I ask her to tell me her story. The elderly woman recounts how she walked with her daughter and grand-daughter from Goma, a city in Zaire, to Ruhengeri in Rwanda. The journey took them over 12 hours, and they did it barefoot because they didn't have shoes. The mountains they crossed were volcanoes. I've always known volcanoes to be majestic, eye-catching, cone-shaped structures. I didn't know they were made of volcanic material that feels like a mix of broken glass and razor blades. Walking on such inhospitable hosts must have been excruciatingly painful. The old woman had no choice but to bear the pain. After reaching level ground, she and her family continued walking, but this time on gravel roads. The gravel in these parts is not your round, polished pebble, riverbed variety, but the raw, crushed, rugged one with jagged and cutting edges. Walking on this terrain would be hard in shoes and practically impossible with bare feet.

How did they get to Goma in the first place? The woman explains that during the massacre, she and her family, along with hundreds of thousands of other Hutus, fled for their lives over the border to Zaire and settled in Goma on the border. After some time, however, the authorities told them that they overstayed their welcome and needed to leave. So they left.

This family of three now has absolutely nothing except each other. I look at them and then at their feet. I look at the youngest of this trio. She is barely eight years old and still so innocent. It took great courage to come to me and ask for help. They were once a proud people, standing tall and able-bodied. Now they limp home, not knowing what they will find, but certain to find something. Even nothing is something more than what they have now.

The woman's ordeal is heart-wrenching, and it doesn't take a medical degree to make the diagnosis. She just wants a safe place to rest her feet for a while. She doesn't say it, but what she wants is a little tender, loving care. I get it. Finally, I can make a medical diagnosis with relative certainty and put into place a meaningful plan of action—one that matters.

I grab the keys to the pickup truck and invite my esteemed guests inside. We exit through the hospital gates and then drive into the tumult of the town, where thousands of other grannies, daughters and granddaughters march in single-file lines back to their homes. Everywhere we look, there are displaced people on the move. Some walk with purposeful gaits; others are lost somewhere between oblivion and no-man's-land, while others saunter from side to side, going essentially in circles. Most are tentative and fearful, anxious and traumatized. No one cries. No one has any tears left; they dried up long ago. Buckets of them became rivers, became lakes, became oceans, became deserts. Today, only shells of souls remain—souls that walk about like zombies, leaving nothing of themselves behind because there is nothing left.

Grandma sits high in the front passenger seat, looking at all the people passing by. The people look at Grandma sitting high—regal in her chauffeur-driven pickup. She has never been in a car, van, truck, pickup, semi, or any other moving machine before and will certainly never again find herself in a luxury vehicle like this one. It is fascinating watching her watch the world through a windshield. People pass by her window at the speed of a jet. She has never had the chance to go faster than her own two feet, so imagine the exhilaration and excitement she is feeling, right about now. Grandma listens intently to the music on the radio and is fascinated by the speakers. She stares at them, touches them cautiously, and tries to figure out how the singers miniaturized themselves to fit inside. It is a joy seeing an elder see the world for the first time, like a newborn child.

I drive directly to the United Nations depot, where many supplies are available for all returning refugees. Giving people provisions is the only way we can entice them to return to their homes. And provisions they get: flour (350 grams per day per person), beans, soap, salt, linens, casserole dishes, and jerry cans filled with potable water—a priceless commodity in these days of dire. Multiple stalls filled with goodies are placed around an open field. We make the circuit together to collect everything available. Using my influence, I bring them to the front of lines that would otherwise take hours to pass. My skin once again gives me license to cut lines and make the entire process easy and fun for them. All they have to do is stand with their arms extended as I load them up. They are dazed, dazzled and bedazzled. When they can carry no more, I escort them back to the *limo*.

Instead of taking them to the UN semi-trucks assigned to transport people further into the interior of the country, I take my esteemed VIP guests of honor back to the hospital, order meals for them, and arrange a private suite for their sojourn.

"Stay here as long as you like," I say sincerely. "Let this be your home. Rest and be safe."

They can say nothing and don't need to either. It feels so good to give!

7 November 1994
Monday

My Dearest,

Karin, our pediatric physician, and Hannah, our pediatric nurse, are special people with enormous capacities to care. We have become family through all this adversity. When we come together, we leave all the day's duties, disappointments, and failures behind and just enjoy being in each other's company.

Today, our motley trio took the pickup and did the strictly *interdit* [forbidden]: we deliberately strayed off the beaten path and got lost in this marvelous tropical paradise. We just couldn't help it. The volcanoes were beckoning us, and the sounds of little life forms you can't easily see, like birds, frogs and insects, performed a concerto that needed our audience. So what could we do? Instead of going left at the intersection back to Base Camp as required, we had an intentional lapse of memory and went right. And what a wonderful turn it was! Three in a pickup, ready for the world! We sang out loud, danced in place, and watched the world go by. Being attacked by insurgents was considered. Driving over a landmine was possible. Being kidnapped was also an available option, but in each other's company, nothing else mattered. Irresponsibility had seized this occasion, and we were profiting without looking back. The sweet sound of our song and the fantastic feel of our friendship was our special moment today.

My Dearest,

The sounds of machetes slashing the overgrown grass in the garden wake me up. Along with the scent of newly cut greens, my eyes find intrigue in the potato people—those who carry potatoes on their heads to the market. They walk so regally, like African enchanters and enchantresses. They walk through rain and cold barefoot, wearing rags that wouldn't be enough to wipe a wet shoulder after a shower. Watching them make the most of their very hard lives is awe-inspiring.

Yesterday, today, and tomorrow would be paradise here if it weren't for the looming danger and insecurity we each face daily in Ruhengeri, one of the most dangerous regions in the country. Geographically, we are next to the border with Zaire, the place where the masterminds and master murderers of the genocide hang out and prepare for war. When they eventually make their move to retake Rwanda, Ruhengeri will be their first point of entry into the country. Everyone is concerned about their inevitable attack. The question is not will they attack, but when will they attack.

Last week, two French nationals were attacked at gunpoint and robbed of everything in their house. As one of our houses has already been raided by the military, we live in limbo, waiting to be attacked and robbed with guns pointed at our heads. The organization will not evacuate us until someone is killed. So we wait and wait and wait. Living every day under such stress and uncertainty prompts me to pause. Being amid hostile fire from insurgents who orchestrated a genocide of biblical proportions in the cradle of our civilization in the twentieth century forces me to pause some more. How will history be told later when all is forgotten or frankly denied?

How has our human species gone so awry? Did the serpent that enticed Eve to chomp on Eden's apple poison it, leaving her offspring—us—damaged? How did we get so lost and divided?

209

9 November 1994
Wednesday

My Dearest,

I'm feeling more balanced thanks to meditation, which has become my best friend. Sitting quietly seems to show me the friendship in the things that go wrong. It reveals the light hidden in the darkness, so I can appreciate darkness as well.

The people in the project have become ever dearer to me. When we first started working together, everyone was on their best behavior to get along with each other; living in such close quarters with strangers in such adversity could push buttons, flare personalities, and lead to irreparable rifts in the team. Thankfully, our concerted and diligent efforts to listen, yield, and compromise have paid off. We are now a strong, close-knit family. Despite coming from many different countries, each with unique histories and traditions, it somehow works. We are one—a community in unity. We live together, dine together, sleep, laugh, dance, and giggle together. And life is good. Our world here may be simple and confined to a small compound amid chaos, but we have each other. We may be surrounded by violence and hostility, entwined in political pandemonium, and subjected to ruthless power struggles, but we have each other. There is an abundance of *bad* at our doorstep, especially death, which seems to come not in steps but in stampedes—but we have each other.

Speaking of death, the first person in line today at the clinic is a woman who presents with abdominal pain. Initially, I think she has viral hepatitis. She should be so lucky. After a more thorough examination, I fear she has liver cancer. The woman is only 36 years old and may die soon. She doesn't know this yet. And I'm not going to tell her. Two other people also come in today complaining of abdominal pain. They both test positive for HIV. They have an ill child with "diarrhea." He is only 15 months old. He not only has HIV but the virus has led to full-blown AIDS. Mom, dad, and baby will all die. But they don't know this yet. And I'm not going to tell them.

10 November 1994

Thursday

My Dearest,

Today, I discover the hospital staff are charging patients 100 Rwandan francs to enter the hospital gates. It's a free hospital, free for all. So I have a free-for-all. I've had to grow eyes in the back of my head to monitor the underhanded methods people use here to survive and get ahead. No matter how clever I think I am, they are always one step ahead of me.

Speaking of free-for-alls, I had another one with my most challenging medical assistant. Unlike conflicts we have had in the past where he stepped down, today he stands tall, digs his heels into the ground, and reprimands me for reprimanding him. "We've already gone through a lot!" he says boldly. He was referring to the war between Hutus and Tutsis, but subtly, he is referring to the war I am endlessly waging on the ward. I actually like and respect his courage to confront me. After all, I'm his boss, his bread and butter. He needs his job, and there are many others waiting to snatch it from him. I appreciate his perspective. I am demanding, and my expectations for patient care are almost unachievable. But what am I actually asking for? I want respect and compassion for all patients. What the staff deliver is anything but compassion. They are selectively careless, dismissive, and downright passive-aggressive with the Hutu patients. Why? Because the staff are predominantly Tutsi. and many of the patients are Hutu. The people who killed the Tutsis were Hutu. The problem now is that I ask the Tutsis to care for the Hutus, some of whom were the killers themselves. How do you care for your mother's murderer? How do you show any compassion to your father's executioner? How do you have anything other than hate for your child's killer? It is good to forgive, but time must pass—lots of time—before the raw, open, gaping wounds can start to heal. I can't plaster the pain, graft the gap, or bandage the bleed. I can't put blinders on people with 20/20 vision or convince them to forgive and forget. They can't forget. Those who lost their precious parents, children, brothers, sisters, and

211

friends never forget because every second of every hour of every day of every week of every month, they wait for them to come home. But no one does. And no one will.

I have been forcing reconciliation since I arrived without much success. There is nothing wrong with reconciliation, but there is something wrong with my pace. I want everything done yesterday. Pushing people to put the past behind them yesterday is just not realistic or healthy. People need time to process, to mourn, to pain, to deny, to be angry, to be steady, to let go, and let live. Forgiveness is a gift that comes only after people have gone through the emotions it takes to be human. Yes, there is something wrong with my pace, and it is costing everyone dearly. When I am rough with the staff, they do deliver, and I get what I want, but they are left deflated and demoralized. This is not what I want. I have come to build capacity and empower the people, not degrade or disempower them. Yet this is what I do time and time again. And time and time again, I berate myself for failing to create a safe, peaceful place for the people to heal. How can I possibly expect my staff to treat their parents' killers with compassion?

11 November 1994
Friday

My Dearest,

Just minutes down the road from Ruhengeri perches its neighbor, Uganda. "Perches" is an appropriate word because the country is like a perched bird suspended on a tree branch: still and steady, sound and secure. The Rwandan genocide was about the extermination of a particular group of people. It was not a territorial dispute, so the Ugandan border was respected and not breached. This makes Uganda the perfect place for a much-needed R&R to decompress. Uganda will be our Club Med moment in Africa—home away from home for an entire weekend. 2 days, 48 hours, 2880 minutes, 172,800 seconds!

Crossing the border into a place of peace after being visited by death day after day for far too long means more to us than any outsider could ever appreciate. The actual Rwanda-Uganda border itself is nothing more than an imaginary man-made line without much flair, fanfare or flamboyant flags. There are, however, the usual patrols and procedures, as well as the all-too-common arrogance that comes with people in self-made, authoritarian positions. Today's powermongers are particularly aggressive. They begin with their interrogations, followed by a near-strip search of our personal belongings. As the patrols haphazardly rip through Hannah's possessions, her intimate apparel becomes a point of contention. She feels they are examining her black brassière with too much intrigue and immediately puts an end to it by snatching it right out of their hands. They don't like this and start getting more aggressive. Something needs to shift and shift fast. To lighten things up and defuse the patrols' fury, Hannah does a quick 180 degree and brilliantly simulates a little striptease act by swinging the brassière above her head like a lasso. The border patrols are not amused and threaten to block our entry into the country. They revel in the power they have over us and savor their authority to determine our fates. We have no other option but to change our approach and humbly deliver an assortment of obsequious apologies and undeserved flatteries. Nearly down on our knees begging for forgiveness, the patrols soften and finally stamp our passports. We are on our way.

Uganda is geographically similar to Rwanda. Politically, however, they are worlds apart. Uganda had its moment in history many years ago when Idi Amin slaughtered thousands of innocent people, along with 90% of the country's wildlife. Unlike in Rwanda, I do not see any soldiers, military convoys, displaced people, or slivers of souls on the brink of breaking.

We make our way to a lovely lodge by an even lovelier lake. It is calm here. It is quiet. The moonlight is bright, and the sky is dappled with scintillating stars. It is magnificent. I stare at the sky and know I am ready to move on somewhere far away from Rwanda. But as soon as I get this clarity and certainty, an equally clear and certain inner voice speaks up and convinces me to trust and stay the course.

12 November 1994
Saturday

My Dearest,

We aren't in Kansas or Oz. And we aren't romping around with munchkins or encountering cowardly lions somewhere under, next to, or over any rainbows en route to see a wizard in an emerald city. No, we are off to see gorillas in the wild in Uganda. The ones living in Rwanda were killed, trapped, or fled across the border during the genocide. We are now looking for them. Trekking through bamboo and very dense jungle brush, we are on a mission: we want to be face-to-face with a gorilla in the wild. Gorilla sighting is a lucrative tourist adventure that costs us $140 for the opportunity. As part of the package, we are accompanied by a single guide who walks stealthily with a rifle that he uses not to protect us from the gorillas, but to reassure us that we are in good hands. The guide is frail and thin, like the barrel of his rifle. I hope the gorillas recognize him and yield to his meekness.

Today seems to be unusual because our guide cannot find a single gorilla. Our luck, the gorillas are in hiding or on strike. We are determined, though, so we persevere. Finally, after one and a half hours of walking and stalking in grime, mud and drudge, the guide spots some gorilla … that's right, poop. He assembles us around a mound of *brown* and proudly smiles as if he has successfully found us a gorilla. We stand around the precious poop, sweating, panting, impatient, and begrudgingly appreciative. We are obviously disappointed, but no one dares to bark. When the guide begins to conclude the tour and heads back, I decide to be the mouthpiece for the group. We are not paying $140 to see poop. "Excuse me, Mr. Guide, we want to be eye-to-eye with the real deal—a gorilla—something brown and hairy, not something brown and smeary from his backside." The guide is exasperated but agrees to continue.

The jungle vines make it impossible to walk upright, and after a while, I find myself walking like a gorilla. It is actually more natural and jungle-friendly to climb in and out, around and under the brush when you walk somewhat hunched over. Primates figured this out. The bamboo deceives stalkers by pretending to be fragile. Its lightness and flexibility, however, are only façades covering an impressively strong and robust natural native. Mess with it and you will find yourself rivaled by its coat of imperceptible, fine, hair-like prickles that irritate the palms of anyone daring to touch it. It is remarkable how even the flimsiest flora commands respect in these parts.

The jungle is not user-friendly and does not invite us with open vines. Instead, its vines do everything to entwine and disturb us from reaching the gorillas. The jungle is not only user-unfriendly, it is downright hostile toward us. Humidity, heat, thorns, stickers, insects, and more insects make this place uninhabitable. Hot, thirsty, itchy and sweaty, I lose patience and my ecological consciousness. Get me out of here. I start ripping through the jungle's unending webs and tentacles. The guide is unsympathetic and reprimands me for the assault I am inflicting on the jungle's offspring. I apologize and again do the jungle dance, sometimes slithering like a snake on the ground and at other times bent over like a gorilla. I may settle for gorilla poop after all and call this off. To make matters worse, I am reminded that no air-conditioned lodge awaits us with cold beverages and pretty postcards at the end of it all.

We are under the jungle's jurisdiction; it is the judge and jury now. Reluctantly, we jiggle and jostle our way forward at a snail's pace. Then it happens. Thump! Suddenly, dropping from the sky, there's a small ball of black hair inches in front of us. Standing all of three feet tall, a baby gorilla clenches his fists and pounds his chest like a miniature Tarzan, screeching his first words: "uh, uh, uh, uh." He is cuter than the beloved Pillsbury doughboy popping out of his cardboard tube. He is absolutely awesome! Babies, human or animal, are precious beyond description. And like baby humans, baby gorillas are never too far from Momma. Sure enough, Momma appears and is a lot bigger than baby. She clearly lets us know in non-negotiable terms to mind our distance from her precious one. How does a non-English-speaking gorilla say this to English natives who don't speak "Gorilla," assuming that is the name of their language? I can't explain it, but she does, and she does so eloquently. We gladly accept her terms and conditions and are not offended by them. She is just doing her Momma duty.

No sooner do we settle into Momma dearest's space than a sight beyond description casts a shadow above our heads: a silverback—the head of the household and the king of the jungle—comes strolling by. We drop to our stomachs and lie stiller than still, emulating death. The guide tells us to stay still and avoid eye contact with Mr. Kong. My heart thumps, my breath stops, and my mantra changes from the primordial "OM" to a simple primal plea: "Please don't eat me!" I know gorillas don't eat meat, but what if this one has a bad sense of smell or poor vision and mistakes us for a banana or a piece of palm? To connect with Kong, the guide starts grunting gorilla garble—"uh, uh, uh, uh, uh." It sounds just like the baby gorilla garble that we heard seconds ago. Upon hearing these grunts, this stunning human kin is reassured that our visit is solely a peaceful one and that we have no ill will or unsavory intentions. We are only wishing to be part of his family for a moment. Mr. Silverback passes peacefully by us at an unnerving distance of about 30 feet. He is taller than an elephant and makes King Kong look like Minnie Mouse.

I have never seen such a large animal. The gorillas in zoos are dwarfs compared to this one. What a gift to see such magnificence in the wild. What a treasure to experience first-hand the demure nature of this beautiful being in the jungle. Unthreatened, Kong sees no reason not to share his space with us. How wondrous that our closest relatives remember us as family! How is it that we, Homo sapiens—supposedly with the most advanced brain of all living species on the planet—have forgotten this? Man is the gorilla's only enemy. We hunt their skulls for paperweights and use their hands for ashtrays. After these amputations, the rest of the carcass is left to rot in the obscurity of the jungle. Anyone interfering in this heinous transaction is doomed to join Dian Fossey and the *gorillas in the mist*.

13 November 1994
Sunday

My Dearest,

Our driver asks to take our vehicle for the evening to visit some relatives who live near the lodge. For security reasons, the team feels the vehicle should remain with us. I offer to accompany him: he can drive to his relatives, and I will drive the vehicle back to the lodge—at least, that is the plan.

Uganda is muddy, and the roads here are unpaved and ungraveled. The only way to recognize that they are actually roads is by seeing other modes of transport on them—in this case, feet. Today, the roads are practically unrecognizable because it is raining. As the rains rain and the roads get wetter and *puddlier* they not only become more unrecognizable but also less passable. This doesn't stop the driver, however, who makes a right-hand turn off the main road and slithers down a path carved in the side of a mountain. The path is clearly not suitable for automobile traffic. Sliding like a snake from side to side, he manages to gain momentum and eventually reaches his relative's house. He should never have taken the vehicle down what barely qualifies as a footpath—a precarious one at best. Anyway, I bid him farewell, take hold of the steering wheel, and proceed through the mud bath. To be honest, though I have a license, I'm not authorized to drive the vehicle because of security and insurance reasons. But what harm is there in bending a few rules? What harm could a simple trip in a truck do, anyway?

I carefully inch down the path at the *speed of snail,* ranting to myself about how completely inappropriate it was for the driver to enter this footpath with such a big vehicle. The path agrees with me too, as it suddenly gives way and collapses. The path completely crumbles, rendering itself null and void, lost for good in a mini-mud avalanche. And what happens to the vehicle—the one with me inside? First to go is the rear right tire, then the front right tire, then the body, followed by the entire vehicle, which inconveniently flips onto its side, taking yours truly—me—with it. Everything happens so very quickly, and I find myself in a state of shock, incoherent, and immobile for what feels like forever. I am now horizontal in the vehicle's cabin, which is on its side, halfway submerged in the mud. Fortunately, the path collapsed onto a terrace of cultivated land just eight feet below. Miraculously, I landed on it instead of being hurled hundreds of feet down the mountain.

My mind works—barely—but I do know I should send an SOS to base with the car radio. Unfortunately, I forgot how to use the darn thing. Well, to be honest, I didn't forget; I never learned how to actually use it. Why? I never attended the mandatory emergency preparatory course, which included radio instruction. Who knew I would ever fall down a mountain one day in a pickup truck? So, here I am holding a worthless piece of mandatory metal that looks like a proud lifeline but fails to act like one. I convince myself that I can figure it out. After all, it's just a radio. Great, there's a radio manual in the glove compartment. I frantically try to figure out how to use the radio to call for help, but not to my surprise, the manual is written in Shakespearean English, and I am not conversant in that tongue—never was and never will be. Oops. Completely unprepared, I can only think of the repercussions I will face for destroying the project's brand-new $40,000 vehicle.

Villagers gather outside and stare at the overturned vehicle lying on its side. They smile and wave at me through the windshield. Embarrassed, I wave back at them. All I can think of is how I am going to be blasted when I return to the lodge. My personal safety and contused arm don't concern me.

With the grace of a goose and some fancy maneuvering, I manage to make my way through the passenger seat door, which resembles a submarine with its hatch opening upwards. Finally with my feet on stable ground, I gloat over my accomplishment. Dozens of villagers in tattered rags stand around me barefoot, shaking their heads in disbelief. Without a common language, I can only shrug my shoulders and say "Oops" once again.

I am sure no one here has ever seen such a sight in their remote and uneventful village. I never have either. What am I going to do? There is no radio, no way to communicate, and no prospect for a solution or plan of action. So I do the only thing there is to do: shrug my shoulders again, abandon the vehicle, and mosey myself down the muddy footpath in search of some help. I am not surprised to find there are no tow trucks, gas stations, telephones or even electricity anywhere. But there is a boy on a bike. He is happy to help me and rides me part of the way back to the lodge. I walk the rest of the way, which takes several hours to reach the team at the lodge.

Everyone is relieved to see me. They were worried about my whereabouts. "I am so sorry. I'm so very sorry. I thought I was doing the right thing by bringing back the vehicle," I say apologetically, then recount the details of the day.

I conclude my eventful saga the best I can, minimizing the fallout—the fallen vehicle. Every time I mention the damage, I painstakingly preface my words with "I am so sorry. I am so very sorry." I sound like Polly the parrot. To my surprise, no one cares about the pickup truck. They just care about me.

"Forget the vehicle! Is your arm okay?" they ask in unison.

I completely forgot about my arm. It is the least of my worries. I wonder how long this support will last once they realize we are all stranded in Uganda without a way to return to Rwanda.

We make our way back to the site of the mishap and Africa smiles at me. To my utter amazement, over 200 villagers have congregated around the fallen metal contraption and are in the process of restoring it to its rightful position. Before our very eyes, they collectively start raising the vehicle using rags they gathered and tied into a number of cloth chains. With a rag chain on each of the four corners, the villagers heave and hah and together as one raise the two-ton monstrosity, returning it to its place on the footpath. They have done the impossible and beam bright at the sight of their success. I am overjoyed by the unconditional love and support these people offer me in my time of need. They want nothing except the satisfaction of seeing me happy.

And happy I am. I am ecstatic. Actually, I am so ecstatic that my body spontaneously starts jumping up and down like a kangaroo in an Australian bush. I can't control myself—neither can the people. My jumping seems to spark a public frenzy, and everyone starts jumping up and down like kangaroos in the same Australian bush. After jumping together, my arms start to flail about. Everyone is infected and does the same flail. Picture the sight of us together: one people, one voice, one love. Minutes pass this way, and then everyone stills and starts hugging one another. Witnessing this pure-hearted and unconditional human solidarity is like a rebirth for me. I am once again reminded how remarkable people can be and how profoundly connected we are to one another. It is clear that these 200 strangers are my guardian angels. With them by my side and on my side, I can never fall or fail.

14 November 1994
Monday

My Dearest,

We are finally safely back in Rwanda. Once again settled in, I reflect on our time in Uganda. The diversion was divine, and the overturned truck story plays nonstop as a symphony of sensational sounds. Seeing all those people jumping up and down, flinging their arms from side to side in celebration of their accomplishment, was truly a pivotal moment in my life. They actually lifted a truck with their bare hands, together as a community in unity. They joined forces and lifted a two-ton vehicle. And they did it selflessly for whom? For me! They wanted nothing but the joy of being of service. Hmm! Their hugs were exactly what I needed at exactly the right time. At first, I was upset that the driver put me in harm's way, but now I realize his recklessness was a blessing in disguise.

Returning to Rwanda brings the familiar pristine panorama punctuated with military men patrolling the town. Stories of more deaths, shootings and lootings replace the peace and calm we just enjoyed next door in Uganda. We are briefed on the security situation and informed that some unidentified men in a car passed by one of our houses today and asked our guard a myriad of questions. "How many people live here? Is there a television set on the premises? How much money is in the house?" Naturally, I am concerned. Who was the person? What do these questions mean? Will we be robbed or attacked tonight? Expecting the unexpected makes this place writhe in unwritten pain. The subtle stress of the unknown, in addition to the imminent dangers and unavoidable terror, all weigh heavily on me. My nerves are immediately unnerved and start firing random impulses that leave me shaking. I struggle to settle myself. I've been here before—actually, too many times to count since my arrival to Rwanda. Living in a perpetual state of fight or flight is not what I signed up for. I don't recall it being mentioned in my job description. Just minutes over the border in Uganda, gorillas gallivant freely in the wild. Gallivanting here, in contrast, is bound to leave one limbless from landmines, abducted, shot or butchered to death.

Prior to returning to work at the hospital, I set an intention to be optimistic, flexible, and gentle-mannered with the staff. I set the intention as a test to see if I could deliver. Well, I couldn't; I didn't stand a chance. Nothing was worthy of any optimism, flexibility or gentleness. The intravenous perfusions were hanging, but there was no fluid in the bags. The patients weren't given their medications. A number of patients refused to be discharged, and new, healthy "patients" mysteriously settled in on the ward and demanded services as if the hospital were a five-star hotel. Seeing all of this, I lost my better half and unleashed Mr. Hyde. Needless to say, I failed today's test. I failed miserably. Luckily, I have all day tomorrow and the next days to retake it. Thank goodness for tomorrows and next days. Whenever I fall or fail, there is tomorrow to try again— no judgments, no complaints, no questions asked.

15 November 1994
Tuesday

My Dearest,

A woman with end-stage AIDS is brought to the hospital by her sister, who can no longer care for her. The sister did all she could and gave her dear sibling all she had. Now, she literally has nothing left to give: no soap, no soup, no scraps. Honestly speaking, there is nothing more to give or do. Sure, we can give a warming hug and a soothing smile, but neither of these will fill an aching, hungry stomach. Neither of these can change the course of this woman's destiny. She is now just skin and bones—skin and bones. At this point, her skin barely wraps around her bones. And all we can do here in the hospital is watch this poor woman wither and slowly disappear like a piece of butter on a warm biscuit.

The cry of a person being consumed by this voracious virus can be compared to the cry of gladiators being eaten alive in a Roman lion's den. It's horrifying. What can I do to help, even if it just leaves an infinitesimal dent? I can't rearrange the skin on her bones. I can't wave a magic wand to miraculously heal her. I can't prolong her short life with a pink, yellow or blue pill because there are none against this rabid virus. There is nothing I can do except perhaps to make her remaining days more comfortable. Yes, I can make her more comfortable. This I can do. I will try my best to help this woman with AIDS defy her murderer. If the virus is intent on ending her life, then let her life be brilliantly violet and color-filled for the time she has remaining.

Again, I break protocol and make the city circuit of all the other organizations offering assistance to the poor. The people at the Red Cross are quite moved by this woman's plight and decide to make her last breath a deep one. They shower her with 180 pounds of flour and more than 100 pounds of beans and rice. I match their generosity by taking her and her sister "Christmas shopping" in our storeroom. Again, I become both Robin Hood and Santa and bring down the chimney an equally celebratory bounty of goodies, including cups, plates, towels, detergent, washbasins, blankets, soap and first-aid supplies. The two young women bloom with joy and become a bouquet of flowers for a few moments before they part ways for the last time. For today, they are happy.

"Can we have two more blankets?" they ask timidly.

"Of course," I hum.

What I need to do is give someone something every day. It is not only nice for patients, but it is fantastic therapy for me—a brokenhearted aid worker who thought he could change the world.

16 November 1994
Wednesday

My Dearest,

Jamuel has been a constant challenge for me. His nursing skills are the best of anyone of the staff. He is clever, smart, competent and resourceful when he works. The problem is his work is shoddy and his attitude is poor. Furthermore, he is antagonistic, oppositional, recalcitrant, and often indifferent to the patients. He just doesn't seem to care anymore. Today, he cracked his callous exterior and shared his excruciatingly pain with me, along with many tears. In his own words:

> *"One day, our people went mad. Our neighbors started killing us. People ran to protect themselves in their houses. I was with my mom and brothers and sisters in the house when they came to our door. Being the oldest and biggest, I managed to climb up and hide in the ceiling before they entered. My Mom and sisters and brothers were screaming, screaming in the room below me. The men beat them, beat them all, and then cut them into pieces with their machetes. I was in the ceiling and watched ..."*

I can't continue.

18 November 1994
Friday

My Dearest,

Hannah, Karin, and I sneak away after work in our getaway cruiser for our unmentioned rest and relaxation jaunt through the inconspicuous paths carved through tropical greens. We go nowhere in particular, just out and about. Our high-tech truck is fortified with an anti-mine plate that supposedly protects us if we inadvertently drive over a mine. It is also fueled with diesel, which doesn't explode like gasoline; so, if a mine explodes, we won't—in theory. This super-safe vehicle is so safe we don't consider the inherent danger in our little off-the-record outings. Besides, danger is so common here that it has become our new norm; without it, we would feel sort of slighted. So, like brave warriors going to battle, off we go.

These excursions are strictly forbidden, and we would be harshly reprimanded if we were caught. To protect ourselves and our *rendezvouses*, we tell no one and do our best to make ourselves invisible. In the bush, however, we are anything but invisible. Away from our team leaders and the military, we morph into three Swiss yodelers yodeling at the top of our lungs in a land cruiser, cruising along at the *speed of tortoise* with windows open as banana leaves brush against the sides of the vehicle. I think they are checking us out to see if we are real. The local villagers also weigh in on the wonder and attentively give audience and appreciation to us for our mobile performance. They will not forget us.

The terrain is exquisite with lush greens of every shade. The leaves are as diverse as the configurations of clouds in the sky, and a smorgasbord of serenity soothes the Self infinitely. Mother Nature is magnificent. She doesn't get trapped by the follies of us humans. She just lives and lets live. The sun shines on everyone equally, regardless of race, religion or tribe. The rain does the same. The wind mimics the others, while the radiant greens of the fields touch the souls of ants, worms and butterflies, too. It is this that we feel.

Just up ahead, nestled among and between the greens, is some sort of celebration with little people. We head in their direction to check out the festivities. Coasting down the path now at the gingerly *speed of idle*, we are beyond surprised to find ourselves smack dab in the middle of a military camp where dozens of children—barely seven years old and four feet tall—march single file in perfect line formations to the whistle of their miniature commander. Draped over every miniature's shoulder is a not-so-miniature rifle, which seems to be more than a plastic toy. I recently read something in the international press about children in Rwanda being abducted and forced into the war machine, but until I had seen it myself, the reports were only political commentary. Now, with our own eyes, we see children being prepared to fight this war of hatred. Are they Hutus or Tutsis? Who is being trained to kill whom? I'm told there are obvious physical differences that distinguish Hutus from Tutsis. Hutus are said to be short and stout, while Tutsis are tall with long facial features. These children, however, are still miniatures, and any differentiating features are not yet apparent, at least to an inexperienced expatriate aid worker who disregards ethnic differences and naïvely lumps everyone together as one people.

All eyes are on us. Are they hostile or friendly, intrigued or irritated? It is hard to tell by looking at them through the windshield of a vehicle that sneaked up on them and nearly deranged their line formations. It is overwhelmingly clear that we are where we aren't supposed to be—out of our station and out of our minds to venture off this way. It is incontestable that this was a very bad idea and that we need to disappear and disappear quickly. There can be no trace or memory of us left behind. What if they recognized us or our vehicle? What does their military manual say about intruders who discover their illicit activity? We immediately reverse course and drive away as fast as we can, pretending not to have seen what we were not supposed to see. And naturally, we can't mention a word of this to anyone back at Base Camp because we weren't supposed to be on this path in the first place.

19 November 1994
Saturday

My Dearest,

Today is a day of rest. With nowhere else to go, the team hangs around the house. Hannah compliments me on the work I'm doing at the hospital, but notes that I am doing the work of three people and rapidly burning out. She recalls that when I first arrived to the project, I was energetic and full of life. Now she notices that I have become weary and exhausted.

"Fill the ward with your loving energy, Cary," she says. "This love of yours will stay in Rwanda and serve the people in many ways after you leave the country. Be your love; give your love again," she tenderly mothers me.

Hannah is very supportive and protective of me. In fact, the entire team is very kind and supportive of me and my needs, moods and confusions. They are always close by when I need to lean left or right. There is always a hand to hold and a kind word when I'm down. I'm so blessed to have them in my life.

Hannah is right, I've lost my footing. But where do I put my feet? Somewhere between a killing field and a landmine? The weight of all this death and destruction is oppressive as it hovers alongside me, tenaciously refusing to let go, burrowing deep into my skin like a rat scouring for something to eat. My nerves are shot, my mind is mad, my heart is breaking, and my spirit is in freefall. Essentially, I am falling apart. I need an immediate *life lift*, a pick-me-up, a veritable new beginning.

Karin brings lunch and makes a fire. The random dancing flames flicker in a rhythmic way that mesmerizes us, and we are at last at peace. We break bread together and eat in silence, not because we have to, but because our friendship needs no banter to sustain it. We eat and then fall asleep on the couch. It's nice when something good happens. The simplest things mean so much to me now. Walking, talking, breathing, and seeing the light of day are all magical gifts we are given. We no longer take these things for granted.

21 November 1994
Monday

My Dearest,

Rwanda is a tough place. With death constantly in my face, at every corner, step, hospital gate and hut, I can't help but confront my own mortality. While I would prefer to ponder the great pearls of wisdom that come to me each day in deep reflection, my mind gets snagged by the incorrigible monster, death, which rapaciously grabs at anyone, at any time, at any place. With death so close to everyone here, why am I not included? Why am I spared, or am I?

Since coming to Africa, I notice my body decaying before my eyes. The tough times here have clearly taken a toll on my health. Since the day I arrived, I've been sick numerous times. Back home, I was the epitome of health, so I am not used to, familiar with, or even comfortable confronting illness at my relatively young age. Suddenly, I am forced to accept that my body is not permanent; life is actually time-sensitive and ends. In spite of this awakening, I continue to defiantly insist that I can still move mountains. I know that eventually I will have to accept that this invincibility is nothing more than a child's fairy tale. For the moment, I'm not ready yet.

The brutal reality that I'm actually fallible and will die like everyone else seems unfair to me. But if my death opens up a spot for someone else to take my place and experience the joy of life and the privilege of living, then it is okay to pass the baton and give that someone a turn. It will take time for me to accept that I am fallible and feebler with every passing day. Is this what they call a midlife crisis?

22 November 1994
Tuesday

My Dearest,

The rumor is that there will be war by November 30th, eight days away. The rains have stopped, and insurgents can now mobilize themselves. We wait … eight days!

23 November 1994
Wednesday

My Dearest,

6:30 AM. I am awakened prematurely by the crassness of the sound of stomping military troops exercising in the streets of the neighborhood. Children cry hysterically at the sight of them. Haven't the little ones gone through enough? Hasn't everyone gone through enough?

No one understands this war. Frankly, I think those who masterminded it don't understand it either. A question comes to mind: How did man—father, grandfather, brother, husband, friend, neighbor, uncle, boyfriend—conceptualize, create, and execute the grotesque and contorted atrocities that occurred during this genocide in the name of ethnic cleansing? What could be so offensive or repugnant about a person's ethnicity? How could the height of a person be grounds for slaughter? How could the dimensions of someone's nose justify a death sentence? How could the shade of a person's brown skin be a determinant as to whether they live or die?

The troops stomp by in their full glory, strutting their male stuff. The earth takes the beating beneath their boots as dust takes flight. The children bawl as I lie here in bed, unable to soothe their tears. They've seen this before and most certainly will see it again, because another armed conflict is inevitable. My questions are many: When will it happen? Where will people run for safety? Who will attack who? And how will it end? Will the Tutsis do to the Hutus what the Hutus did to them? If so, blood will flow like water from a sink faucet.

I often wonder what motivates us, aid workers, to come from faraway places to cesspools of hatred where scavengers scavenge and avenge the living long before it is their time to die. What draws us to serve in these conditions, remain in this absurdity, abuse our bodies, neglect our health, break our hearts, torture our minds, and sacrifice our souls? What is the driving force behind our madness? I haven't found the answer yet, but when I do, I will settle … finally.

24 November 1994
Thursday

My Dearest,

An 18-year-old girl comes in lifeless, barely breathing. She looks like she's nine months pregnant. On closer examination, I notice that her belly is distended with fluid, most likely from some angry internal process that has extended to her breast and obliterated it. Mom stands hopeless next to her daughter and wails. The daughter lies helpless on a bed next to her mom. She doesn't wail. What can I offer her at this point? There is nothing left to give: no hope, no help, no time, no nothing. Does she have breast cancer? It is highly unlikely at her age. Does she have liver cancer, an abscess, or perhaps a parasitic infestation? Many diagnoses could account for her signs and symptoms. Laboratory studies could conclusively determine any number of possible diagnoses, but nothing would make any difference.

In industrialized nations where resources are plentiful and manpower is abundant, left-brained inquisitives rack up big bills as they problem-solve with sophistication. CAT scans (computerized axial tomography), MRIs (magnetic resonance imaging), USs (ultrasounds), and UGIs (upper gastrointestinal series) are like appendages that can reach farther and wider than our eyes, ears, hands, and imaginations to give excellent visuals of what is happening on the inside of us. Doctors shine with these modern, sophisticated machines, and patients feel a sense of relief because someone is doing something about whatever it is they have. We tinker with these state-of-the-art toys to satiate our need to know, but realistically speaking, when a person has a fatal disease, there is usually little that can be done to alter the course of their prognosis.

Death is an eccentric intruder that has a life of its own. It is an unwelcome guest that comes when it wants, regardless of people's plans, schedules, commitments or intentions. When it is ready, it barges in without knocking, sometimes passively and sometimes aggressively, sometimes gently and sometimes abruptly. It pays no attention to a person's age, race, religion, sexual orientation, financial standing or social status. It does not discriminate. It touches each and every one of us. In this way, it is much like the rain and the sun, treating everyone equally. But there is a significant difference between them: the rain and the sun give. Death, on the other hand, takes. Its appetite is voracious and insatiable. Its proclivity to destroy is ruthless and unrefined. Why death chooses this 18-year-old girl to consume today, I do not know. I will never understand. From a Hindu perspective, she did something wrong in a previous life and accumulated bad karma. Now it's payback time. From a Buddhist's perspective, everything in life is impermanent, and the more she is able to detach from her attachments, and the cause and effect of all things, the freer she will be from misery. From an atheist's perspective, this woman's suffering proves there is no God, for if God truly existed, He, She or It would never have allowed such misery to decimate one of His, Her or Its beloved children. From a spiritualist's perspective, everything is perfect, predestined, and simply an opportunity to grow and be reincarnated into a more advanced state in the future. Personally, I think … Actually, I don't know what I think. I need a bit more time to figure it out, but not now. I have more important things to do, like attend to the young teen who is dying just a few feet away from me in bed number four, next to her mother, who is drowning in her own tears.

In another bed just a few more feet away, there's a 36-year-old woman dying the same way as her neighbor—prematurely. She is also lifeless and barely breathing because of the same abdominal swelling. The woman's mother stands at attention next to her bed, looking at her precious child for the last time. She doesn't want to miss one single, solitary second with her daughter, given the few grains of sand remaining in the girl's hourglass. Both patients are mirror images of each other. Both mothers are mirror images of each other, standing in puddles of tears.

26 November 1994
Saturday

My Dearest,

The banana bushes stand still and strong, unfettered by anything near or far. Their green is luminescent, even at night under a waning crescent moon. Tonight's serenity is like the lull of a landscape before a twister. Something is brewing. Political tensions are rising, military actions are intensifying, and something is going to happen.

At this time, the Tutsis are in power. They are a formidable force, but so are the exiled Hutu militants. Both are hot and reactive, like molten lava that moves and clears anything in its path. Both are volcanic, ready to blow. When they do, where do we go? Kisoro, a city over the border in Uganda, seems to be the most logical destination. It is only 25 miles from here, but 25 miles is farther than the farthest planet in the universe if the road is blocked. And if the road is blocked, how will we make our escape?

Our team starts to unravel and mirror the political and military climate on the outside of the compound. Once sturdy and determined, we are now disjointed, confused and angry. With the increased tension in the country, our group intention has become more tenuous. The team, once family, cuddly and close, is now crumbling to pieces. Our individual fuses are shorter, and our coping skills have degraded as the country is invaded by more and more insurgents surreptitiously crossing all fronts. No one is at their best. Rachel, the head of our project, is angry with everyone; Hannah is pissed with Doug; Roland dislikes Claus; Fred and I have some conflicts; and Jane .... well, somehow, she remains steady and still. I like steady and still, so I spend most of my free time with her.

It is now late in the evening. I sit in front of the fireplace and try my best to settle. It feels good to befriend silence in the company of this mysterious force of nature. It is reassuring to see how easefully the fire's light dominates and displaces the dark. The light is good for me. There is going to be war.

231

27 November 1994
Sunday

My Dearest,

Today, Jane, our revered British midwife, got a letter from her father. Let it be recorded here for all posterity to cherish.

Dear Jane,

This is just to say I am very sorry I am not around to spend this evening with you. I know Mummy and you will have a good gossip together this evening. I'll call when I get home.

You know how much we support you in what you are doing. The home team is right behind you. To dedicate yourself to helping others, particularly those living under appalling conditions whether by virtue of poverty, politics or war, is very much your mission, and we appreciate it.

You obviously have all the skills and knowledge necessary to cope, although I expect you will have some tricky moments, and your confidence in yourself is an essential component of undertaking a somewhat unknown task. It will be a real test of all you have learnt over the past years, and I'm sure you'll come through with flying colors.

We will all be thinking a lot about you. We'll write and look forward to hearing from you. We could photocopy your letters around the family.

We love you very much and look forward to welcoming you back when the time comes. You'll be very successful and gain greatly from your experience. Take great care of yourself— you must eat! Your life will demand a lot of your physique and like any complex machine it needs fuel and good fuel! Don't take unnecessary risks. You are not among totally friendly people—one side may be supportive and the other might be just the opposite.

Enough lecturing. Enjoy the challenge and the experience. We love you and our thoughts and prayers are with you. We are very proud of you. Love, Daddy

28 November 1994
Monday

My Dearest,

The Zairian military attacked refugees rioting in one of the camps in Goma. Fifteen people were killed and over 50 others were injured. Zaire's government was never keen on receiving refugees from Rwanda's genocide, but one day, over a million people just showed up at their doorstep. The refugees are Hutus who fled from the Tutsi military that took control of the country. Some of the refugees participated in the killing of Tutsis, while others remained peaceful. All fear reprisals.

Goma is situated just on the other side of a volcano that imposingly stands guard at the border between Ruhengeri and Zaire. In anticipation of more bloodshed, we have been asked to send blood to Gisenyi, a town near the Zairian border, to help any wounded.

The UN published a report this week stating that the security situation is rapidly becoming "concerning." This is a euphemism for "war is imminent." If war breaks out, we have two hours to escape, which is the amount of time it will take the insurgents to reach our location. The one road to Uganda is our only way out. This road is paved and in good condition when conditions are good. But if there is an evacuation, we will not be the only ones using it. We may be the only ones with vehicles, but those on foot will surely not curtsy to the left or move to the right to let us pass. They would be best to block our convoy and use us as human shields.

The only reliable ally we have is the volcano. It is the sole impediment that blocks the insurgents from reaching us. Unfortunately, volcanoes have no appendages to grab, snatch, or stop two-legged killing beasts. While volcanoes may look big and ominous, they are just pussycats without claws. But in all fairness, they do have lava, which is a force to be reckoned with. But then, volcanoes rarely resort to spitting up, and this one, which is supposedly protecting us, is not expected to blow for several years. I wonder if the insurgents know this.

233

1 December 1994
Thursday

My Dearest,

We encounter an overturned vehicle on the road. Alongside it, a man lies on his back with a towel over his head. The towel is saturated with blood, and the blood drips drop by drop onto an already rain-wetted concrete road. The man's children sit motionless alongside him in utter shock. Dozens of people congregate around the fallen man and his children. No one takes any initiative to help him, possibly because they have all seen so much death during the genocide that another casualty does not faze them. Our team takes charge and lifts the lifeless man into the back of our pickup truck, then takes him and his children to the hospital. The children sit near their father and say nothing.

Imagine one fine day, a dad goes to his field to pick some potatoes to feed his children. On his way home, he is killed on the road. No one will ever be the same.

I remove the man's watch and give it to his children after I clean off his blood from it.

2 December 1994
Friday

My Dearest,

I have a dream.

In our hearts is love to give to one another.

I have a dream.

In our minds is the will to help one another.

I have a dream.

In our palm is a place to hold another.

I have a dream.

In our lives is the time to make a difference.

3 December 1994
Saturday

A letter home

Dearest Mom and Dad,

I haven't written in a while. Sorry. I'm safe and doing well. The hospital, on the other hand, has its perpetual problems. There have been many deaths on the ward, and after each assault, I can't help but blame myself for failing to save them. I feel overwhelmed, intimidated, and helpless when confronted with death's omnipotence and the non-negotiable stance it has here. It is unforgiving and stubborn, to say the least. When death comes, it usually leaves with the person it wants. I'm highly inadequate against its force and conviction.

Death seems to be more rabid and insatiable in this part of the world. No one escapes it, and everyone seems to have their firsthand experience of its antagonism, either through the loss of a friend, parent or child. In a resource-poor place, people seem to surrender more easily to life's counterpart—death. Giving up without a fight is not our way in the West because, in places of plenty, we have something to fight with and often have a lot to fight for. Here, sadly enough, there is nothing to fight with and little to fight for: there is a lack of food and water, electricity, shelter, education, healthcare, comfort and security. Escaping the squalor that unilaterally befriends people here is simply an impossibility, and one might ask, "What's the point?"

My day is spent resolving problems that create themselves without hesitation or invitation. If I'm not at the hospital, it hobbles. If I'm not on the ward, it limps. Initially, my vision was to train the personnel to work independently so they could manage their own affairs; unfortunately, they aren't motivated to learn right now. They have many other pressing matters to contend with as they try to heal and rebuild their lives after the genocide. The government is also overburdened as it tries to regroup and rebuild the country. It looks like our medical services will be needed for a while.

Regarding our services, we see many people with AIDS. In fact, at any given time, up to 40% of our patients are HIV positive. Illiteracy plays a powerful role in protecting the virus. People know nothing about this dreaded killer and take no precautions to prevent its spread. As a result, the massacre of over a million people in the genocide will be, unfortunately, rivaled by the next massacre orchestrated by HIV. Currently, a 15-year-old girl on the ward has end-stage AIDS. She was raped by a soldier. Believe it or not, infected soldiers remain a significant vector for the virus because they rape so many women. There is still no effective treatment for HIV here or anywhere, and there are no social service programs to help those infected. This means once people are infected, they simply suffer and senselessly succumb.

Overall, we see a lot of critically ill people, though many also come with feigned illnesses to get hospitalized. I can't blame them for wanting to come and stay. It is safe, clean, and comfortable here. Why not be and remain a patient? For the most part, the patients are wonderful. They are kind and respectful, friendly and gentle-mannered. Many struggle with trauma from the genocide and require intense mental health support. It is not uncommon to see patients lying all day in their beds, sleeping apathetically in their own excrement, and refusing to shower or care for themselves. It is hard to reach these people, who have essentially given up and opted to die rather than face memories of the genocide. They need time to heal and put their lives back together again.

Sometimes, when times are tough and I despair, I think of a woman who came to the hospital destined to die. I did my best. And she lived. I can't claim to have saved her life, but I did help her heal. I never thought I had the ability to make such a difference in someone else's life. It is beyond words to see someone walk out the front gate who would have, could have, and should have died. This woman was hanging on to life by a thread, and now she is alive. What a privilege it is to be a doctor! Thanks. Thanks for putting me through medical school and making this all possible. I love you. — Cary

6 December 1994
Tuesday

My Dearest,

A glorious day! Four long letters from friends and family arrived! Four letters! It doesn't take much to make me ecstatic. These letters are my lifeline. Being reminded that people love me means so much. Four letters are four terrific gifts. Getting briefed on the lives of special people in my life realigns me with the nearly forgotten world on the outside. It's easy to lose perspective here. Without telephones, newspapers, and barely any mail coming in from the outside world, we get out of sync with the rhythms of the lives we once lived and the people we once lived with. Being away from all that is dear and familiar forces us to find surrogates for kindness and love. But these surrogates are only temporary, holding us over until we can return home to those we love. I am beyond grateful to have a life that is so generously endowed with the most amazing people. Because of them, I am.

7 December 1994
Wednesday

My Dearest,

This evening, we all sit together around a campfire and talk about our futures. Some say humanitarian work is meaningful but leads nowhere. Not only is it dangerous, but it comes with no perks or benefits: no salary, job security, pension plan or guarantees. As a result, very few expatriates return to the field for a second mission. Personally, I want to make humanitarian service my career. Everyone tells me to return home, get a real job, meet someone, and live happily ever after. While this all sounds enticing, I feel I am on a sort of path, some quest or mission that will unfold in its own time. All I have to do is avoid distractions that could derail me. I wish it were easier, though. At this juncture in my life, I am a blind man walking without a walking stick, stumbling, tripping, and sometimes falling. If I only had an inkling of where I'm going and what I'm supposed to do, I would be grateful.

237

8 December 1994
Thursday

My Dearest,

I receive two unexpected pats on my back from the staff today. The first pat is surprisingly from Jamuel, the most gifted yet toughest, recalcitrant, and resistant member of the internal medicine team.

"You really taught me a lot, Dr. Cary," he says. "I feel I am now able to do medical consultations because of you. Our ward is the pearl of the hospital, and officials come to see our work and leave impressed by us and what we do. I understand now why you have been so hard on us. *Merci*!"

Wow, I didn't expect that. I've been exceptionally hard on Jamuel, trying to break through his hardened exterior, so such touching words are especially meaningful. After months of wrangling with the staff, they begin to see themselves shining among their colleagues on other wards. They see their medical skills improving, their clinical judgment sharpening, and their capacity to manage the ward increasing. They now understand that I sincerely care about them and that everything I do is to help them take control and manage their own affairs with confidence and pride. Wow! How do I feel? I feel fantastic!

The second pat comes from Odette and the entire hospital administration. Some weeks back, I discovered that our local outpatient doctor was stealing medications from our pharmacy and selling them on the black market. When I became aware of this, I informed the head of the hospital. Since exposing the doctor, he has been planning his retribution against me. A few days ago, during an administrative meeting, which I did not attend, the doctor denounced me. He assumed that such an attack against me was safe because I wasn't present to defend myself. The head of the hospital, however, understanding the source of the doctor's anger, reproached him and demanded he make a public apology. After the meeting, the heads of all departments discreetly gathered and unanimously confirmed their support of me. They then went a step further and decided not to mention the incident to me because they felt it was vindictive and would hurt my feelings. I never knew anything about the meeting, the comments, or the team's decision to protect me from the doctor's venom. Today, Odette gently takes me to the side and briefs me about the incident, saying, "It's important to respect everyone's unique specialness." Odette is a big lady with a gargantuan heart. Competent and self-assured, powerful and maternal, no one messes with her. I don't know the details of that meeting, but I feel honored to know that so many people rallied around to protect me from what they believed was an unjustified and hurtful assault.

Given Rwanda's precarious political climate today, people are reluctant to draw attention to themselves or act in ways that might be considered contrary, critical or dissenting. Given the changing of Rwanda's political guard, people practice silence and bear injustices without getting involved. It is safer this way. Today's show of support highlights an emerging courage, strength, and willingness among the locals to stand up for what they believe is right. To be defended by the staff is heartwarming. Knowing they will not allow anyone to hurt me is literally *breath-taking*. Wow! Wow! Ask me how I feel. I feel breathless.

9 December 1994
Friday

My Dearest,

Yocham, our Dutch logistician, finished his contract and will leave soon. Tonight, he said something unexpected and moving to me: "I am going to miss you, Cary, and all the wonderful times." Yocham is not an overtly emotional guy, and he is quite awkward in the communication department, so his few words are particularly potent and meaningful. If his words had a particular flavor, it would be bittersweet. The sweet is the flavor of friendship. The bitter is the stark reality of parting. As people leave the team, which has become like a very close-knit family, there is a melancholic mourning that happens, similar to when someone dies.

We humanitarian aid workers are tossed together as if we were some sort of garden salad. Sometimes it is not easy to get along. Actually, sometimes it is nearly impossible. Complete strangers from all corners of the globe are unduly expected to live harmoniously under one roof. Confined in close quarters, our survival is predicated on our ability to remain cordial with one another and find commonalities among ourselves. Often, this can be quite challenging because of our different cultures and backgrounds. In addition, our priorities and perspectives are oftentimes as different as night and day. Yet despite our differences, somehow, when least expected, magic comes and does its thing, and we are one: one people, one family, one heart. Magic has been exceptionally generous with us and has given us much attention. This can easily be seen in the way we depend on each other, support one another, look forward to being together, bond at a bonfire, and give and get hugs.

There is a disquiet that overcomes me when faced with the inevitable reality that our "family" will soon disband and each of us will go our separate ways. While some will beat the odds of separation and stay connected, most will return to life in the real world, and our paths will never cross again. The same goes for everything we did in Rwanda—not a trace of us or what we did will remain behind. And what will remain with us of this time in Rwanda? What may endure the test of time are some photos tucked in a drawer or shoved on a bookshelf, a few letters stashed in a storage box in a garage, a memory or two or three, and a number of traumatic flashbacks that will surface spontaneously when least expecting them. We may share this and that with audiences on the outside, but it would only be a nonintersecting, parallel conversation. We could never find the words to convey in any meaningful way details of our unique bond or collective experience because there just are no words. What happens around a campfire or in front of a fireplace here remains among and within us, like in a secret society; all is off-limits for public viewing or scrutiny. We know this, and so we hold this time precious and cherish it quietly to ourselves. In the end, everything will fade away.

12 December 1994
Monday

My Dearest,

The early morning African sun graciously invites all the colors to make their day's debuts. Blue never looked so proud and confident. Yellow never called out with such promise. And green never seemed so loquacious before.

People line both sides of the road with their meager goods, hoping to sell enough to buy a plate of rice or whatever to take their hunger away. Whether it is organic, biologically sound, or preservative-free doesn't matter. If it is edible and gives reprieve from hunger, it is much appreciated. The people are without shoes and carry their lives on their heads with exquisite grace and extraordinary resilience. The heat and cold don't deter them. Their dire lives don't daunt them. The struggle doesn't faze them. They have so much to teach me.

13 December 1994
Tuesday

My Dearest,

Doug, the manager of another humanitarian organization just down the road, brought his satellite phone over and gifted each of us two minutes. I jumped at the occasion and called Grams and Gramps. Within seconds, they were on the line. They sounded healthy and are still very much alive. I miss them so much. What a treasure—two whole minutes.

Connecting to the outside world with such ease makes the remoteness of Rwanda less oppressive. At any time, I could leave, cross the border, fly to Nairobi, and make a major life change. It's all in my hands and easily done, like the swiftness of a satellite call to a destination across the world. That said, it is not in my character to give up or jump ship. I am here now, and I will remain as long as I believe I can be useful. While I often question my usefulness here, there are moments when I know I do matter, especially when I can give someone food.

Food is a lifeline. While I cannot give life or do much to negotiate with death, I can sustain people's lives by giving them food. Giving, however, can create complications, as I have discovered firsthand from bringing food to our house guards each evening for the past few months. When I first started bringing them plates and platters steaming with palate-pleasers, they would bow reverently and humbly extend their hands for the offering. These physical gestures were a kind of traditional African dance to show respect. The guards would then eat with reverence. At the end of their meal, they would wash their dishes and again bow to express their gratitude. This was before. Today, there is a different dance. The guards now expect the food and no longer acknowledge me when I come with a hefty platter. Instead of greeting me, they ignore me. Instead of cleaning up after themselves, they leave their dirty dishes strewn about for "maid me" to collect and clean. What happened to their gratitude? How has their behavior shifted so much and so quickly? I don't know, but in a way, I feel that I am responsible for the change.

There is a fine line to tread when doing humanitarian work. The human heart is generous and begs to give. I would argue that it needs to give and that giving, like breathing, sleeping and eating, is a basic human need. Giving is good, but it has to be done responsibly because it can create dependency and unintended expectations. Furthermore, giving can derail and disempower people. Perhaps a course in the *Art of Giving* should be part of every school's curriculum. Personally, I need to learn how to give, what and when to give, and if to give.

The first time I came to Africa in 1987, I made sure that I wasn't empty-handed. In preparation for my trip, I went from shop to shop asking for donations for the poor. Merchants enthusiastically gave me all sorts of supplies to give to the most destitute. My backpack was stuffed with tuna, granola, pens, cologne, trinkets and money. Upon my arrival to the continent, I was eager to emulate my dear friend, Mr. Claus. Instead of going down chimneys, I walked among the people in the most remote locales to find those with the greatest need.

It was easy to find the poorest of the poor, but it was hard to discreetly give my goodies to them without other people seeing. While I did my best to blend in, my skin color readily gave me away, and my discreet offerings became large public spectacles with untold challenges. For example, one day a woman came to me and said, "You gave my friend a gift; now give me something too." I did. And she was happy. But I wasn't. Many more people approached me with the same demands. When I said I didn't have enough for everyone, they started mauling at my bag. "Give me, too!" they shouted. "Give me! You owe me! Give me!" The crowd then pushed me on the ground and ransacked my backpack, leaving it empty and me full of regret. I quickly learned that my formula for alleviating poverty was flawed.

In Mali, I stayed one evening at an impressive Catholic mission. The priests worked hard there and tended a garden that grew fragrant flowers, fruits, and vegetables in the middle of arid, unproductive land. I asked them why they didn't teach the local people how to create such abundance on their parched and barren plots of land.

"We have been here for 25 years," they recounted. "And for 25 years, the people see our garden giving all the fruits of the earth. We explain how to cultivate the land, but the people hold tight to their traditions that were carried down from their respected grandfather's father's father. Their tradition says to throw seeds on the earth when the rains come." The priest continued, "We explained to the people how to space their seeds, time their planting, and care for their crops. And for 25 years, the people watch our gardens grow as they watch their barren plots of land bear nothingness. When you ask them why our gardens grow and theirs don't, they say, 'God wishes for the White man to have food and for us to go hungry.'"

And so it is: the priests have flowers, fruits and vegetables, and the locals run out and spill seeds on the earth when it rains.

18 December 1994
Sunday

My Dearest,

A treasure trove of toys and other goodies arrived today, including several bicycles. Wheels! We have wheels! Like the excitement of an adolescent taking the family car on their own for the first time, I couldn't wait to grab a two-wheeler and bond with it. Since the main road has been de-mined, we are free to roam the *one-mile* stretch. This short distance may hardly seem noteworthy, but when you are practically under house and hospital arrest, as we are here in Ruhengeri, one mile of freedom is enormous. One mile is twice as long as a half a mile and four times longer than a quarter of a mile. An entire mile to roam! Wow!

I set off like a child and have a glorious time. Children come from every direction and run next to me with surprising speed. They are completely captivated by the chrome and *shiny* on the contraption from the modern world they have heard so much about on the outside of their country. Some have never seen a bicycle before, and none of them have ever ridden on one, so this is my chance to give them their first chauffeur-driven handlebar extravaganza. To magnify the moment for them and make it bigger than big, I put my headphones over their little heads and play music from my Walkman. They are startled and start looking up and down, left and right, and behind themselves. They ask where the music is coming from. It dawns on me that they have never seen a Walkman or headsets before. I point to the little yellow box and do my best to explain that the music is coming from it. Befuddled, they examine with suspicion and intrigue the plastic casing and every crease, crack and corner. I can't imagine what they are looking for. Then I realize they are trying to find the musicians inside the little yellow box. Like the old woman last month who looked for the people singing in the radio speaker, the children try to figure out how in the world I managed to miniaturize the musicians and stuff them inside my little yellow plastic box. They enjoy and so do I.

The children here are so pure and uncomplicated. Few have anything but rags, and some don't even have them; no one has shoes either. Designer clothes and the latest fashions would be of no use to these children. Their games are not sophisticated, computerized gadgets like in the West, but rather handmade creations of exceptional, innovative genius. Bananas, for example, are accessorized with twigs and Coke bottle caps to create banana mobiles, which are proudly paraded down the street for all to see and admire. The children also make toy cars that are carefully crafted from aluminum cans and rolled down the main road without motors or strings attached. They strut their stuff to show they are alive and well in a mirage of magic. Soccer balls are also among their toy treasures, the most prized of all. The balls are made from either plastic bags or socks filled with newspaper. They are strong and robust and rival the standard air-filled ones that professionals play with in places of plenty. The children's resourcefulness is impressive, as is their creativity and imagination. They could easily start their own non-profit and call it "Brains Without Borders."

The opportunities to find myself amazed and inspired by the children are never-ending and without borders. Sometimes I spend all my free time on the street sewing their clothes and attaching buttons to every strip, strap and flap. In this way, they are beautified. Not that they need to be made more beautiful than they already are, but renovating their rags gives the children more regal stature. Clothes with buttons, pockets, collars, and sleeves make them feel like real royalty. In their new regal attire, they immediately go from being paupers and peasants to princes and princesses. They have nothing, yet they have everything. When I watch and listen to them, I am reminded of Porgy from George Gershwin's *Porgy and Bess*. Porgy says he's got plenty of nothing, and nothing is more than enough for him. The children are my Porgies, who, time after time, remind me how abundant my life is.

As I ride the last child on my handlebars, the children shout in unison, *"Umuzungu neza* [White man is good]*!"*

24 December 1994
Saturday

My Dearest,

Tonight is Christmas Eve! I'm excited because this is my first Christmas celebration. Judaism has Chanukah, which is a joyous celebration, but Christmas is by far glitzier and more grandiose. Judaism does have a lot to celebrate, but its history is filled with pain and riddled with expulsions, mass graves, pogroms, ghettos, gas chambers and genocides. The Jews and the Rwandans seem to have a lot in common.

Christmas has become a symbol of universal love for all people. This single day invites us to see not the differences that separate us from one another, but the similarities that bond us together. Christmas reminds us who we are and what we can create collectively for the greater good. Imagine everyone as one big family celebrating each other. Imagine our world without borders, free of racism, class distinction, or any other divisive division. How spectacular it would be!

And since we're on the subject of spectacular, we are having a spectacular Christmas party this evening. In preparation for tonight's extravaganza, the team decorated the front room smashingly. What was once an unfurnished, barren space is now a palatial paradise that can be put on display and flaunted. Without much of anything in our possession, we call on our creative juices to lend us a helping hand. Candles are placed here, there and everywhere, and heaps of flowers are borrowed permanently from our gardens and tied together not with string, but with the next best thing—surgical thread. Our Christmas tree is not the customary spruce or evergreen but a mini-majestic tropical shrub. For snow, cotton balls are pinched from the surgical ward, and tinsel is created from foil packaging that once wrapped medical supplies. The room is angelic, as is our menu, which is beyond divine with a little help from friends in high places in Nairobi who procured wine, salmon and Champagne. All was sent to us via special envoys through channels too guarded to divulge. MM MM!

My Dearest,

Christmas Day! Playing Santa Claus never felt so good. The military men at the checkpoint get a bag of candy, and an elderly, disabled man on the side of the road gets a ride in our Toyota pickup *sleigh*. Transporting locals is highly out of order and strictly against all our rules and regulations, but what would Christmas be like without bending and breaking rules? Does Santa Claus have a driver's license to steer his sleigh or permission to go down people's chimneys? Does he knock before he breaks into people's houses and prances around their dens, toying with their trees and stockings?

Giving—I love it. You don't need to have anything to give something special to someone. A smile, a hug, a handshake, a kind word, and a thank-you are all wonderful and priceless gifts we have in abundance. Give them all away for free.

The giving is a two-way street. Odette, for example, gives me the best Christmas gift when she asks me to extend my contract so I can remain with the staff. It is hard for me to believe she is serious, but she means it.

"Odette, you can't be serious," I say kiddingly. "I've been so miserably strict and demanding that I can't believe anyone would want me to stay."

"You know, Dr. Cary" she says, "it is like a mother who tells her children she doesn't mind if they're out until all hours of the night because she doesn't care, versus the strict mother who is mean for the benefit of the children because she cares." She continues, "The staff know you care about them, and when you are cross, it is for their own good. You know, the doctors who came before you were nice, but the staff got away with everything and nothing improved."

Odette goes on to tell me all the things she has learned while working with me. Her list is long and impressive. I am profoundly touched.

The bounty continues to overflow when Doctors Without Borders in Holland sends every team member a care package filled with goodies from all over Europe. The best part of the package is a heartwarming letter thanking us for our work and sacrifice. The letter also includes the Christmas story of the organization's birth. Here is my version with some personal embellishments: Once upon a time, it started not in a manger but as a dream to alleviate human suffering beyond man-made borders. Then came not three wise men dressed in robes, but rather much doubt that anyone would share this same dream. After all, who would leave their families and comfortable lives to go beyond borders where death befriends the living, and the terrain is so toxic that hatred grows like weeds in the people's gardens? Fortunately, the dreamers—the founders of Doctors Without Borders—miscalculated the human heart. To their surprise, they were touched way beyond the borders of their imaginations to find others, too numerous to count, aching to realize the same dream. Over the years, many enthusiastic and dedicated professionals have served tirelessly to provide medical care to people in need. And what do they get in return? They get the gift of giving, the joy of loving, and the satisfaction that comes with making a difference.

Finally, for the grand finale, we bring Christmas to the children at an orphanage we sponsor just outside Ruhengeri. Volunteering as little Santa elves for *Elves Without Borders*, we decorate the facility with handmade delicacies baked with tons of love. We cover the orphanage with loads of cakes, candies. and cookies and put balloons and bubbles in every nook and cranny. The only thing missing is the gingerbread man. When the children are finally brought into our magic menagerie, their eyes are as wide as super gumballs. They are speechless, wondering how something so special could really be happening to them. After all, they only recently lost their entire families and everything dear to them in the genocide. They never imagined being remembered by anyone ever again. Watching the children stuff their faces with food, get showered with gifts, and blow bubbles for the first time in their lives is indescribable. This is their special day. Finally, they can be children again. Their only care is to figure out how to hold their balloons, slurp their sodas, eat their food, unwrap their candy, and open their gifts all at the same time with only two tiny hands, ten little fingers, and one minute mouth. Merry, Merry Christmas, precious ones!

26 December 1994
Monday

My Dearest,

The spirit of Christmas quickly crashes to a halt.

"This is a human being, not an animal!" I bark. "What if he were your brother, your father or your son? Would you let any of them lie in their urine, all wet and cold?"

I am out of control. At one o'clock in the morning, I check patients on the ward and see a 20-year-old boy crying, writhing in pain, saturated in his own urine, shivering and cold. The staff pass by his bed and pay no attention to him. Earlier in the day, he was shot in his pelvis, and his bladder was ruptured. As a result of his injury, a steady flow of urine passes from his body. Without a bladder to hold his fluids, he will leak for the rest of his life. I lift him up and have his body cleaned and dried, then find him a fresh sheet and dry blanket.

I am immediately volcanic and erupt. "Look at this patient lying in his urine on a cold, smelly sheet!" I spew. "He didn't receive his medicine, cries out from pain, and lies here disregarded like rubbish. Are you proud of this work? Would you do the same if your mother were lying here like this?"

Each staff member stands at the foot of his bed and looks down at the floor. Maybe I am too hard on them; after all, many of them can barely read. But they are human beings and don't need to read or write to understand the problem here.

"This is a person—a living, breathing, feeling human being. You don't treat people this way!" I continue roaring. "This boy has dreams and hopes like you and me!"

249

Everyone stands at attention without daring to move and watches me suffocating on my own words, gasping for more breath to continue my tirade. I keep scolding them with each new breath I can muster, but it doesn't feel like enough has been said. I wipe the boy's tears from each eye and walk away.

I believe the intentional neglect of this patient brings to the surface the staff's hidden animosities that still haven't been resolved or evened out yet. The medical staff is Tutsi and this patient is Hutu. Once again, I am confronted with a recurring dilemma: How can I expect the staff to respectfully serve the very people who may have killed their own families? But how do you know who committed the heinous crime of murder? Not every Hutu is guilty of genocide. Is there any way to know who has killed by looking in their eyes, listening to the coarseness of their voices, or feeling the callousness on the palms of their hands or on the soles of their feet? For me, it doesn't matter who did or didn't do what. I'm a doctor, not a lawyer, judge, magistrate, policeman or soldier. My job is not to determine or assign culpability. My job is to see the best in people and show them the best in themselves.

I recall a time when my own survival instincts took me by complete surprise. I never knew that I had the capacity to be so aggressive. One day, some rowdy threatened my beloved grandmother. My grandfather, who was well over 80 years old at the time, came to her rescue and risked his life to defend her against Mr. Punk. If I had been there, I would have done all and anything, including *everything* in my power to neutralize him. In other words, threaten people I love, and I will go into a fight mode that could potentially put the assailant out of commission permanently. So who am I to judge my staff for leaving a man shivering in the coldness of his urine? Could this be their own survival instincts taking them by surprise? Maybe this is their own silent Judgment Day and the justice they need to avenge those who massacred their families. Maybe this is their way to heal. Who am I to judge them?

27 December 1994
Tuesday

My Dearest,

Military personnel use their guns to steal whatever they want: a meal, a woman, money, or a piece of furniture. And no one can do a thing about it. They traumatize the locals with their little handheld toys. And no one can do a thing about it.

We are reminded that our house may soon be raided by the military. They've already raided the other houses in the area, including an expat's house. This took us by surprise because aid workers are supposed to be protected by the military. But then, the Geneva Convention and the purported immunity it affords us from military actions mean nothing to those holding the guns. The military is looking for arms—not human ones, but weapons. I say not human ones because human arms are already readily available on the beaches from the massacre. No one wants any more of them.

28 December 1994
Wednesday

My Dearest,

Over the past few months, I have been conducting a weekly medical education program for the medical staff. Initially, I would select a topic and review it with them. Now, they ask if they can also give presentations. They believe they are ready to assume more leadership in the hospital, and would like the opportunity to strut their stuff in front of their colleagues. I am overjoyed. What a good idea! Turning the program over to them is the perfect next step. Why didn't I think of it? In a way, I have become the wizard of Oz, waving an imaginary wand and bestowing upon downtrodden people who feel lost, hopeless, and helpless without greatness, a certificate from an invisible bag. "*Et voilà* [And so it is]. By granting you this certificate of outstanding achievement, you now officially have greatness." And full of confidence, they walk across the floor without touching their feet to the ground.

As the staff compare themselves with their colleagues on other wards in the hospital, they do indeed shine. Their ward has become the five-star wonder of the hospital. It is clean, organized and provides excellent care to patients. Their ward has also impressed the hospital administration. As a result, all dignitaries and government officials who come to visit the hospital are directed to the internal medicine ward, which has become a showcase for the staff's hard work and medical expertise. Applause and accolades consistently come from visitors as the medical staff stand tall with their heads held high and their faces plastered with smiles that are bigger than big. I, too, smile a smile that's big for my face. When I leave, a steady, strong, and competent medical team will remain to carry on. I am so proud of the staff. They have come a long way—a very long way. My contract ends soon, but I am going to extend my service a bit longer so I can enjoy their glory.

29 December 1994
Thursday

My Dearest,

Today we have a meeting of many minds for many hours, with many differing approaches and opinions. This mind mess will generate more questions that, unfortunately, will not come with any answers. Endless brainstorming, soul-searching, and heart wrenching leaves us all exhausted, feisty and furious. This is the beauty of medicine: it is a science, it is an art, it is provocative, illuminating and unapologetically imperfect. The purpose of today's meeting is to determine the fate of many thousands of ill people. Essentially, we are deciding if people should be given a chance to live or be condemned to die. In short, we are playing devil's advocate with Hippocrates, the father of Western medicine. He allegedly said, *"Primum non nocere* [First, do no harm]." Shakespeare also weighs in on today's important discussion, posing his infamous quandary: "To be, or not to be—that is the question …." In the context of our conversation, this translates to "Do we treat people with tuberculosis, or do we let them die?"

Tuberculosis is a major killer worldwide. It was initially called "consumption" because, over time, the disease literally consumed people. Actually, it still does. Untreated, people with this dreaded consumptive disease watch their weight steadily decline as their bodies waste away. Eventually, they die a slow, miserably prolonged, and degrading death.

Tuberculosis is notably more virulent in Rwanda because the disease attacks and thrives in malnourished hosts. What is the connection between malnutrition and Rwanda? Well, the genocide wiped out generations of farmers and able-bodied people who can no longer plant, till or cultivate fields that once fed the population. Without this workforce, there is less food to eat. As a result, malnutrition is rife in Rwanda, and it is a dominant player on people's plates today. Without food, particularly protein, the body's immune system cannot sustain itself. When the immune system is starved, people are more vulnerable to opportunistic infections, like tuberculosis. In other words, tuberculosis is best of friends with malnutrition, and malnutrition is best of friends with tuberculosis. Both feed off each other in a symbiotic relationship that is mutually parasitic: tuberculosis needs malnutrition to flourish, and malnutrition needs tuberculosis to flourish. In this way, they are linked.

Today, our humble group of humanitarians debates whether we should treat people infected with tuberculosis ... or not. Back home, the mere question would be considered medical malpractice and serve as grounds for a major lawsuit. Here in Rwanda, however, this question requires extensive discussion, compromise, surrender, blind eyes, and a hardened heart.

Those in favor of treating people with TB say that, as health professionals, we are obliged to save lives. They further add that treating those with TB will also prevent other people from contracting the disease, since it is spread through the air and is highly contagious. They point out that we have the money in our project budget to fund a TB program, enough people to run it, expertise to provide good quality control, and outstanding logistical support to ensure a steady supply of medications, so that there would be no treatment interruptions. This is important because medication shortages and treatment interruptions often lead to the emergence of resistant strains that no longer respond to treatment.

Another argument in favor of treatment is that tuberculosis is often found in patients with HIV. As more and more people are infected with the virus, the number of cases of tuberculosis will also increase. In other words, more HIV means more TB. Since tuberculosis is so contagious, failing to treat it will lead to more TB-related deaths in the general population. It is, therefore, imperative to commence the project immediately.

On the other side of these arguments, a number of people present opposing opinions that expand my understanding of the complexity of practicing medicine here in Africa. People opposed to starting a TB program say that we have a limited amount of money in our budget to do endless necessary work. Do we want to use our precious resources to buy expensive medications to save the lives of a few people when the same resources could be used to set up orphanages to house the thousands of street children who miraculously survived the genocide? Why not give these children a chance to live a full and satisfying life with love and guidance, education and the joy of a safe childhood? All this, of course, requires significant sums of money. The opposition presses for investing in preventive education for HIV/AIDS, which kills far more people than TB. Preventive healthcare could deter people from engaging in unsafe sex so they don't get snagged by this wicked butcher—HIV—which leaves its victims disfigured, disregarded, and literally disembodied. Some team members propose setting up basic schools with our funds and helping people create sustainable income-generating projects so they can exit poverty. "Why invest in the dying when we can empower the living?" they ask.

Other people opposing a TB program say we should use our funds to feed our guards when they are hungry on night duty, as well as invest in the children's feeding center. Why not fund an increase in the children's daily food rations from 1500 to 2500 calories?

The opposition continues when someone expresses concern that if we establish a TB program to care for infected people in Rwanda, the government may shirk its responsibilities and ignore its obligations to establish, fund, and maintain its own national TB program. Someone else notes that tuberculosis treatment is a long-term commitment that would obligate us to remain in the country longer than the organization's official memorandum of understanding with the government. So now, what do we do?

What is the best thing to do? What is the right thing to do? Deciding who should live and who should be left to die is something out of this world for many. But in this particular world where the cradle keeled over, we are forced to make these decisions and live with the repercussions of our resolve and actions.

Do I have the power to appoint life? Do I have the tools to make these decisions without feeling responsible, reckless or guilty? I don't know who should live or who should die. If it were up to me, I would treat everyone who has tuberculosis. We have the means and medicines sitting on a shelf in a storeroom nearby as infected patients sit in an adjacent waiting room, begging us for a chance to live. It would be morally criminal not to treat them. Let's begin the TB program, and if orphans come to us, let us find a way to help them. If we have an extra moment, let us talk about HIV transmission and prevention, clean people's fingernails, and tell them how to safely manage their toilet waste when they go to the bathroom. Treating a mother who has TB will enable her to live and care for her children, so they can also live. By implementing this program, we don't have to decide who should live and who should die. That decision then goes back to the *One* in charge. Deciding who should live and who should be left to die is not in any of our job descriptions.

30 December 1994
Friday

My Dearest,

We had a party for the staff this evening, and everyone had fun. It is fascinating to watch two parallel worlds intersect. Our worlds share the same sky, but they are as different and divided as night and day. Our worlds are like the sun and moon: one warm and blazing with light, the other cold and dark. I can imagine, once upon a time, the Rwandan people were robust and radiant; their families were flourishing; their fields were full, and their communities were resilient—before colonization, before slavery, before poverty.

I wonder what the locals feel when they see us *Umuzungu* [White people] living lavishly. I wonder what they would think of our lives back home with our wall-to-wall carpeted floors, microwaves, air conditioners, fireplaces, fully occupied two or three-car garages, ice cube makers in the doors of jam-packed double-door refrigerators, washing machines that self-time, ovens that self-clean, dryers that fluff the final cycle, and plastic credit cards that mysteriously make money obsolete. I wonder how they would react to cash machines that dispense all-you-can-spend sums of money for whatever, whenever and wherever, and water faucets that deliver hot and cold potable water. And picture the looks on their faces when they see their first shopping mall, where you shop till you drop, and their first smorgasbord, where you eat all you can eat. Finally, picture their faces when they see their first flush toilet flush: now you see it, now you don't—going, going, gone! Where does it go, and how does it do that? I wonder what they see and feel when they look at me.

Food, food, food, along with chocolates, beer, soft drinks, and then some, are on tonight's menu. Everyone eats dinner as though it were their last supper. They practically inhale their food, stuffing as much in before the pot runs dry. But it never does. In fact, they have seconds and thirds and then go wild when they are served second, third and fourth courses, too.

What a magical evening! Watching the staff eat and enjoy is a real gift. They might not have this bounty ever again, but at least tonight they have a taste of our world. Maybe one day our worlds will merge, and we will all have the same.

After the party, the magic of the moment ends, and I drive everyone home. It is against protocol to circulate after dark because it is too dangerous to be outside at night, especially for women. I have been in Rwanda for several months, but I have yet to see how people live outside the hospital. We are not the only ones living under house arrest. The locals appear to be incarcerated in their homes as well. But no one among them complains because, in the dark of the night, dark things tend to happen. So, the incarceration is welcome.

As I drive through residential areas, the streets are dark, dingy, deserted and uninviting. The houses have no light, and I am only able to see what the vehicle's headlights allow me to see—just bits and pieces and slivers of slaughter. The desolation of the place speaks louder than words. I recall the day I arrived in Kigali and there was no one to be seen for miles. The ravages of genocide may no longer be visible, but they are obvious nonetheless in that which is not seen. This "invisible obvious" will remain alive and unwell in the hearts and souls of every generation of every generation.

31 December 1994
Saturday

My Dearest,

New Year's Eve is a second chance. It is a time we can put everything behind us and begin again. It is the perfect time to forgive ourselves and make new and improved resolutions to replace the ones we made and broke the year before.

Every day can be a New Year's Eve because every day is a chance to change. Every day can be a new beginning if I choose to change. In this way, life is tremendously generous and forgiving. No matter what we do or how we fail, we have a chance to amend the moment and try again and again. The universe offers us an infinite number of opportunities to right the wrongs and correct our actions. In this way, we can move forward with no regrets. In keeping with the New Year's Eve tradition, I will make the following resolutions: I will be more organized, avoid negativity, temper my temper, refrain from gossip, and meditate. Wish me luck for the umpteenth time.

Later this evening, Rachel and Denis, Jane and Tom, and Linda and I will have dinner together. It will be just the six of us on the exquisite setting of our porch, surrounded by the simplicity and grace of our beautiful garden. Tom, our logistic magician, will perform yet another magic trick and procure rare and delectable delicacies from Nairobi, including shrimp, roast beef, Caesar salad, Yorkshire pudding, and crème brûlée, not to mention French wine and … Champagne—the staple of any *Umuzungu* soirée in the heart of Africa.

It is easy to feel guilty knowing that just outside our fence are people without food. How do aid workers deal with this? They hide behind the shrubs and pretend for a while that no one is there. Having a guard helps too, as he is responsible for shooing away anyone who tries to sneak a peek at us through the foliage that was probably originally planted to separate the haves from the have-nots. It is awkward dining with candles and fine wine in our garden as villagers look at us through that fence. Hopefully, in the silence and darkness of the night, no one will stand on the other side of the fence tonight.

Speaking of feeling guilty, I recall one day, while traveling in Mauritania, I found myself packed in a public transport vehicle with dozens of locals, driving over mammoth sand dunes in the Sahara Desert. There was nothing to eat or drink for hundreds of miles. I was hungrier and thirstier than I had ever been in my entire life. All I had was one bottle of water and a single tangerine that I clutched for dear life. These two things were the gateway to life itself. A very pregnant woman sitting next to me reached for my tangerine. I thought for less than a nanosecond, then shook my head apologetically from side to side, holding tighter to this single, solitary speck of life. The woman then reached assertively for my water bottle. Severely dehydrated, weak and withered, I needed not a milli, nano or split second to reflect. With parched lips that cracked open when I tried to speak, I again shook my head from side to side and clutched tighter to the bottle. This time, however, I was considerably more mechanical, less apologetic, more resolute, and less concerned with the woman's well-being. It is frightening to see what human nature becomes when it's just you, the sun, the sand, a tangerine, a water bottle, and a neighbor. When it comes to one's own survival, there is no room for guilt, apologies or second thoughts.

Back to our soirée: Linda and I oversee the decorations. Tom isn't the only one who makes magic. We do too. With a little creativity and a lot of imagination, we transform our veranda into a veritable palace. First, dozens of candles are delicately displayed on and around everything the eye can see. Then silver tinsel is placed on everything the eye can and can't see. It sits like snowflakes on tree branches. Next, the table is made beyond beautiful. Because tablecloths are at a premium in wartime, we use a newly pressed 100% cotton bed sheet from China. It can easily be passed off as a high-end textile from a chic boutique on the Champs-Élysées. Purple flowering vines decorate the cloth and hug each wineglass, which is bathed in a bed of blooms plucked from the branches of the most fragrant plants in our *private* garden. Palettes of petals, the colors of rainbows, add a final tantalizing touch to tickle the table, and a floral centerpiece intimidates and humbles any rivals. Without Styrofoam, it takes a bit of ingenious ingenuity to find a stable base to secure the flowers, but we do have bushels of baby bananas. They do the trick. In addition, each place setting is adorned with a bouquet of miniature flowers placed in vases, which we create using empty plastic camera film containers that we cover in tinfoil. Finally, to make things more intimate, we drape an African textile around an exposed light bulb hanging from the ceiling to cast an orange glow on our masterpiece. It is breathtaking, if I do say so myself!

Dinner is served ...

Tom's magic is magnificent. Michelin would be in awe and envious. Crickets play in the background, and the candles do their flickering thing elegantly. The evening is perfect, as is our friendship. War does bring out the worst in people, but it also brings out their best. Tonight, we are at our best. We hold onto one another and make an important difference in each other's lives. We all know and acknowledge this. Gosh, life is good.

Happy New Year, My Dearest!

1 January 1995
Sunday

A letter home

Dearest Mom and Dad,

Happy, Happy, Happiest New Year! I just received your letter posted November 4, 1994. Two months is not that bad, considering the lack of any official postal system and your letter's trajectory. This time, the letter you sent to France was forwarded to Holland, then flown to Uganda, where it was hand-carried to me here in Ruhengeri. So, while your letter may be a little late, it is nothing short of a major miracle.

You wrote that you have a role as parents to protect me and respect my need to follow my dreams and passions. Well, I assure you, I'm fine—more than fine; I'm the luckiest person in the world. Seriously, I have never been happier. I've fallen in love. Yes, finally, I'm in love ... with ... life.

You wrote that you worry about me being psychologically scarred by the things I have seen. The bulk of the bodies were cleaned up, the stench of rotted corpses was gone, and the horrendous horrors were hidden before my arrival. Sure, I saw my share of things no one should ever see, but there seems to be some kind of protective shield that comes between me and the ugly. There is something that happens to aid workers here that can't be explained or understood. It feels as if we are living in a pseudo-comatose state, going about our lives without getting involved with our own thoughts or emotions. On the outside, we appear to be cool, callous and indifferent, numb, dumb and unable to feel, but this is not the case at all. Somewhere, there is something waiting to come out. Where have all the tears gone?

Working in the hospital and seeing people die regardless of what I do for them is devastating. For my own survival, I have no choice but to surrender and trust wholeheartedly that those who die prematurely are being taken to a better place for a higher purpose.

It is very hard to make a difference in these people's lives because by the time they come to the hospital for help, it is already too late: their bodies are exhausted, their hearts are broken, and their spirits are unrevivable. Without immunity, strength to fight, or hope to believe, there is little left to save. And so they accept their fate and die. Yes, it is a quiet affair between them and death. And then it's all over. Those who are left behind, loved ones and family members, stoically bear the brunt of the loss. They also do it quietly. Yes, it is a quiet affair. Most pass this moment without showing the slightest sign of emotion, as if they are convening with some higher power. Seemingly unmoved and unaffected, I wonder if they are also in a pseudo-comatose state that I so often find myself in.

Remarkably, I have managed to stop beating myself up for things that go wrong. I had no choice but to resign myself to doing my best; otherwise, I wouldn't have been able to survive here and serve the people. The constant self-flagellation was so emotionally devastating and self-defeating that, in the end, I had to accept the fact that I could not give or take life. What I could do was do my best and always serve with love.

Happiest New Year to you both! Remember how quickly life passes, so take hold of its miracles and make every moment wonderful. Befriend life, take a bite out of it, and then fall in love with its deliciousness. I love you, Cary

2 January 1995
Monday

My Dearest,

Sometimes, something unexpected happens that stuns the soul and changes a person's life forever. Today, one of those things happened.

A patient's tear touches my heart and leaves it and me broken. No number of letters assembled into words in any configuration on a page in my diary can do justice to this single tear, but this man's hardship deserves a sympathetic ear.

A roadside accident killed 15 people and left many others permanently maimed. The accident happened when a semi-truck, going in one direction, collided head-on with a public bus going in the opposite direction. I was asked to join a group of volunteers to help reassemble the body parts at the scene of the accident. I declined the request and chose instead to stay at the hospital on standby. There was no medical necessity for me to go and be scarred for life by things better left unseen.

When the group returned from the accident site, I was convinced that I had made the right decision not to go. Those who went to assist returned completely shattered: no one could talk; no one could focus; no one could engage. Judging from everyone's demeanor, they will not recover from this road trip. I feel sad for them. Sometimes, there are things you just shouldn't see. With gentle prodding, snippets of the scene leaked out like pus from a hideous wound: "A child's head rolled across the road; its decapitated body no longer looked much like a decapitated body." Someone adds, "A man's abdomen was blown open, and all its contents were scattered over the road." Someone else reluctantly shared, "A head with its contained brain was no longer contained. Body parts were everywhere." I am so grateful that I chose not to see what could never be unseen. Such horrific images will come time and again, by day and by night, in sleep and in nightmares, for the rest of their lives.

A man, an ordinary man, a simple man, a man like all other men, miraculously survived the accident. I am asked to see him. Tragically, he sustained a back injury and subsequently was immediately and definitively paralyzed from the waist down. The man is only 27 years old. Boarding a bus to visit his brother, he never anticipated his visitation rights would be irreversibly revoked.

I enter the ward and see him lying alone, in pain, with beads of sweat dripping from every pore of his body. No one attends to him. A Foley catheter is in place, and an attached bag is filled with cloudy urine. As all systems below his waist are permanently retrenched, his bladder is now and forevermore an external tube and plastic receptacle.

The staff are busy. No one looks at the bag. No one looks at him. He looks at no one except himself and his worthless life and his worthless legs, which now serve no other purpose but to get in his way. His mother, wife, and children still do not know he has even been in an accident.

I change his catheter and look at him as he stares blankly at the ceiling. His face gives nothing away. He is elsewhere. How degrading it must be to need someone to assist with the basic, intimate requirements of being human. Self-care and hygiene are taken for granted when the body is the way it is supposed to be—functional. Unfortunately, this man's life will be, from now until forever, without function and, in his mind, without purpose. I am sure that in the blankness of his newly bleak world of dependency and isolation, he will struggle to find meaning. What will his wife and children do when they see his uselessness?

The man's urine drenches his sheets, and a foul smell of ammonia from a long-overdue bed cleaning is intrusively humiliating. I clean him as a mother cleans her own child, for without the kindness of strangers, he will not survive. The ward nurses stand at the foot of his bed and casually discuss his medical management. They look around the room absently and fail to connect the data from the patient's roster to the actual man before them. It seems he has lost his name and has been downgraded to a collection of numbers on a page. I look at our patient and sense his utter desperation and hopelessness. With nothing else to offer him, I take hold of his hand. Until this point, his gaze is free of *blink* and fixed on the ceiling above. He is distressingly absent. I stay silent, respecting his need for privacy and honoring his wish to be anonymous. For now, he must hide his vulnerability and helplessness to get through this ordeal. Minutes pass. Each minute is an eternity with a man present in the flesh but absent in mind and spirit. I can do nothing but keep his silence company. Then, to my surprise, his grip tightens. In his grip, he silently tells me everything, not through talk, not through touch, but through tears—actually, just a single tear. From the corner of his left eye coyly comes the slightest wetness, so slight that it could be missed or mistaken for a drop of dew, like the ones that sit so still on the surface of a green leaf in the morning. In this tear, he peels back the layers and dares to let me in. Traversing skin color, culture, and every other difference between us, he generously shares the unabridged account of his very sad story with me. It is beyond space and time. It is a moment you will remember all your life. I lean forward and discreetly dry his tear. No one needs to see him so exposed, so vulnerable.

4 January 1995
Wednesday

My Dearest,

The man I saw yesterday with paralysis, really touches and troubles me. I think of him. I think of his thoughts. I think of his life. I went to see him this afternoon to reassure him that everything would be okay. Somehow, someway, things would work out. To add to the reassurance, I gave him my watch. He was so happy. *Happy* makes doctors happy. He smiled. Smiles make doctors happy too. If money could bring back his "lower life," I would find funds for him. But it doesn't work that way here. What will happen when he first sees his wife and his wife first sees him? She still knows nothing about the accident or what has happened to her husband—the father of her children. She will soon come to know that her man has been retrenched from the living and emasculated. Once strong and able, head of the family, ruler of the roost, her man is now relegated to a position somewhere between worthless and burdensome. He will not be able to tend the fields that once fed the family or carry potatoes to the market in exchange for some oil or sugar. How will his wife work the fields, care for their children, manage the market, and now carry her man?

5 January 1995
Thursday

My Dearest,

The man's single tear continues to sadden me. It is as if his pain and suffering has become my own pain and suffering. I find it hard to move on from his tragic ordeal. If only I could do something substantial and meaningful to help him. But I can't. And he will tragically suffer for the rest of his life.

Speaking of tears, when will I break and shed one? Since my arrival, my well has been dry. I constantly ask myself why. Months into my time here, I still can't answer this question. Is it depression, denial, disbelief or disengagement? Do I have some deep-seated psychological block or a fear of being weak and overly exposed if I cry? For me, crying over the butchery of this genocide is an admission that evil exists and that some people could be inherently evil. Admitting this unearths my foundation and leaves me with nowhere to stand. I don't want to go there. I want my feet on firm ground, a place from where I can pivot and step forward with grace and confidence. Take my ground away, and you might as well take my breath away. I want to believe—I must believe—that people are good but sometimes do bad things. Rwanda has pushed me to the brink. I don't know what I believe at this time, so I exist somewhere between denial and denial. I find myself conflicted because the atrocities people committed in the name of ethnic cleansing were downright evil. As a result, I am in a *state of stun*—numb and mute. Maybe this is why I haven't cried in Rwanda.

265

6 January 1995
Friday

My Dearest,

There is chaos in the delivery suite. In the States, "suite" conjures up images of an inviting, luxurious accommodation with plush furniture, a private shower, Egyptian cotton linens, creams and gels, specialty soaps and all the other amenities, not to mention a window with a view that exceeds expectations. Our suite is something less lavish. The delivery bed is an iron frame that houses a metal wire mattress that is covered with a pad barely thick enough to call it a towel. The "bed" looks and feels like something that would be used in a veterinarian's clinic. Our hospital suite is basically an "un": undecorated, uncomfortable, uninviting and uninspiring. Despite the décor, I continue to call it a suite because of the *sweet* obstetrical staff that work together tirelessly to bring beautiful baby beings into the world. Jane is at the helm of the suite. She is caring, compassionate, and adored by everyone on her team. Besides delivering babies, Jane trains her staff in the art of birthing babies. In this way, she hopes to eventually make herself redundant.

Today, a woman comes to deliver her baby. Her delivery is anything but normal; both she and her baby go into distress. Anything that can go wrong does go wrong, miserably wrong. Pandemonium takes hold of the obstetrical suite, and everyone clamors in all directions to save mom and her baby. The only way for either of them to stand a chance of survival is if mom agrees to have an emergency cesarean section. To convince a woman from a small rural village, who cannot read or write, that we have to cut open her abdomen to remove her baby to save her life and the life of her baby is no minor feat. Time was not on her side, and such a decision was already long overdue. Fortunately, after much insistence, she agrees.

The surgery begins. Once the baby is delivered, Jane works furiously to reanimate the near-lifeless newborn, wrestling with death head-to-head. She refuses to give the infant up. She is determined to defeat death and break its clutches on this little being. The staff stand to the side mesmerized by the stork bearer's mastery and dexterity. They are awestruck by her insistence to save the newborn and astonished to witness what a woman's will can accomplish despite tremendous odds against it. They never witnessed a miracle before. But they do today as they watch for the first time the defeat of death by the small hands of a petite English woman. Yes, Jane wins and sends death to hell empty-handed. The staff are ecstatic! Now that they see that the impossible is humanly possible, maybe they will also dare to dance with death and snatch away its next meal, or at least give it a try.

8 January 1995
Sunday

My Dearest,

It is Sunday. The project manager asks me to take the day off so the staff can begin managing the ward on their own. I reluctantly agree. Eventually, our project will come to an end, and they will be responsible for running the hospital on their own. Becoming redundant was my stated objective from day one, but it is hard for me to make the transition from being needed to being unnecessary. At this point, they can manage the ward by themselves, so I have no other option but to pass the baton and give them the honor to run with it.

With a day off, I happily relax in our garden and watch our newly acquired black and white rabbits run around, nibbling here and there, to their delight. The flowers in the trees don't seem to mind the rabbits below. The volcanoes just over there don't seem to mind either. I wonder what they think of us.

The sun blazes, and birds of every color combination comb the sky, looking for their place in it. I wonder if they conquer or claim any part of the sky for themselves, or if they follow the laws of nature and share it for all to enjoy. The birds seem content to just watch us from there. I also wonder what they think of us. How do they all get it so right? How do we all get it so wrong?

10 January 1995
Tuesday

My Dearest,

Amos, an Israeli surgeon, joined our team for a few weeks. He is an orthopedic surgeon but has been asked to do general surgery. He does his best and saves lives. Amos is not bitter-sweet but tough-sweet, like a prickly pear, a unique cactus fruit that is tough on the outside and sweet on the inside. When he first arrived to the project, people were unimpressed with him because of his coarse exterior, but to know him and see him in action is a real privilege.

Amos is extremely generous and spends his free time giving gifts, passing out money, and granting everyone their wish lists. Admittedly, the smiles he brings to people's faces are something to see. "I have it now. They don't. So why not help them?" he says. And so he gives. Though remarkably generous, I chastise him for giving gifts indiscriminately: "You're taking away people's dignity and encouraging them to beg for handouts," I protest. "You give false impressions about our lives and our financial resources and exaggerate our ability to help them. You are creating dependency!" Then, with my next breath, I find myself raiding the stock closet and quietly giving away everything within reach to those around me. I know it's not right. I know I'm a hypocrite; Amos is right; we have it now and they don't, so why not? It's a win-win for everybody. When we give, their smiles are set on fire, and we feel ecstatic seeing them ablaze!

The long-term impact of dependency is just an intellectual argument that gets in the way of living in the moment. In the not-too-distant future, we will all leave Rwanda because we won't be needed here any longer. The people will return to living their lives; new children will be born, and eventually, these children will bear children who, in turn, will have their own offspring. And in this way, life goes on in perpetuity. So why not seize the day and be a secret Santa, quietly staging little Christmas parties when no one is looking?

11 January 1995
Wednesday

My Dearest,

Given the intensity of this mission and the confinement we are subjected to, the organization requires each expat to leave the country from time to time for rest and relaxation. It always seems like an unnecessary indulgence since we are so well provided for, but I have to admit, it is easy to lose one's better judgment and objectivity when working too long under these conditions. So once again, I go to Uganda to recalibrate.

Uganda is renowned for its extraordinary wildlife, but I wouldn't know. The elephants in the distance are supposedly elephants because someone with binoculars tells me so. I don't see them or the giraffes! There are crocodiles, but they don't really count because they only lie in one place and do absolutely nothing. They don't walk, talk, swim or attack. They could be dead, for all I know. I'm told hippos are not sweet, like the ones I came to know and admire in the cartoons of my childhood. Peter Potamus was a peculiar, purple hippo with a sense of sweet humor. The Ugandan variety is aggressive and easily agitated. But I wouldn't know because I don't see anything resembling Peter in purple or anything else from the Potamus family. After an exhaustive search, I am told they are hiding somewhere under the water.

The Ugandan people I've met have been very kind to me. They are quite curious and often stare at me with so much intrigue, trying to figure out what I am. Most villagers have never seen a white person before and are fascinated by my lack of black and my hairiness. Compared to their marble-like, hairless skin, the closest I come to anything remotely familiar to them is their highly esteemed national treasure—the gorilla. Some people think I'm an albino gorilla. I remember my own fascination and surprise when I saw a person with black skin for the first time in my life. I was in first grade, about six years old. When I saw him, I stared at him with great intrigue. I also didn't know what to make of him.

18 January 1995
Wednesday

My Dearest,

It's my first day back at the hospital after a week away. I feel refreshed, my energy is replenished, and my enthusiasm is recharged. Everyone is happy to see me; their many smiles tell me this is so. I am glad to be back with my Rwandan family and eager to see how they managed without me. In the past, when I was away, they struggled to keep things clean and organized. As I enter the ward, all eyes are on me. The staff wait nervously to see my reaction. I am astonished. They immediately beam brightly. The ward is impeccable. The patients are well cared for; the charts are complete, and the room is spotless. They have done an exemplary job.

While I was away, a French doctor discovered 20 newly massacred bodies. He was quickly forced out of the country by government decree to avoid publicity and Western media meddling. Deny it or not, there is fighting between Tutsis and Hutus on the border, as well as Hutu unrest in refugee camps in Zaire. The authorities there are demanding that all Rwandan refugees be repatriated immediately to Rwanda. The current Rwandan government is divided over the issue of refugee repatriation. Some officials accept reintegrating the estranged Hutus back into the country and beginning the process of reconciliation. Other officials categorically refuse to acknowledge their very existence and want them permanently gone.

A similar divide seems to exist between the international community and the current Rwandan government. After all, our history as colonizers is not so prehistoric that it has been forgotten. While we have come as humanitarian aid workers this time—not colonizers—there is and will likely always be an imbalance of power between the two sides. As long as there is dependency, there is domination. As long as there is a reliance on support from outside sources for the basics, there is leverage. Time will either heal or redeal another deck of cards for another game of ... Who knows?

My Dearest,

My Ugandan R&R seems to have been nothing more than a distant mirage. Did it ever happen? Was I ever refreshed? It has only been two days since I've been back, and once again I find myself thrown headfirst into a cesspit. I'm due right about now for another R&R.

A child weighing a mere six pounds at five months old is rejected from the feeding center. She unquestionably meets the criteria for admission, but for some strange reason, she is not admitted. The poor child fails to thrive and needs nutritious food desperately. The administration refuses to let her in or take her on. They claim she doesn't stand a chance to live. I'm infuriated that the child is refused a second chance to enter the land of the living. I don't believe this child is destined to die. And I don't accept that her destiny is our destiny to decide at our discretion. We have the food, skills, willingness, and expertise to do the job, yet she is not considered. Why does this child need to be left to die when we still have so much fight left in us, not to mention the resources and manpower? The feeding center is an autonomous entity that has its own protocols and independent leadership. While my authority is limited outside the internal medicine ward, this doesn't stop me from protesting and raging. Unfortunately, nothing I say or do makes any difference. The powers in charge charge straight ahead like bulls taunted by red flags. I'm the matador without legs, trying to curb the beast. The bull is clearly the more powerful of the two of us. I'm nothing compared to its force. So I surrender, and the innocent, defenseless little child will wilt away like a shoot in a desert under a scorching sun. I am defeated and demoralized. Why does it have to be this hard?

Playing patient advocate, I become reactive and lose the better version of myself. I am burning bridges while I am still standing on them. There is enough burning and exploding in this country without me adding to the violence here.

21 January 1995
Saturday

My Dearest,

An eerie afternoon stroll…

I jog down my usual route along a footpath in between plantations of green. It is quiet. Eagles soar and scour the sky, perusing the pastures for something to eat. I'm curious today and decide to turn down a new path to explore the yet to be discovered mysteries of an alternative route. Without a care in the world, I trot through thick tropical foliage, following dirt paths that were carved out by generations of bare feet before me. Feasting on Mother Nature, I go deeper into unexplored territory, first left, then right, then straight into a cul-de-sac, where I find myself in an affluent residential area with quite impressive ornate houses. There are no huts or grass roofs as far as the eye can see. This is clearly a place of privilege for the privileged.

Quickening my pace to a steady gallop, I explore these new surroundings. With my Walkman blasting my favorite tunes, I am captivated by this intriguing site. It is surprising that such an affluent enclave exists in a country that is so impoverished. As I continue exploring the surroundings, I am struck by a curious finding. There aren't any people around. There are no children playing in the streets, no moms in the kitchens, or dads tinkering in their gardens. Actually, the entire area has been abandoned. Something feels wrong.

I slow my pace to a near standstill and notice shredded clothing, bronze-colored bullets, shell casings, and strands of human hair embedded in the mud. I wonder what happened here. What caused this ghost town? Were the affluent people Tutsis, and did they flee or were they abruptly butchered? This place reeks of rage and terror, and there is nothing left but an eerie silence. In some inexplicable way, this silence seems to be sharing its story with me. How can silence speak? How can this uninhabited, barren spot speak to me? I don't know, but it does. It's like a silent movie with a cast of actors and subtitles in Braille. I ask my many questions and feel the answers as sadness and profound sensations of sorrow. I can honestly feel the slaughter.

I am overwhelmed with grief and distracted by a mind in crisis. Before I realize it, I have strayed off the path and find myself in no-man's-land, where an abundance of man-made *toys* are surely somewhere in the soil. These toys bemuse and diffuse the toughest, roughest and most robust. They stop at nothing, sparing nobody, to get their job done. Living limbless was not on my agenda when I set out jogging today.

I stop. I stiffen. I freeze. "Help!" I shout, hoping someone will come to rescue me. No one is remotely nearby. Even if someone were, I doubt they would come and risk their life to save mine. I am not sure I would want anyone to come and put themselves in harm's way to help me. Confronted by the real possibility of stepping on a mine, I stand as still as a statue in the drizzle, with my shoes sinking deeper into the mud. How will I get home? Will I ever get home? When landmines are activated, I'm told, they make a clicking sound. Unlike a trap set for mice, a landmine goes off only after you release your weight from it. In other words, once you hear the click, it will truly be the last thing you will ever hear.

Man designed landmines to destroy and kill. During the genocide, they were haphazardly placed around Rwanda for maximum population extermination. The problem with them is that they have no eyes and cannot discriminate. Not only do they kill the enemy, but they kill the ally and the innocent, too, most notably children—lots of children. How do mines have a particular penchant for children? That's an easy question to answer. Children climb mountains, play hide-and-seek, and run between the raindrops. The raindrops make mud, and the children slip and slide in it. It's fun. The mud, however, sets sail to mines that then move about freely and change the game from hide-and-seek to hide and explode. The children who die are the lucky ones. Those who live, on the other hand, suffer the brunt of the blast. It happened this way to a little boy who was just playing tag down a little path with his little buddies. They had done the same day after day, week after week, until they knew the pebbles on the path by heart—at least until the rains came and altered the course of a mine that altered the course of the little boy's life forever. There was nothing little about what happened next. His legs were completely blown off seconds before I saw him in shock, staring intensely at his splintered appendages.

"I am not that little boy. I am not going to step on a mine. I am not going to lose my limbs," I say with conviction in an attempt to convince myself. I must weightlessly get to safety. How do I do that with a 160-pound body? If the mines are activated by pressure, then all I need to do is become a master mud slider and slide my way to safety, making sure my shoes are below any mine in my path. Slowly, at the pace of a three-legged sloth, I start sliding my shoes through the thick mud, millimeters at a time. I'm not far from the main path, but it's far enough for me to lose my limbs or life. I slide and listen. I slide. I listen. I listen intently for a click—the last click.

24 January 1995
Tuesday

My Dearest,

Rwanda's neighbors are demanding compensation from the government to pay for the clearing of Rwandan bodies from their tributaries. The too-many-to-count corpses are apparently clogging their waterways.

Officially, 11,400 bodies were recovered from the rivers in Tanzania. I wonder how many bodies were consumed by the crocodiles before the official count was made.

Speaking of numbers, it is difficult to determine the exact number of people killed in the genocide. If an entire family or community is butchered, who is left to report it? Grandma was last seen peeling potatoes; mom was hanging a wet shirt on the line; baby was watching a butterfly with delight; and now they aren't. Bits of bones are many, but they don't add up.

My Dearest,

A 25-year-old woman comes to the maternity clinic today. Her chief complaint is, "I still have not had my period." It was never an issue until she got married. A married woman is essentially an indentured servant; some might even call her a slave. She is expected to clean, cook, collect firewood, fetch water, tend the fields, sell at the market, and then some. She is also obliged to satisfy her man. Oh, and most important of all, she is required to produce offspring. Childbearing is not a woman's choice, decision or right, but an obligation, duty and requirement. It has been several years now since this woman has been doing her *wifely duties*, but despite her heroic efforts, she has fallen short in the reproduction department. This is tragic because in Africa, infertility is like a crime against humanity. Without a baby, a woman's value is without value.

The woman appears to be in good physical shape and wears a dress that conforms well to the contours and curves of her body. Her hair is short, which is often the way of women in these parts, and she has a broader chest than usual, which is not particularly noteworthy given the heavy physical labor women do here. What is noticeable is that when she removes her headscarf, she looks more like a man. But then, what makes a woman: lipstick, polished nails, high heels, and legs garnished in leotards or pantyhose? Men and women often look similar in these parts. The only distinguishing feature between them is that women hold the babies in their arms and on their backs, the laundry on their heads, and somehow the field's harvest somewhere in between, while the men either walk ahead empty-handed or are absent altogether.

On physical exam, the woman has ambiguous genitalia, which in layman's terms means she has underdeveloped and partial genitalia of both a man and a woman—she has no testes or ovaries, hence she is infertile. Anatomically, she has no problem urinating, but intercourse would be catastrophic.

The vaginal vault is nearly nonexistent, and anything of any size introduced into her would be akin to rape—a painful and violent act that would be physically unbearable and psychologically traumatizing.

I feel sad that she endures untold endless pain every time her husband chooses to take her. I feel sad that she embraces this pain to fulfill her lot in life as an African woman. I feel sad that she will never have a child and will eventually lose her husband's interest. When news of her infertility is public, her husband and the other villagers will see her as damaged goods—an unfit woman. Without children, she shames her husband and family and disappoints her community. Infertile, she has little to no value and is considered a noncontributing liability—a burden. And in the end, she will be banished from everything dear to her: her husband, her family, her house, and her community. As a result of this great loss, she will face crippling destitution and end up being pitifully poor. African women who cannot bear offspring are brutally abandoned and unfairly forgotten. This woman's future is a road map to hell.

There is absolutely nothing I can do for this poor woman. This is a genetic aberration, and no medication will alter it. Since there is no treatment, it doesn't make sense to say anything about my findings, so I don't. But I do tell her gently and apologetically that she will not be able to have any children this time around.

28 January 1995
Saturday

My Dearest,

Today is a good day. I like good days. During rounds this morning, the nurses tell me about a new admission: an 18-month-old child with measles. When we enter his room, I see the child lying in bed with his father, who is cradling him tightly in his arms. You can see he loves his son very much. When the father sees me, out of respect, he jumps out of bed and looks around the room to find something to cover himself; he is not wearing a shirt. Reaching into a plastic bag near the bed, the man pulls out his "shirt." I put "shirt" in quotation marks because there is nothing shirt-worthy about it. The thing he takes to cover himself doesn't look like a shirt, button like a shirt, or cover like a shirt because it is a rag, nothing more, nothing less. One could argue that it fails to qualify even as a rag. In fact, if it were tossed into a rag bin, chances are the other rags in the bin would, without reservation, reject and dispose of it in a rubbish bin. It is that tattered and useless. Come to think of it, I'm not sure the rubbish in the rubbish bin would accept it either.

I don't know how many children this shirtless dad had and now doesn't have, or hopes to have in the future, but I can see he is concerned about this son. Since we do not speak each other's language, Dad relies on my body language and facial expressions for clues about his son's imminent future. "Will he live, or will he die?" is written across his forehead.

Dad is poor—very poor. His shirt, which has no buttons, sleeves, collar, back or shoulders, embarrasses him, but he can do no better; it is all he has. I am greatly affected by his plight in life, and moved nearly to tears, I take off my shirt and place it around his shoulders. He probably has never had such a nice shirt before. And he probably will never have another one in the future. He will most likely use this shirt only for the most special occasions. After all, wearing something too much will wear it out, so he most likely will not wear it too often.

With a simple shirt on his shoulders, he looks like he has just been granted eternal life or received a million dollars. He smiles, then looks straight into my eyes and, in silence, tells me more than I could ever recite in a lifetime. His heart is filled with joy and gratitude. His transformation is astounding. He is finally a man standing tall.

Today is an exceptionally good day. At last, I was able to do something meaningful. Today, I finally made a difference in someone's life.

29 January 1995
Sunday

My Dearest,

United Nations observers came to Rwanda to document the atrocities committed here and bear witness to history before it is changed, buried, forgotten, then most probably denied by future generations. They work rigorously and expeditiously to uncover the real facts and figures of this Rwandan genocide before the government cleans it up and hides the crude truth about what happened between its people. The government feels ashamed and violated to have observers and journalists expose certain truths about its people. After all, it isn't in their best interest to have its citizens' savagery paraded in public; hanging dirty laundry out for all to see is humiliating.

I wonder if the shame that the Rwandan people have isn't collectively shared and felt by all people around the world. After all, genocide is not unique to any one clan, tribe, nation, ethnicity or religion. I wonder if this is why the international community pays millions of dollars to bury millions of parts of people here. These burials lay to rest a tragedy for, by, and about humanity. If humanity is directly or indirectly part of any genocide in some form or another, then it is everyone's culpability and responsibility to right the wrong.

Those who committed this genocide were sloppy and left their killing fields untidy in their haste to exit the country. Perhaps their untidiness was intentionally left behind to show the world their victory. Perhaps it was done intentionally to boast about the efficiency of their killing machine. Speaking of killing machines, I remember Claude Lanzmann's film, *Shoah,* where a nazi boasts about how Germany's efficient killing machine could exterminate 12,000 - 15,000 Jews a day.

Speaking of extermination, some of the United Nations observers have come to our humble abode this afternoon. Their coming is a pleasant surprise. They want to show us some footage they filmed of their findings in the field. We are eager to see their work, especially after they tell us this is a private showing for VIPs only. Who doesn't want to be a VIP, even if it is just for pretend? They tell us this movie will not be shown to the public, but since we are aid workers, they think it is important for us to see firsthand what they have uncovered. Needless to say, we feel privileged to be privy to private and classified information and quickly assemble in the front room, each of us competing for the best viewing spots in front of the television set. How very exciting! Sunday night at the movies is a welcome diversion from the monotony of the lives we live here. The only thing missing is the popcorn.

"The footage you are about to see is what we saw during our investigation here," one of the officers authoritatively announces. Without further ado, he loads a videocassette into the player. Our entire team sits attentively, like well-behaved schoolchildren, waiting eagerly for the movie to begin. And then it does. The opening scene is an impressive aerial view of Rwanda's awe-inspiring landscape of a thousand hills. We all recognize the innumerable shades of green of the tropics, the majestic volcanoes, and the simplicity of the African village décor. Seeing Rwanda on television makes us feel like exotic movie stars on a movie set with a backdrop that is stunningly drop-dead gorgeous. At this point in the mission, most of us have been in Rwanda for several months and have become part of the terrain we see so passionately displayed before us on the big screen. An air of greatness creeps upon us as we begin to feel a bit exceptional. But just as we begin to feel pretty unique and special, a curious thing happens. Without warning, the scenery changes, and the movie goes from a travelogue with a G rating for general audiences to a horror picture with an R rating only for very mature viewers. Without narration or commentary from the UN officer, the backdrop dramatically changes from enchanting tropical landscapes to images of bodies with detached feet, stills of skulls with cracks the width of machetes, and fields of pus and pestilence from rotting flesh. The movie continues with the showcasing of mass graves that are filled to their brim with thousands of limp, contorted, dismembered, and decapitated bodies.

We all remain motionless, riveted to a television screen, startled, stunned, shocked, shaken and comatose. No one acts or reacts, grimaces, blinks or breathes. We have all checked out somewhere and left our bodies behind. Sudden sensory overload has caused our brains to completely shut down.

During the genocide, people believed churches were safe havens where they would be protected from the slaughter happening everywhere on the outside. After all, the churches were hallowed homes where people went to commune with their Lord to pray and sing His glory. It was comforting and safe there. Communities would traditionally gather in these abodes of God and exalt the miracles from the week before. All God's children were welcome and equal, praised and protected, celebrated and forgiven for their transgressions. When the mass slaughter began, people naturally ran to their beloved churches, their heavens on Earth—God's home—for protection. Once the people entered the womb of their Lord, however, the doors were locked and their heavens were set ablaze. And who lit the flame that ignited the blaze? Hutu priests, believe it or not. They were often the torchbearers.

The UN movie continues...

Church walls are wallpapered from top to bottom with blood, smeared like a child's finger painting in kindergarten. You can feel the pulse of the people's pierced arteries in the images on the screen. Bones are charred beyond recognition, identical to the remains of Jews in the concentration camp ovens. And skeletons with and without their flesh are arranged in configurations that are too grotesque to describe. And ... in the corner of the womb, by a pew, with her back toward the wall, a child—about preschool age—is crouched down with her arms tied behind her back in a fetal position, like the one she was in inside her mother's womb, and burned alive. Her body is charbroiled. She came to life in a fetal position and returns from where she came in the same fetal position. In this way, the cycle of life is complete. The pain and suffering is no more. The search for the meaning of life and death begins.

The VIP movie abruptly ends, and the television screen goes blank. The UN observers eject the videocassette, place it in a black briefcase, and leave without saying a single word. When the observers came, there were no hellos, and when they leave, there are no goodbyes. And us? Hmm. We all sit at attention, speechless, breathless and emotionless. No one knows what to do, how to act or react, or where to find the chunk of ourselves that has just been assaulted and excised. Our innocence has been robbed from us without our consent. In some inexplicable way, many of us were holding onto the possibility that the genocide never really happened and that what we see with our eyes day after day and hear with our ears day after day wasn't real. This illusion was shattered by the stark visuals we just saw, and we are all of a sudden face-to-face with humanity's inherent evil.

The remainder of the day is spent being angry, not against the perpetrators of the genocide, but against the UN observers who showed us a film with images our minds could not credit to Hollywood. This film will haunt us with horrific, indelible nightmares for the rest of our lives. The raw reality was too raw, too real, too much. Too much hate. Too much death. Too much blood. Too many bodies. Too many bones. Too many babies. Before the screening of the video, the UN officials could have warned us. After the screening of the video, the UN officials should have given us some kind of counseling. They should have also asked for our consent and permission to take away our innocence.

The soul is a curious companion. It can't be seen, but it sees. It can't be touched, but it feels. It can't be smelled, but it senses, and it can't be heard, but it listens. The soul is a trusted and reliable companion that loves and protects us. It's the soul that brings life to love and love to life. It is here with us, for us, in us, and as us. I believed that the soul was infinite and immutable. I can now say with certainty that this is not so. After today's experience, I can say with confidence that the soul is a sentient being that can think, feel, cry and die. How do I know? Because part of mine did today.

30 January 1995
Monday

My Dearest,

Yesterday's horror show continues to agitate me. Paranoia of someone hurting us seems to be the flavor of the day and my renewed preoccupation. If ordinary people here have the capacity to murder family and friends, as documented by the UN, what is stopping them from rising up against foreign aid volunteers? After all, we Whites were the enemy who pillaged their continent, enslaved their men, women and children, and dominated their people, land, and culture for centuries. Why wouldn't they raise the machete against us now in retribution for their suffering and the suffering of their ancestors? What do they have to lose by leveling the playing field? Fortunately, they need us right now. We provide healthcare and infuse vast amounts of foreign currency into their broken economy. We also provide employment and opportunities that can advance their nation locally and internationally. But what if revenge is sweeter than all these elusive benefits? There is nothing we can do if they should choose to act, react, and dismember us.

While jogging, I have repeated flashbacks of the images I saw on the big screen yesterday. As a result of those images, villagers passing me on the side of the road become potential killers. Children returning from the fields with their machetes in hand become potential hackers. People's once sensational smiles become potential ambushes, and my dear friend—the jungle—is now the perfect place to hack me up and dispose of my pieces. I am out of control. My mind is driving me insane, and paranoia has taken a toll. Until yesterday, I was enchanted with the Rwandan people. They have been remarkably kind and considerate—the perfect hosts—generously endowed with good hearts and abounding compassion. Now I find myself maintaining a safe distance from them. You never know. I also find myself intentionally avoiding any eye contact with them. Who knows if they will suddenly find my gaze threatening or antagonistic. Anything can happen at any time now. My white skin, which was once a privilege, is now my greatest liability.

31 January 1995
Tuesday

My Dearest,

Things are tough at the hospital. Just when I think I have a handle on death and feel immune to it, invariably, someone dies and shows me how ill at ease, unprepared, and clumsy I remain around it.

A little boy plays with a bullet and it explodes in his hand. Now, he is handless. Another child comes in with intractable abdominal pain. His blood work shows he has leukemia. I take the boy's brother to the side and say, "We cannot help your brother. Maybe you can take him to a traditional healer?" This is my way of saying he will die. He does die a few hours later.

I go to see a sick child on the pediatric ward. I ask the ward nurse if there are any other concerning cases that I should see. At first, she says everyone else is fine. "Really?" I press her.

"You could take a look at the child in room number four," she casually says to oblige me.

The nurse leads me to the room and says the child is resting comfortably. When I enter the room, I see a 2-week-old infant resting peacefully in an incubator, with his mother and father standing attentively and affectionately at his side. I greet them as well as I can, using my hands and face to speak in a crude sign language, then proceed to review the infant's vitals and medical records. Everything is in order. I smile at the parents to reassure them. I check his intravenous solution and it is also in fine working order. Again, I look at the parents and smile. They smile. The child is indeed resting comfortably. They smile again. The nurse is reassured and steps out of the room temporarily to attend to other patients. I hesitate to examine the infant because he is resting so comfortably, but how will it look to the parents if I don't do an examination?

Bending forward ever so gently, I put my stethoscope on the infant's chest. It is difficult to locate a heartbeat. I check for his peripheral pulses. It is difficult to locate them as well. I check for chest expansion. To my surprise, there is none. The infant is not breathing. In fact, he is dead. Leaning over the infant with my back to the parents, I find myself in the most awkward position of my entire life. I have just affirmed repeatedly to them that their baby is doing well, and now I must tell them that their beloved child is dead.

I have absolutely no idea what to do next. What is there to do? Nothing! I can do nothing. So I do nothing. I just remain bent over the infant with my back to his parents. I stay this way for what feels like lifetimes. What am I going to do? I break out in a cold sweat. Compose yourself, Cary! I could stand upright, smile, and again gesture that all is fine, then walk out of the room. I could tell the nurse to tell them later that their baby has died. In this way, I wouldn't have to deal with this excruciatingly tragic and awkward moment. But I could never do such a thing. My mind races a million miles an hour in all directions, trying to find a way out of this. As I race around, going absolutely nowhere, I remain hunched over a lifeless, beautiful baby boy in a crib as his loving and attentive parents wait politely behind me for an update. What do I do? What do I say? How did I get myself into this mess? Beads of sweat flood my forehead and run into both eyes. The sweat stings. There is nothing I can do but bear it. It doesn't seem fitting to wipe anything away. It doesn't seem fitting to move, to act or react. So I just continue standing, bent over baby. Under normal conditions, a stethoscope is nothing more than a doctor's necklace. It has little to no noticeable weight and just hangs around the neck without calling much attention to itself. In this situation, however, my stethoscope weighs more than the iron anchor from the Titanic. It suddenly is an oppressive noose that is intent on strangling me, then sinking my body with its intolerable weight. As I contemplate my next move, Mom and Dad wait for the good doctor to move and finish his examination. There is nothing more to examine. Their baby boy has gone upstairs, and they think, as I initially thought, that he is at peace and resting comfortably in his bed. What am I to do? What can I do? What should I do?

Finally, after what feels like forever, the nurse returns to the room. I am still hunched over the infant. "Nurse," I mutter awkwardly from the corner of my mouth, "Nurse, this baby is dead." The nurse is not moved one way or the other. She says nothing. She does nothing. "What do I do? How do I tell them?" I ask her, begging to be rescued.

Without elaboration, the nurse casually turns to the parents and says, "Your baby is dead." Completely stupefied by the nurse's announcement, I slowly stand upright and look at the parents, pretending I don't know what she has just said. The parents just stand there looking at us. They have no reaction—not a sound, not a shrug, nod, flinch or tear—nothing—just nothing. I wonder if the nurse misunderstood me and failed to translate my exact words to the parents. I mutter again from the corner of my mouth, "Did you tell the parents that their baby is dead?"

"Yes, I told them," she answers.

The silence is deafening. It is so quiet that you could hear a grain of salt hit the floor.

Several minutes pass this way with the mom, dad, nurse, and I standing mute, waiting for someone to do something. So someone does. The nurse walks out of the room. It is like a scene out of a bizarre horror movie, with an attentive, wide-eyed audience waiting for something to send shivers down their spines before they scream. And then it happens—the shriek of a mother who has just come to know her baby is dead. It is a sound like no other. It is a plea, a prayer, a pain, a *beg*, a *fit*, a *no*, a nightmare, a "take me instead." The shriek of a mother who has just come to know her baby is dead is all of these and then some. Mom is inconsolable. Dad wraps his arms around her and holds her tight as her body quivers. Her tears torment me. Her grief is a public lynching that parades my impotence before the world. I am humiliated. I take this all personally. I shouldn't. I know. But I can't help it. All I can do is stand at attention like a defiled, incompetent soldier who has been stripped and flogged, shamed and ashamed. After what seems like forever, all I can do is gently put my hand on their shoulders. This offers neither of them any consolation. They don't want me around. I failed their child.

Feeling unwanted and unwelcome, I reverently leave the room slumped over with my head inclined toward the ground. No sooner do I enter the hallway than a young boy is brought in because his leg was just blown off by a mine.

1 February 1995
Wednesday

My Dearest,

Some of the day's top stories …

I enter the internal medicine ward this morning. The water in the sink is running full force. I ask the orderly standing next to the sink, "Why don't you turn off the water?"

"I didn't turn it on," he answers.

One of the nursing assistants says he does not want to clean the patients. He says cleaning is beneath him. I do it, and he lowers his head in shame.

Four people were attacked and killed today. This is the third attack this week. Security guidelines have been revised once again to meet the increasing need for vigilance. It is easy to forget the dangerous reality here, as we are seduced by symphonies of sweet sounds from Mother's songbirds flying under stunning, white, puffy clouds floating over a terrain that is transcendental. The seduction is unfortunately short-lived, as machine guns, mines, and machetes, dominate our lives.

Back at home in America, lives are crumbling. People are dying, others are getting divorced, and Grams is becoming increasingly fatigued. And then there is dearest Gramps. He is discouraged because he lost his job. He wants to continue being a productive, contributing citizen and goes for job interviews, but is repeatedly rejected because of his age—88 years old. And how is Cary doing? Well, I am still very much in love with life. Despite all that collapses around me, I am flourishing on a precious path. How blessed I am to have found my calling.

2 February 1995
Thursday

My Dearest,

My work here finishes at the end of this month, and the staff are preparing themselves emotionally for my departure. Some share how I played a special part in their lives and how much they are going to miss me. Over the past several months, we have gone through a lot together, some good and some bad. But for better or for worse, we are family. When someone in our family leaves, everyone feels the brunt of the move. When someone leaves, we all lose a part of ourselves. It is going to be difficult to say goodbye, especially knowing that we will probably never see one another again.

On a brighter note, Linda, our project medical coordinator, tells me that I am a valuable asset to the organization and that she has officially recommended me for future missions. I am touched. Warm fuzzies, pats on the back, and kind words make me happy. Gosh, when it rains, it pours, and when it pours, it feels really nice.

3 February 1995
Friday

My Dearest,

Cataracts are a common cause of reversible blindness that affects millions of people all over the world. In the West, cataracts are nothing more than a temporary nuisance, handled in a matter of minutes as an outpatient procedure in a day clinic. Here in Africa, cataracts are a permanent nuisance and serious disability because not all people are welcome in the day clinics. Rwanda has a number of ophthalmologists who are qualified to do the surgeries, facilities to accommodate the patients, and the resources to remove cataracts, but only for people who have money. As the saying goes, "no money, no honey." Once again, we are face-to-face with an unfortunate contradiction in our human ethos. All men are created equal, but not every man is treated equally. This reality is sadly ever-present and very real in Rwanda.

Last week, I saw a woman in consultation with bilateral cataracts. Her condition was so advanced that she was blind. Her blindness, however, could be surgically corrected. In fact, if she had both cataracts removed, she could potentially have 20/20 vision. I referred her immediately to an ophthalmologist at an eye care center. The woman returns today because the doctor refused to see her. Why? She didn't have money to pay his consultation fee. Another patient has cataracts and needs a referral to the same eye care center. I am sending him with a letter, hoping for a more compassionate response this time:

To Whom It May Concern:

I am sending this gentleman for an ophthalmologic consult. He recently presented to our rural health post and was transferred to our medical facility for further investigation. Given our limited diagnostic capacity, I am referring him to you for your appraisal.

Last week, I sent a woman with bilateral cataracts to your facility. You refused to see her because she did not have 200 Rwandan Francs (200 RF = $1) for your consultation fee. I am not familiar with your medical ethics here in Rwanda, but in my country, we swear to uphold the Hippocratic Oath before being allowed the privilege to practice medicine. Perhaps because of all the recent commotion and civil upheaval, you have lost or forgotten this valuable document. If you would like, I can send you a copy. Thank you for your attention.

4 February 1995
Saturday

My Dearest,

I have plenty of powerful pills to help a lot of people, but from my vantage point, none of my pills, liquids, and potions are as powerful as soap, water and food. I have plenty of tools, syringes, needles, and spools of thread, but none are as powerful as reading, writing and arithmetic.

5 February 1995
Sunday

My Dearest,

A child is brought to the hospital from the feeding center. She is severely malnourished and short of breath. Her body cannot get enough oxygen because her blood does not have enough red blood cells to carry the oxygen she breathes. As a result, she is suffering from suffocation. The child has been critically ill for the past six days, but no one in the feeding center noticed her. She was just one child among many and was too sick, weak, and exhausted to cry. So no one paid any attention to her. The same thing seems to be happening to her on our medical ward. The girl is gasping for air while the staff sit on a nearby bench chatting. No one notices her. No one comforts her. No one cares. Inwardly, I condemn the workers for their indifference and insensitivity. But they have seen so many dead and dying children that another case of the same is not especially noteworthy.

The child needs blood and needs it immediately if she is to have a chance to live. I take charge and contact the lab over the walkie-talkie. I know for sure they have one unit of blood left. *"S'il vous plaît, venez vite et prenez un hématocrite en urgence en salle neuf en pédiatrie* [Please come fast and take an emergency hematocrit in room nine in the pediatric ward]!" I plead. Before the lab tech can respond, I hear Jane calling the lab from the maternity ward, saying, *"Venez vite et prenez*

289

un hématocrite en urgence en maternité [Come quickly and take an emergency hematocrit in the maternity ward]*!"* The hematocrit is a laboratory test that determines the quantity of red blood cells in the blood. A very low hematocrit requires an immediate transfusion.

"Jane, I have a six-year-old child with severe anemia who will die without an immediate transfusion within the hour!" I shout over the walkie-talkie.

"Cary, I have a woman hemorrhaging in active labor who is hypotensive, pale and crashing!" she roars.

Who in the world do we try to save? We play tug-of-war with each other, wrestling to save our patients' lives. Jane and I are our patients' only advocates, their tokens to the admission park of life itself. Deciding who should or could live is not one of our strong points, but the two of us fight with all our might for what we think is right for our patients without even knowing what is right.

Prior to this very ill, anemic child coming to us from the feeding center, I was working with a 27-year-old man who tried to commit suicide by drinking battery acid. Battling to keep him alive, I now have to make a life-or-death decision. Sorry to say, I don't have the staff, time, or knowledge to save someone who wants to die, while others who desperately want to live are dying. In the end, I don't have to make the decision. The young man gets his wish and dies, despite our attempt to go against his wishes.

In the end, I figure Jane's patient should have our only unit of blood because saving the mother will also save her baby. In other words, two lives for the price of one. My little person is sacrificed, and I sit still, watching death do its thing.

6 February 1995
Monday

My Dearest,

In Rwanda, patients are expected to come to the hospital with their own caregivers, who are usually friends, spouses, or other family members. Because hospital resources are limited here, these attendants care for the patients while they are in the hospital. They clean and feed their loved ones, assist them with their toileting needs, fan them when it is hot, and huddle close to warm them when it is cold. They quench their thirst with spoonfuls of water, wipe the beads of sweat from their foreheads, and rub oil into their parched skin. Watching this exchange of love and friendship is exceptionally moving. Such attentiveness is not often seen in Western cultures, so it is a real gift to see it here.

7 February 1995
Tuesday

My Dearest,

Two prison guards bring a pregnant woman to the clinic for an evaluation. They want us to determine if she is in active labor. We are told she is a prisoner, and make it none of our business to find out more. This way, we remain neutral and can treat the patient without bias, prejudice or judgment. This doesn't stop me from wondering why she is in prison. Did she perhaps murder someone during the massacre? Or was she raped by someone important who wants to take the baby from her?

The "prisoner" is *very* pregnant; anyone can see this. You don't need to be a doctor or have any medical training to see that she is carrying a full-term infant. The woman appears withdrawn and depressed. She refuses to talk. Jane asks if she is having contractions. The woman shakes her head from side to side. With the patient seemingly comfortable, we ask her to rest and remain for a few hours for observation.

Since the woman is resting comfortably, Jane and I go to lunch. When we return 45 minutes later, we find the woman in the bathroom squatting in a pool of blood with her baby's head head-down in a toilet hole. Her newborn is still attached to the umbilical cord, and the placenta is still undelivered. The newly born is newly dead. And the woman? She just squats there, unmoved and unaffected. Did she kill her baby? When she came to the hospital, she was actually in active labor but concealed it. How can a woman bear the contractions of labor, which are so painful, without making a sound? She did. She did because she didn't want this baby. What happened to this woman? Forensics would find a full-term infant conceived nine months earlier, in the middle of a genocide, during which women were raped. She must be in excruciating emotional pain. What can we do to help her, and how can we gain her confidence so she will accept our help? Nothing. We can do nothing. We can say nothing. We can offer her nothing, not even a human hug. She is quickly taken away by the two prison guards—without her baby.

8 February 1995
Wednesday

My Dearest,

This morning, I share with Bart, our logistician, the story of little Joseph and how he was dumped on the hospital steps and abandoned. He starts to cry. He asks me if I have cried since coming to Rwanda. A bit embarrassed, I hesitantly say, "No." He is surprised. "I cry often," he says.

Why haven't I cried in Rwanda? I keep asking myself this question. When you see a father dump his dying child on the bare ground and walk away …. When you hear about people hacking their friends, neighbors, and even family members to death for having narrow noses and long legs …. When you are called to help a bleeding child whose legs were just blown off by a landmine …. When you are in front of a young girl who got AIDS from a monster who intentionally raped her to rid himself of the virus …. When you care for a pregnant woman who murders her baby by shoving his head down a toilet hole, it doesn't take long before the body, heart, mind, and soul shut down. In shutdown, I am no longer anywhere—not here, not there. In shutdown, life's text is redacted, so I am spared the reality in front, in back, and all around me. In shutdown, what I see, hear and feel, I don't see, hear or feel.

9 February 1995
Thursday

My Dearest,

We ran out of intake forms for the in-house patients. I go to the prefecture and ask them to make photocopies of it for us. They refuse. I explain how important this form is for us to monitor the patients in the hospital. "It's not our problem," they say haughtily. Have we overstayed our welcome here? The government's overt passive-aggressive posturing toward aid agencies is discouraging. We are now their enemy. I think that in the not-too-distant future, we will be asked to leave the country. When it happens, I hope it will be done respectfully.

10 February 1995
Friday

My Dearest,

Rainbows come with their spectacular colors at the end of thunderstorms, when we least expect them. They will continue to come when we least expect them because we are the rainbows and we are the storms.

11 February 1995
Saturday

My Dearest,

When I first came to Rwanda, one of my greatest concerns was having my everlasting faith in a higher power fractured. Believing in something beyond and in some all-encompassing force is easy when the going is good, but would I continue to be a believer when the going got tough? Today, I am tested.

293

Anne manages the outlying dispensaries. She escorts a man that she has been treating to the internal medicine ward.

"Cary, I know this is breaking protocol, but can you do me a major favor?" she begs. "This gentleman is 31 years old and has intractable pain. I have been managing him with injectable narcotics in the field, but he needs constant pain relief, and his wife is not comfortable with injections."

The man appears to have an advanced case of purulent necrotizing fasciitis extending from his testicles into his groin. In layman's terms, his tissue is rotting, and he is literally being eaten alive. This man's rotting tissue is not only grotesque but has a stench that is beyond anything I have ever encountered in my life. It is so repugnant that I have to step away from him several times during my examination to breathe. Adding to his misery, he is in excruciating pain, which is more painful than a woman's labor. This is a case that has gone very wrong. It's too late to do anything meaningful. It's too early for him to die. It's too sad to see his future. It's too tragic to comprehend.

Moved by this man's plight, I put him in a private room and try to creatively find a way to debride his wound. We need to submerge his body in warm water to remove the dead and infected tissue, but the hospital has no bathtub or hot water. "How can we make a miracle?" I ask myself. After a while, I get a good idea. And it's so easy too … or so I think.

I commandeer a vehicle and take the patient and his helper to my house, which has two bathtubs and lots of hot water. Transporting the man to the house is easy. Moving him from the vehicle into the house, however, takes a lot more time and patience than I had anticipated. He can barely walk and needs support to remain upright. Each step he takes is accompanied by a cry of unbearable pain. Each twist and turn causes him and us agonizing distress. Fortunately, after numerous hurdles, we manage to reach the house.

At this point, we are only at the front door. Getting him to the bathroom and into the bathtub is ever more challenging and causes him even greater pain. It is terrible to see the extent of the fallout from this man's consumptive disease.

Eventually, we successfully get the patient to the bathroom. Once in the tub, we submerge his body in warm water and painstakingly remove the dead tissue from his wound, wash away the pus, and restore his dignity.

When the man is clean and his wound is properly dressed, we return to the hospital and put him back in his bed. There is a glimmer of awe in his spirit and lots of appreciation in his heart. He knows that what we did is only palliative, a noble attempt to comfort him, a temporary step before his final one. He doesn't deceive himself by believing this fix is anything more than momentary, and he understands his condition is beyond repair. Even though what we did was insignificant and added little to the remaining days of his life, there is an astounding change in his attitude and demeanor. A simple bath gives him a sense of being human again. He no longer has to contend with people passing by and gagging from the putrid stench of his wounds … at least for a while.

Later in the evening, I am burned at the stake by my housemates, who heard I had treated a patient in the house.

"How dare you bring a patient into our house? How dare you?" they howl.

I am stunned.

"This is our private living quarters, and it is off-limits to patients!" they blast.

I fight back and furiously defend myself and my actions, saying, "The man needed debridement, and only with a bath and warm water was this possible."

"That's not our concern," they growl. "You wouldn't bring a patient to your house in America, so never do it again here!" They attack me from all sides, like a pack of hyenas.

"This isn't America, and the medicine we practice here is a world away from the way medicine is practiced there. Back home, when patients need care that can't be delivered at a health center, they are transported to another facility that can," I counter. "Our hospital doesn't have the facilities to properly care for this patient. We do in our house. Are we not morally obliged to do everything in our power to get him proper care? Is it not our duty to share our fortune to alleviate people's suffering?" I ask imploringly. "Would you not hope, expect, and demand that everything possible be done for you and your loved ones if you were in a similar situation?"

My words fall on deaf ears. They report me to the director, who scolds me, claiming that I overstepped the boundaries of appropriate medical care. I am forbidden to bring any other patients to the house for treatment. I am dumbfounded and ashamed of my colleagues. They are nurses themselves and committed professionals. How could they deny treatment to a man on his deathbed, especially when we have the resources at hand to defy death a bit longer? This man will die soon. Doesn't he deserve a day of dignity? I wonder how they look at themselves in the mirror and like what they see.

12 February 1995
Sunday

My Dearest,

Someone in the team finds a VHS movie among a stash of trash. Before we can blink, we are all around the television set. Judging from our excitement, you would think we were from the Middle Ages, seeing a movie for the first time. Such treats are rare here, and we gobble them up.

The Hollywood extravaganza is teeming with limousines and fancy people wearing high-heeled shoes, designer glasses, and handbags to match, of course. There is nightlife under strobe lights in chic clubs with super sexy outfits that are color-coordinated with sports cars, Rolex watches, and Gucci buckles to boot. It is all super entertaining, but everything seems so frivolous, decadent, purposeless and unfair. How can

I ever return to that channel? How will I ever partake in "the good life" again when I know that somewhere people walk barefoot in the rain without umbrellas over their heads, shirts on their backs, or food in their bellies?

The disparity between the world's classes is too great for me to digest, and I'm afraid I will return a stranger to what once felt right and familiar. What is most familiar to me now is the sight of kindhearted people walking to market with their goods on their heads, without shoes or socks on their feet, determined to survive until tomorrow. They are good people and simply ask for enough to make it just one more day. The people may be poor, disheveled and lacking a college degree, but so what? They are strong and resilient, hardworking and resourceful. They carry the world on their shoulders and say nothing about it. There is no time for that. There is also no time to notice the rain, the cold, or the rocks cutting their feet. They are on a mission—to survive. If, by chance, someone passes them on the side of a road, despite their plight, calluses and hunger, they will always manage to bring light to their faces, along with unsolicited, sensational smiles and heart.

How am I going to go back home to the West and eat when I know the people here are hungry? How did I get to be one of the lucky ones to live in the "land of the free and the home of the brave?" How did I get the privilege to prance around in planes bound for here and there and roam where the lands are overflowing with milk and money?

13 February 1995
Monday

My Dearest,

As I attend to patients on the ward today, I am unable to find the man we bathed and debrided two days ago. I go from room to room and bed to bed, but he is nowhere to be found. The ward is quite busy, and with all the patients, caregivers, workers, new admissions, and daily discharges, it is possible to get lost and disoriented. But how could a patient go missing? I brace myself for the worst and walk reluctantly to the nurse's station. I have to know what happened to him, but I don't want to know if he died.

"*Bonjour*," I say nervously to the nurse. *Bonjour* means "good day." I wonder if it is going to be a *good day*. "You know the man with the groin wound? Did he pass away last night?" I ask, knowing it is probably so.

"No, he's still in his room," the nurse replies.

"No, he's not. I just checked; someone else is in his bed."

"That's strange; I just saw him," she says.

The nurse goes to see what has happened. Seconds later, she returns and says, "*Monsieur docteur*, he is in his bed."

Once again, I go back to the room and peek inside. I can't understand what is going on. He is not there. I return to the nurse's station. "Was the patient moved to a different room? He is not in his bed; someone else is there," I insist.

"He has not been moved; he is in the same room, *docteur*," she says politely.

I'm totally confused. "Can you do me a favor and take me to his room?" I say sarcastically. I am convinced she is going to take me to another room or realize she is wrong.

The nurse leads me to the patient's room and then points to the man sitting up in his bed.

"*Voilà, il est là* [Here he is]," she says.

I look at the man. I don't recognize him, but he smiles when he sees me. I stand there stupefied. Just days ago, when he was admitted, he was human rot, carrying a stench that was so vile the staff refused to enter his room. Now, in front of me is a man who is radiant and alive, full of life and vigor. Wow! It is truly amazing what a little soap and water and care can do.

My Dearest,

Rwanda is landlocked. It is not blessed with a border on an ocean, but it doesn't matter because life here is like riding waves. Sometimes, it feels like a tidal wave has drowned me. Other times, I'm surfing and riding high. Today, I'm riding high. No wonder it's Valentine's Day.

Saint Valentine seems to be exceptionally generous today. His magic comes to us surprisingly at a surgical team brawl. How? A group meeting is called to allow the surgical team to vent their feelings and frustrations over the ever-burdensome workload thrust upon them. Casualty after casualty pours into the operating theater needing immediate attention. As a result, the staff are beyond exhausted. Working nonstop under such adverse conditions, the surgical team members lose their way and start attacking each other like a school of piranhas. At the meeting, a subservient orderly, a domineering nurse, and an overbearing surgeon declare war on each other. No one from any other medical ward dares to interfere as the trio battles it out with outrageous fury. They must find their own balance for the operating room to continue functioning. The surgical staff has clearly been overworked, overburdened and over-extended. The problem could easily be solved by reducing the number of surgical cases. But this, apparently, is precisely the problem: the surgeon refuses to turn anyone away. He is a die-hard medical professional who is physically powerful and mentally masterful. His capacity to perform is extraordinary and far exceeds that of all others on the team. The problem is that he expects the others working with him to keep up with his pace.

Since Amos, the surgeon, joined the surgical team, he has been a recluse and positioned himself on the periphery of the team. This intentional or unintentional distancing has led to misunderstandings and harsh judgments against him. This is especially true of those who work directly with him on this team in the operating room. In the past, no one dared to cross him. He was, after all, the surgeon, and everyone working in the surgical suite was assigned to support him to do surgery.

Tonight's feud is a ruthless public lynching of Amos. Not only do his assistants vilify him, but they refuse to work with him if he continues to insist they work around the clock to accommodate all the patients coming for help. As their battle intensifies, the surgical staff unite their voices, hoping to gain ground. As expected, the stronger his weary and warring staff become, the more Amos holds his ground and resists their assault. Then, in an unexpected turn of events, this Herculean warrior suddenly starts to cry. Everyone is stunned by the intensity of his emotional breakdown. He is obviously in great pain and racked by internal turmoil as never before. For all on the sidelines watching this battle unfold, it is excruciatingly difficult to see this man's pain. We have just watched a public lynching of a man with a golden heart that has been broken and then ruthlessly crushed in front of us. Everyone, including his own team members, wants to reach out and comfort him.

"I know I'm responsible for wreaking havoc in the team. I know I'm pushing everyone to work more than is humanly possible," he bawls, "but it destroys me to turn anyone away, knowing I can help them. At the expense of my life and the lives of my staff, I push forward, wishing and wanting and needing to save yet another and another and another patient. I'm sorry. To you all, I'm so sorry," he continues. "When I sit alone, away from the team, in my own little world, it isn't because I'm antisocial. I'm simply trying to figure out how to turn the patients away the next day! I'm sorry. I'm so sorry!"

His tears touch and silence everyone. No one knew his inner turmoil. By raising the white flag and suddenly falling to the ground, he admits defeat. The war is over. Yet the staff don't win. No one wanted to break the man with the knife who brings life to so many lives who are hanging on by a thread. No one wanted to hurt him or make him cry. The staff only wanted a little pause to deal with their own inner turmoil.

Initially, they too wanted to give above and beyond to serve the surgical patients, but they realized early on that they were only human, after all, and being human has its limitations.

What you see here is not necessarily as it appears. We all try to cope. On the outside, we wear suits that look good, but on the inside, we wrestle with our tears, holding them back so we don't appear to be weak or fragile. Seeing this surgeon, a veritable pillar of strength, fall before my very eyes brings me nearer to the wonderment of the human heart hidden behind the all-too-familiar inhuman façade. People really do have an extraordinary capacity to care and do good.

How does a surgeon—a simple man—decide who to rescue from the clutches of death and who to let go, knowing people will go to their deaths without surgery? How does a human have the right and the power to decide another person's fate? When I'm thrust into such a predicament, I freeze. I loathe having to hold the scalpel and I resent manning the guillotine. The burden of determining the fate of a person's lifeline is too heavy for me to carry. Like Amos, I am equally incapable of making the final decision—the final cut. Like Amos, I could not make the decision and would subsequently push myself and my staff over the edge, unwittingly burning them out trying to save yet another, yet another, yet another.

Seeing Amos's tears is a heartwarming gift, but at the same time, it feels like Saint Valentine's heart is breaking.

15 February 1995
Wednesday

My Dearest,

A profound shift in my understanding of my life's purpose occurs as I walk home from work today. Like every other day, I leave the hospital on foot and walk down the one-mile stretch of road toward the house. I reflect on the day. It was a good day because I accomplished a lot. And so I am happy. But I am not satisfied. I still haven't done enough.

An internal monologue captures my attention. It goes like this: "If I were the manager of the hospital, I could accomplish so much more than I'm doing as a doctor. But actually, this wouldn't be enough. If I were the head of the project, I would be able to set up countrywide systems to help even more people and, in this way, my contribution would be greater, and I would be satisfied." I continue with my internal banter. "But then, if I were the head of Doctors Without Borders at their European headquarters, I would be able to establish a global foundation and touch even more people. And, in this way, I would be satisfied," I marvel, finally getting it right.

As I continue walking home and dozens of children again fight to take hold of just one of my ten fingers, I think, "No, I have to be the President of the United States. If I were the President, I could recruit donors and appeal for funds to help developing countries establish viable programs to eradicate poverty and, in this way, change the world. And then I would be satisfied," I conclude, patting myself on the back for uncovering the definitive solution to cure all the world's woes.

I continue my walk down the road in deep contemplation. I look at Mother all around me, listen to her sounds, feel her contours, and revel in her sheer magnificence. Overcome by her grandeur and greatness, I have a sudden eureka moment. I understand what I need to do in the world to effect the most change: love! I simply need to love. If I become the essence of love, I will touch every person on this planet with the ripples of this love. And in this way, I will finally be satisfied.

My Dearest,

Kabera is an exceptional nurse who works tirelessly in the intensive care unit. Nothing is ever too much, too hard, or too burdensome for him. He truly gives every bit of himself when caring for his patients or comforting those in pain. He inspires me because of his unwavering concern for others and his remarkable sincerity. He must inspire others, as well, because many go to him for his loving and compassionate counsel.

I don't know anything about this man. His past, present, and future are all mysteries to me. What he endured during the genocide is also an unknown because he and I never had that conversation. Our relationship has always been professional.

Kabera is facially fine; one might say he is easy on the eyes. Speaking of eyes, his eyes are warm and inviting, and if the eyes are indeed the window to the soul, then I can say with certainty that in the soul department he is gifted. Gentle and genuine, he puts everyone seeking his care at ease. His heart is warm and generous, and his smile—well, that is where the problem lies. Kabera is a man without a smile. Actually, he has a smile but hides it behind a pursed upper lip and his hand. What exactly is he hiding? An empty space—he is missing a front tooth. It might seem unimportant to have one less tooth, but in this part of the world, most people have radiant smiles with whiter-than-white, sparkling teeth. In contrast, Kabera's smile is disturbingly unsightly. Unfortunately, he knows this all too well and is self-conscious about it.

I liken myself to the little boy who outs the naked emperor in that children's fairy tale of my childhood, *The Emperor's New Clothes*. Kabera is the emperor, who believes that by concealing his missing tooth, it doesn't exist. I am the boy informing him that he is, after all, toothless.

Ever so gently, I tread cautiously, as if nearing a landmine. Bringing up the subject to his attention means his secret is on public display for all to see and know. Bringing his secret to his attention may shame him. He will surely feel vulnerable and exposed, so why do I need to say anything? Why do I need to break his cover? Because I can do something about it. Because I can make it right.

"Kabera, what happened to your tooth?" I ask as gently and respectfully as I can. For him, it must feel like an invasion of privacy. I fear I just shattered his life. There is a pause. Then, with his head down and slightly to the side, he says, somewhat ashamed, "I was in an accident." His words were staccato and measured.

"Why don't you have it fixed?" I prod. My question is a bit ridiculous because it is obvious that he has no money to fix his tooth. I walk on eggshells and try not to break him.

"I do not have the money," he answers.

"How much does a tooth cost?"

Still looking down, he says, "Eighty dollars."

"If you had the money, would you buy a tooth?" I ask.

Still looking down, avoiding all eye contact with me, he moves his head up and down.

It doesn't take me long to do the right thing. I fold up four 20-dollar bills and put them in his hand. "Kabera, this is for a tooth. You cannot buy a bed with it, pay your bills, or even get food. It is for a tooth, only a tooth. Okay?"

Again, he pauses. He doesn't know what just happened and can't fathom the enormity of this gift—his smile.

"Yes, yes—thank you," he finally says, stunned.

He will soon have his smile back, and while 80 dollars is one year's salary here, it is a mere pittance for a smile. What an excellent investment this is, and what a phenomenal return on my money! How many lives will he touch and inspire with his sensational smile?

17 February 1995
Friday

My Dearest,

I'm infuriated. I'm seething. Cary, count to ten and breathe. Go to the kitchen for a cup of tea.

The young man with the groin wound deteriorates. Since the house bathtub has been barred, we haven't been able to bathe him and properly care for his wound. His skin rots, pus pours out of his groin the way blood pulses from a ruptured artery, and once again the stench from his wound is so vile that no one can enter his room without retching. More and more tissue is degrading, and the young man is rapidly being consumed. Without a tub or hot water to thoroughly clean his wound, he will die a miserable death without dignity. I put my mind in the fast lane to find an immediate solution. And *voilà*, I have one of those good ideas. If I can't bring him to the tub, why not bring the tub to him.

I scour the hospital grounds for as many empty plastic pails as possible and drive back to the house to fill them with the only medicine that can help him—hot water. Once the pails are filled to their brims with scalding hot water, I return to the hospital to begin work. First, I scrounge around for anything that can be used to make a tub. With plastic sheeting from here and basins from there, along with pieces of this and that from everywhere, I quickly put together a makeshift receptacle to rescue him. The design is primitive and unattractive, but it will allow us to submerge his pelvis so the necrotic tissue will loosen. I can then debride the area and restore his dignity.

Though in excruciating pain, we do our best to lift him into our makeshift bathtub. Unfortunately, our best has the worst outcome. While pouring the scalding water into the tub, one of the sidewalls suddenly collapses, and the water spills directly onto the man's skin. He screams. He is badly burned. His cry is my cry. I want to shout. I want the expats who did this to be held accountable for denying this man the medical care he needed and deserved. I am beyond angry; I'm explosive.

305

18 February 1995
Saturday

My Dearest,

My replacement arrived this morning, a Canadian doctor. The medical ward is soon to be hers. I'll miss this place and these sensational people, whose smiles made the depravity and deprivation of my time here less devastating. The staff have improved beyond my imagination, and they are now shining stars and miracle workers. I'm so proud of them. In the end, the real winners are the Rwandan beneficiaries who will benefit from their care. I am no longer needed here. As was my intention coming to Rwanda, I have made myself redundant.

The nature of a humanitarian is to be human and care, but out of necessity, we have to let go and let live. When emotions grow strong and begin to cloud one's better judgment, it is time—time to move on. My staff have become my family. I care about them like a father cares about his children. This is not good. It wasn't good when I fell in love with Joseph and left him, and it isn't good that once again I find myself too close to my staff and leave them, too. It's not good for them, and it's not good for me. When I leave, I will probably never see them again. So it is time, time to leave before more people are hurt.

Soon, I will go and leave everything behind. In time, I will forget people's names and their stories. Most will be lost like dust in the wind. Such is Mother Nature. Such is the power of the wind.

19 February 1995
Sunday

My Dearest,

It's after midnight, and I can't fall asleep. With just days left before my departure, a flurry of intense and dreaded emotions surfaces. My head pounds with random thoughts that need to be birthed. I put pen to paper and spend the next several hours cathartically delivering Joseph, the little boy who was left on the hospital steps, abandoned by his family and condemned to suffer. The words just pour out of me, as if they have their own voice and need to tell their personal stories. As the words surface, they regurgitate a meal gone wrong. At the same time, my soul seems to expulse what it no longer chooses to house. The words that come tell a story of a memory that needs to be processed and passed. Much of what I write has already been written before, but I need to vent. I need to purge and expunge this gunk that tenaciously holds me hostage. Perhaps these words are Joseph's last words, his last work to be done here in this world. His life, condensed into a few words on a page, will touch the heartstrings of countless lives. And history will write its own account—its version of today—tomorrow. I wonder how we will be judged.

The words …

A country somewhere on the globe has gone through its own holocaust. Human beings went savage and out of control, cutting each other up with machetes, decapitating people in the streets and targeting children. "Kill the children!" roared over the radio. "You have to kill the inyenzi [cockroaches]," commanded the orchestrators of the genocide in pre-scripted broadcasts that incited a population and left a country in ruin and a population culled. Death delighted as it feasted on furrows of festering flesh. A human arm lying in a field with its tendons and ligaments ripped from its socket was once attached to someone. It all remains a nightmare with visuals that will plague me forever. Whose arm was it? What was his or her cry before the end of his or her life? Why did I go to see that atrocious killing field? Why did I photograph the skulls lying around like pebbles on a beach? Was it to believe the unbelievable, to make tangible the intangible? And here I am thousands of miles from home, on the other side of the world, surrounded by eagles, volcanoes, gorillas, disease, soldiers, and imminent war that one day in the future will make more killing fields over the already existing ones that have already been covered with earth to hide them.

Genocide—it is hideously human. The atrocities committed in the name of ethnic cleansing are too heinous to recount and almost sacrilegious to record in the annals of our civilization. Future civilizations will judge us badly if they come to know what we have done. But do we not owe it to those who follow us? Is it not a chance for them to do it differently by learning from our mistakes?

A Canadian man traveled to Rwanda. He was a good deed doer and came with good and grand ideas to do something meaningful for the people here. He was in Rwanda when the fighting broke out and saw firsthand the grotesqueness of genocide. While trying to flee the city, he got caught in traffic between Tutsis and Hutus. The Hutu hackers spared his life only because his Canadian passport didn't have T-U-T-S-I inscribed in it. His life may have been spared, but his heart was speared and his soul was impaled. He saw it all from behind a steering wheel. With his own eyes, through the windshield, he saw a family removed from their car. First, the mother was raped. Then the father was killed, and his genitals were shoved into his daughter's mouth as she was being raped. Her head was then split open, spewing cerebrospinal fluid from her skull. In the side-view mirror, he saw another child's skull get smashed, this time by a man who intentionally stomped on it with his black boot, relishing the moment of his conquest. In the rearview mirror, he saw people running for their lives suddenly falling to the ground by the slash of the Achilles tendon, intentionally "two-ed" by a machete in the hand of another human being who hated.

The crocodiles on the riverbanks are too fat to take float, for their bellies over-feasted on the festering flesh of what once was a mother, a father, brother, friend, lover. Ending up a crocodile's bowel movement along a riverbank somewhere on the planet might not have been anticipated when a couple teased each other over an ice cream cone on a hot, sunny afternoon between classes one day. But it ended up that way.

The Canadian man came here to help at the beginning of a

very bad dream. He had so much love to give, so many plans to make, so little experience with hatred. He returned home beaten and battered beyond recognition, trashed by what none of us can ever truly understand. Today, he is unable to listen or hear. He is unable to touch or be touched. He is unable to love. He lives alone for always and forever, far away from living things, and deals with the horror of his mind's memory.

A condominium somewhere with a nice car heading down a highway en route to some plush place with a five-star rating sounds nice, no? But what of the little boy I called Joseph, my little raisin, who reached out his arms when I came to look after him day after day while we poured pounds of high-protein milk down his throat with a nasogastric tube, hoping to save his life. He would reach out his arms in front of his marasmic body, which was only an assemblage of skin and bones, wanting me to bring him closer to my body. He called me "Papa" in his own way, without words, because at two years old, weighing barely 12 pounds, he didn't yet know what his tongue was for. For him, it was a useless appendage that served no purpose, because there was no one to talk to and no food to swallow. There was no mommy's milk to drink. She was sliced, diced, and perhaps burned or ripped to shreds by a man's maleness needing a refuse container for his ejaculate.

And I wonder if little Joseph watched his mommy, heard his mommy, felt his mommy leave him forever without a hug, without a kiss, without a little last lick of milk from her soft, enveloping breast that was always there to comfort him—like a best friend. When Joseph's mother was murdered, she didn't say goodbye to him. Saying goodbye to her baby would have been goodbye baby because the mean man with the machete would have known that somewhere there was a child who had to be killed. And the radio fueled the flames: "These people are a dirty race. We have to exterminate them. We must get rid of them. This is the only solution. Kill the children! Kill the children!" And so, mommy pretended there was no child and didn't cry out when she was being butchered. And in this way, Joseph understood to be quiet.

Joseph was deposited quietly on the hospital steps by his daddy's new woman, who wasn't his mommy and didn't want to be either. She knew he would die without her, but she just walked away, anyway. I found her later and told her to take her baby. She replied, "It's not mine, and I don't want it!"

When I found his daddy and asked him to take care of his baby, he said, "This is my baby, and I am his daddy, but I don't want him." And daddy and stepmommy walked away, not showing much of anything.

Stunned, we admitted baby Joseph, fed him, clothed him and loved him. Day after day, he saw me, a figure constant in his short life, someone giving him love, biscuits and bananas, sometimes an avocado, and always more of that precious high-protein milk that would leave a milk mustache and a trickle down his "bibless" rag remnant of a shirt. Nibyeza [good]. Drink not your mommy's milk, Joseph, but a powder that somehow has to be the next best thing. Drink not from your mother's breast but from an orange plastic cup that is too big for your little mouth, but is somehow the next best thing. He came to think I was his daddy. Seeing me, he would come to smile. In my arms, he came to trust me and quietly rested his head on my chest. In the beginning, he did so because he was too weak to balance his little head on his own shoulders. In time, however, he came to like me. He came to trust that my chest would be there when he wanted to rest his head somewhere strong and constant. Papa he thought I was.

Papa pushed little Joseph to take his first step. Though two years old, he never really knew what his legs were for. "Come, Joseph, come," I would say as I put him down. He stood there bent over, balancing himself like a tripod with his legs apart and hands on his knees, crouched over like a little old man defeated by age, weary and worn. Arching his head just nearly high enough to look into my eyes, he would tell me that he was hurting, that perhaps it wasn't yet the moment to see him step forward without still a bit more time and help from Papa. And once again, he reached forward, begging to place his head gently on my chest—that place he found strong and constant.

The only obstacle between Joseph and me was his very distended stomach, something that looked like a nine-month pregnant woman's belly. Instead of there being a baby inside, however, there were countless worms working unsuccessfully to live symbiotically with him. Mebendazole, ciprofloxacin, nalidixic acid and trimethoprim/sulfamethoxazole were all pumped into this little boy's body as we battled to save this besieged thread of a life. Joseph was like an unsuspecting insect struggling furiously to set itself free from a tenacious, unscrupulous spider's web. Miraculously, against all odds, he slowly made it—each hour another ounce, each week another pound, each moment another smile, another hug. I showered him with love as the African nation looked on with intrigue at the sight of an Umuzungu with this sickly, inconveniencing orphan. I walked him, fed him, and bathed his little emaciated body in diluted chlorine, disinfecting ruthless Shigella that mimicked the ruthless behavior of the perpetrators of the massacre that brought dear Joseph to the medical ward in the first place. Marasmus, developmental retardation, bacillary dysentery, rectal prolapse, kwashiorkor, all of the above, none of the above, or A, B or C, etc., etc., etc. Joseph lived and thought I was his Papa.

One Tuesday afternoon, after lunch, a meat meal no doubt with tropical fruit flown in from a surrounding country and transported four hours on a potholed dirt road, specially for the expats daring to serve in such squalor, I went to visit "my son." His bed was empty. He was gone along with his entire wardrobe: an extra-large T-shirt that hung on him like a nightgown and a pair of shorts that he was going to use to tuck in his extra-large T-shirt to prevent him from tripping when he would eventually have the strength to walk without the confident grip of Papa's big, strong, constant hand. Upset, I reprimanded the nurses for discharging him. They told me Joseph was taken to an orphanage an hour down the road.

After composing myself, I went back to the day before when I entered his room and greeted him with open arms as he greeted me with open arms. I recalled carrying him into the field behind the hospital and having a father-to-son talk, telling him how much I had come to love him and how much I thought of bringing him back to America with me, giving a son what a Papa should give his son. But was it right to enslave an African in a land that dislikes Africans? Was it right to pretend everything and everyone would live happily ever after? Was I right to let him rest his head on me and play Papa? I held him tight and walked around the field, surrounded by magnificent, rolling green hills propped up by banana bushes and wind you could feel but couldn't see. Frightened wild dogs scattered as I continued my father-to-son monologue with Joseph. I knew he couldn't understand, but I knew I needed to say goodbye because I couldn't be his Papa because I wasn't his Papa. I was his doctor. And I had overstepped my professional boundaries and grown to love a little African boy named Joseph, which was not even his name. For whatever reason, the abandoned boy was never given one of his birthrights—a name.

I can see myself now with him in my arms, cradling him like a nest holds its little bird, his head resting on my chest, and my eyes purposely avoiding eye contact with his purely innocent eyes. How do you tell a child who has come to love you goodbye? I stammer and clumsily stumble about as I go nowhere, looking everywhere except into Joseph's eyes. But something suddenly doesn't make sense. I know what it is, but I try not to see it. I try to unsee what I have already seen.

A warring soldier in a desolate field sees another soldier in the distance. It is dusk, and the night's fog is beginning to take its position. The warring soldier cautiously moves toward the soldier in the distance, still uncertain if he is an ally or an enemy. As he nears his target, he sees that the soldier isn't a soldier but a tree. And he will never be able to see the tree as a soldier again. Once you hear something, you can't unhear it. Once you know something, you can't unknow it. Once you see something, you can't unsee it.

A skull—a human skull. I look away from what I have just seen. I no longer see a benign-looking field, but rather the remains of a killing field: bones, skulls in their entirety, crushed ones too, shreds of clothing, chunks of head hair, and dozens of dried woven grass bagel-shaped carrying rings, once used to protect people's heads from heavy loads, like 100 pounds of potatoes. Usually, these head rings are worn by the women who do most of the work here in Africa. But in this field, they were not being used. There were no longer any heads to dress because the women were slaughtered. The only reason these head rings remained untouched and uncovered was because the wild dogs in the field had no use for them. Woven grass rings would not fill their hungry stomachs.

One Sunday afternoon, I went to visit my Joseph at the orphanage. Dozens of children, naked and needy, ran to me with runny noses, scabietic skin, worm-infested bellies, and stool under their fingernails. Grabbing at my hands and legs, they seemed to know their passage to some semblance of a home and family was through ingratiating themselves to me. I looked around for little Joseph and found him unattended by himself in his bed. When he saw me, like so many times before, he reached out his arms as I did my own. I could feel him deeply inhale the joy that he once again felt being close and connected to "Papa." The nurses told me that when they took him away, he cried out, "Papa, Papa," from the tongue that had learned to keep silent since the slaughter of his mother.

Why did I come to see Joseph? Why did I come when I knew I would leave a child who dared once more to love? Just asking this question seemed to bring forth his response. Once Joseph realized my coming was my going, those once-upon-a-time purely innocent eyes were, from that moment on, blinded. Instead of looking into my eyes, he looked through them and saw me not. And I doubt he will ever dare to love again.

This all sounds so overly dramatic. The only problem with this story is that it is understated and true.

20 February 1995
Monday

My Dearest,

Jane is stricken with *sad* today. Nothing happened out of the ordinary, and there is no apparent reason for her sorrow. Yet she is down—very down. It is common here to ride the waves of emotions, like a Hawaiian surfer, up and down. On the outside, we appear to be strong and sturdy, easily keeping ourselves together. On the inside, however, we are fragile, emotionally unstable wrecks.

Today, Jane finds herself in a kaleidoscope of disturbing images and painful memories of suffering and death. As the images and memories gather momentum, they creep into her consciousness and cause her to take an extended pause. When everything she saw and did eventually surfaces, it all becomes more real. When this happens, there is nowhere to go and nothing to feel but hopelessness and helplessness.

We healthcare workers work blindly on purpose, without reflection—reflecting would only paralyze and torment us. We have no choice but to put blinders on and go gaily forward to function here. Sometimes, out of curiosity or incredulity, we sneak a peek or allow the blinders to fall to the side. And what do we see? We see a fuller picture of the reality around us: the senselessness is stifling; the despair is disabling, and the mess is maddening. It is best to stay blindfolded.

Jane, like Bart, asks if I ever cried in Rwanda. I shamefully move my head from side to side, as though there is something wrong with me.

"Why?" she asks.

In my defense, I say, "I don't know. I want to believe there is a reason for all this misery we see each day." After some silence and a bit more pause, I repeat, "I want to believe there is a reason." Then I add, "It's just that sometimes I can't find the reason for any of it. And the tears seem to go missing."

21 February 1995
Tuesday

My Dearest,

Government soldiers came to the hospital compound today and arrested several members of our local staff. They took them to an undisclosed location for crimes against humanity. I have worked with these people for months, and now I watch them being hauled away to an uncertain fate, possibly to a prison cell, followed by the guillotine—the machete machine. It is very frustrating that we can do nothing to protect them, but our hands are tied. Defending them in any way could be misconstrued as obstructing justice or would implicate us in whatever crimes these people supposedly committed. How easy would it then be for the government to accuse us of subversive activities and claim we are concealing "weapons," in this case, human ones with Tutsi blood on their hands? Meddling in the government's affairs or interfering in their investigations to locate the perpetrators of the genocide would have disastrous consequences for us. So we say nothing and watch our friends disappear. What have they done? Who have they killed?

22 February 1995
Wednesday

My Dearest,

The UN came to our compound today to report that there was a shootout in the neighboring town of Gisenyi. A local doctor was killed, and three others were seriously wounded. One of the wounded was a 12-year-old boy whose brain was pierced and bits of it were expulsed from his skull.

Besides casualties of war, there is political rancor between the Rwandan government and the international community. Despite millions of dollars being poured into this country from foreign donors, the current government is increasingly hostile toward us. I can understand their anxiety and agitation with outside agencies. International humanitarian aid organizations

315

serve people, not local politicians or governments. They also serve as advocates and shed light on irregularities they see in the field. Criticizing a sovereign state and its power holders makes them enemies of the State. In the case of Rwanda, criticism incenses officials here, who menacingly hurl their power above our heads. The antagonism is real. The fallout is dangerous. We still have some immunity from the military and political powers since they still need our foreign funds and assistance, but our highway is rapidly getting narrower and narrower, which is restricting our movement and ultimately our freedom. We must stay apolitical. But it is a bit too late for that now. The military, which had once been our friend, now treats us with disdain and suspicion. In their eyes, we are their enemy. Who knows when the machete will fall on us.

Leaving Rwanda at this time is for the best. The fields I cultivated are fertile, and the seeds I planted have sprouted. The fruits of everyone's labor are strong, and the staff are able to carry on the planting by themselves. Waiting too long to pass on the farm can cause the fruit to rot.

There remains a palpable hatred between the Hutus and the Tutsis. No international assistance of any kind will harness their hate. The people of Rwanda need to find their own balance and harmony somehow, in their own way, in their own time, and on their own terms. We have not helped in this regard. We can give love, but our love will not heal their hate.

23 February 1995
Thursday

My Dearest,

My replacement started work and took over the ward today. She is a Canadian physician who comes with an open, warm heart, ready and eager to serve the patients and the staff. The staff, to my surprise, are sad. I have to admit, I am sad too. Thadee, my medical assistant, says, "You are leaving us. Your replacement is not like you." He is deeply distressed. And I am deeply touched.

24 February 1995
Friday

My Dearest,

It is customary for expats to host a going-away party for their staff when they leave. I don't want to have a party. It's not my thing. Jane says the gathering is a way of giving the staff an opportunity to thank me and have closure. She says I can also use the occasion to express my gratitude to them. I change my mind and agree to have the party.

In the evening, the staff come to our house for dinner. At first, it is a bit awkward engaging socially with my co-workers outside the ward. But in time, I find it fantastic. We've been with each other for months, but talking with them tonight, I realize we barely know one another. It would take lifetimes to truly know and understand them, given all the hardship and trauma they have been through. They are an impressive and resilient people. What I find most remarkable is that they still can smile and play and find joy in little things. I hope one day they forgive those who lost their way. They may never be able to forget what happened, but I trust they will find their way.

Back to the party—everyone has a good time. They eat and eat and then eat some more. They even eat the chicken bones. Judging from their voracious appetites, I gather they haven't had such a feast in a long time. It makes me happy to feed them. I remember as a child, Mom always told me to finish everything on my plate because of the "poor, starving children in Africa." I never really understood how finishing everything on my plate could feed the poor, starving children in Africa. Nonetheless, I always listened to her and finished every speck of food on my plate. I still do today. Curiously, thirty years later, I am in Africa, seeing firsthand the starving children finishing every speck of food on their plates.

Everyone enjoys. When there is a lull between dinner and dance, Odette grabs the opportunity and stands up to give a short speech. She is big, and when she talks you listen.

"Dr. Cary, thank you. We have all come to like and respect you so much. We are going to miss you. You've changed the hospital. You've taught us and treated us like your children, caring for us so much. In the beginning, we thought you were just trying to push us down, but now we realize you pushed because you cared. And look at us now! We are so proud of ourselves and our accomplishments! Look at us now because of you."

People applaud, and Christine, one of our medical aides, cries. A tear wants to come out of Cary, but I hold it back.

25 February 1995
Saturday

My Dearest,

I am leaving Rwanda on my birthday. How appropriate, since Rwanda has been very much like a rebirth for me—a new beginning. My life will certainly never be the same after these past six months. Swallowed by war, harassed by hate, and living in lack has given me a sound appreciation for the privileged life I live. Now, with this new appreciation, I have fallen in love with living. In the past, a single moment used to pass without notice. It was nothing important or noteworthy. A moment was just something I took for granted. Now, a moment becomes a sublime gift to cherish and savor.

I wonder about my return home. Have I changed? Do I have the capacity to accept other people's changes or lack of them? Many of the things I have seen in Rwanda cannot be shared. Many of the things I have lived through here cannot be relived. What has happened to me during this mission has left indelible stains that can never be removed, even with the most potent stain removers. I hope my trust in humanity remains strong. I will do my best to surrender, let my guard down, and believe in and count on others again. It is easy to forget to forgive. It is easy to criticize and hate. It is critically important now for me to remember how to love and let live.

I am tired. This mission was intense and demanding. Six months is a long time to live with a pistol pointed at your forehead. The constant fear of someone pulling the trigger has exhausted me. The fact that I am alive when so many others have died should be cause for celebration, but instead, I am tormented. Just two days ago, there was an attack on a town an hour from our house. An entire family was killed: a mom, a dad, and their two small children were slaughtered. The week before, UN troops were attacked. The same week, death did its thing again and took eight more peacekeepers when they ran over a mine. Military men are everywhere the eye can see, and peace is nowhere. I will not miss this part of Rwanda.

26 February 1995
Sunday

My Dearest,

In the late 1960s, a civil war in Biafra led to the starvation and death of an estimated two million people, mostly children. Images of swollen, listless, skeletal, and dead children were widely shown to the public. No bystander was innocent. The Biafra famine was a critical time for all humanity. People clamored to defy helplessness, conquer hopelessness, and stop the suffering. Believing in something better, a small group of doctors and journalists forged a way from helplessness to helpfulness. How? They founded a humanitarian organization to provide medical care to people in need anywhere in the world. They called their ambitious dream Doctors Without Borders. The dreamers arduously set out to join hands with all humanity to serve all humanity without borders. What a tremendous idea! Why didn't I think of it? Helping people in need is a very meaningful and noble life.

Ever since I saw those images of the Biafra famine, I have wanted, in some way, to serve the poorest of the poor around the world. In 1978, I went to the office of Doctors Without Borders in Paris and asked the staff how I could participate in their missions abroad. "Become a doctor and contact us," they said. And so I did. I became a doctor and then called them sixteen years later. And what did they do? They invited me to join them. I salute the founders of Doctors Without Borders for their vision and fortitude to go beyond their dreams, beyond their imaginations, and beyond their personal borders. The organization has given many a chance to see what is possible when people believe in something bigger than themselves—something bigger than life. The organization has also shown me, through direct experience, the miraculous power of a community in unity. Nothing has more promise than committed and compassionate people who work together. Doctors Without Borders has truly given me an opportunity to serve humanity as a doctor without borders. I would like to thank all the founders, dreamers, givers, doers, and optimists who helped me find my passion and realize my life's purpose.

27 February 1995
Monday

My Dearest,

I consider my future and reflect on the infinite possibilities for tomorrow. Continuing to do voluntary humanitarian aid work would bring me tremendous joy, but what about my family, friends, Social Security, medical insurance, pension, and all the other obligations and requirements to survive in the modern world? And then there are the dangers: diseases and war, the uncertainty of political turmoil, and the unanticipated twist of events that could "vegetabilize" my life in a nano-second. These all weigh on me with an oppressive fear that crushes and incapacitates my resolve. I can do without luxury, but what about the basics, like peace and security?

I have a theory: We need air, food, water, rest, and shelter to survive. There is one more thing we need: love. We need love—more precisely, we need *to* love. When we love, we not only survive, we thrive, because it is what we were designed to do. It is our true nature. When we are not permitted to love, we are out of our element and subsequently contract, shrivel and stray from our *raison d'être*.

A life without loving is living without life itself. Take love out of life and the soul starves. When the soul starves, we lose sight of why we are here and how we are all connected. When we can no longer recognize each other, we don't know how to act, so we act up and act out.

In today's world, it is becoming ever more difficult to love—to love our neighbors, to love our strangers, and to love ourselves. People have become fearful, guarded, anxious and suspicious of one another. Children are taught not to talk to strangers; teachers are wary of consoling children as touch is no longer permitted; lawsuits for harassment are generously slapped on anyone who dares to compliment a colleague at work for looking good; and doctors are leaving medicine because they can't afford the exorbitant malpractice insurance that protects them from the very people they try to help. And so, it is hard—very hard—to love today. Fortunately, Africa is behind the times. Children are not told to avoid strangers because there aren't any. Everyone is family. Teachers teach students in schools that have no bars, guards or cameras, and doctors don't need malpractice insurance because patients don't sue. Instead, they are grateful—only grateful.

I am awed by Africa because it lets me love. It welcomes my love, encourages me to love, and blesses me when I love. In fact, the more I love, the more the people love me in return. In this way, we are connected—we are One. Is there any better way to be?

Africa is the cradle where it all happened. It is the womb from where we all came. In essence, it is everyone's Mother: the creator, the sustainer and the protector. Coming back here has been like coming home to mom. I can't explain what it feels like to once again be in her embrace because it is beyond words, but what I can say with absolute certainty is that it feels extraordinary.

28 February 1995
Tuesday

My Dearest,

Thirty-six years ago, I made my debut and landed my itsy-bitsy feet on Planet Earth. Today, on my birthday, I embark on an adventure to another distant land. This time, I am going to Planet Home.

Takeoff...

33,000 feet above Rwanda, somewhere over its thousand hills, I see flickering lights. Did I bring any light?

Rwanda … What will happen to her and her people? Only time will tell. Currently, each side of the conflict holds tight to their position and grudges. Each side holds onto their enmity and refuses to forgive for generations. As a result, battles rage from time to time on both sides of the divide, and slaughter and death are well known to everyone. As long as the balance of power shifts from Hutu to Tutsi and from Tutsi to Hutu, conflicts between them will continue well into perpetuity. The Hutu are people. The Tutsi are people. They are all Rwandan. They are all African and have brown skin. They have bright white teeth and red blood. Hutus and Tutsis have love in their hearts and have so much in common. They are brothers and sisters and have the same great-great-great grandmothers and the same great-great-great grandfathers. So they are related. When they come to know this, there will be peace … finally.

I did my best. I learned a lot. I am grateful. I am grateful for the 80 dollars I had and could give away to Kabera to return his smile. I am grateful to little Joseph for giving me a chance to experience fatherhood. I am grateful for the affection of my staff and the support of my family and friends. I am grateful to my parents for the education they gave me so I could become a doctor. I am grateful for being part of history and being able to give it a little love. And I am grateful to *You,* My Dearest, for giving me this time to commune with You. With You by my side, there is no need to count the footsteps in the sand.

Epilogue
25 Years Later

Twenty-five years ago, I flew to Rwanda at the end of a genocide that left over a million people dead. Among those who perished were grandmothers and grandfathers, mothers and fathers, children, aunties, uncles, sisters, brothers, friends, strangers, doctors, lawyers, farmers, dancers, artists, and …

I went to this little, unknown country in the heart of Africa with big aspirations of making a difference in the lives of those who survived a genocide and those who didn't. How do you resurrect lost lives and make a difference? By bearing witness and sharing their stories with the world. In this way, the prematurely muted souls have their full power to express themselves. The stories I heard and recounted in my diary are only fragmented fragments. Their whole truth can only be brought forward by the very sticks and stones that broke bones and the machetes that lacerated tendons and cracked the skulls of men, women, children, and unborn fetuses. The unabridged story of Rwanda's genocide must be told by the people who held those sticks and stones and machetes in hand and heart.

Hatred erupted like an angry volcano in 1994. It was not Mother Nature that was responsible—it was man's nature. It was also not the jagged edges of Mother's volcanic rocks that came tumbling down on the people, but the primitive edges of man's machetes. Instead of toiling the soil, the almighty blade left the soil to bear the burden.

It is with a heavy heart that I now come back to Rwanda. I come back a quarter of a century after the people's genocide to pay homage to those who passed and finally lay the dead to rest. I also seek to lay to rest my own restlessness, for since I left the country, I have not been at peace. I believe my peace will finally come when I see a flourishing Rwanda, full of love and compassion for all and everyone.

When I was last in the country, I was not allowed outside the hospital gates except for a short one-mile stretch of road that led to our residential compound. Expats were essentially under house arrest. Our movement was curtailed because no one in power at that time wanted us to see the truth. No one wanted to parade the nation's dirty laundry in front of the entire world to gawk at, scrutinize or condemn. The savagery committed by many Rwandan people was, after all, a national embarrassment. I want to see what we weren't allowed to see.

When I first came to Rwanda in September of 1994, the people's emotional wounds were too raw and gaping to do anything more than a cursory exam and treat whatever I could, without being too intrusive. It was not the time to ask the people to share their stories. I wanted so much to see, feel, sense and understand what was unable to be seen, felt, sensed or understood. But it just wasn't the time. Out of necessity, I had to be blindfolded to do the job I had come to do—to be a doctor. Being sheltered from the raw realities of the genocide that preceded my arrival had allowed me to deny anything and everything having to do with human suffering and savagery. When I saw an infant's vertebrae on the ground, I convinced myself that they were dog biscuits; a piece of skull on a hilltop was a broken plastic toy; a severed human limb in a field was irrefutably a doll's arm. I fervently chose to believe that man was inherently good and magnanimous and that horror stories were only fictitious flirtations of talented writers, replete with Hollywood endings. Surely, at the end of this movie, a knight in shining armor rides far off into the horizon as the closing curtain falls and spectators finally relax after sitting on the edge of their chairs in a theater with ice-cream wrappers and popcorn scattered about. I now come back to Rwanda at this time to finish the movie.

What do I want coming back here at this time? I want to purge the pain I hold in my heart. I want to let go, let live, and let die what clutches me and holds my mind hostage. I want to be free of the past and leave "hopeless" behind. I want to move forward with hope in my heart. I want to see with my own eyes if the little I did as a doctor on the internal medical ward 25 years ago made a difference, even if it was just a dent. I want to believe that peace grew from the graves and that the Rwandan people are finally united and flourishing as One.

KIGALI INTERNATIONAL AIRPORT

28 July 2019
Sunday

Touchdown ... Rwanda!

After many years, I finally make it back to Rwanda. There is excitement, thrill, and trepidation in my heart. A blast from the past crashes onto my shores like a tsunami as I make my way out of the plane, onto the tarmac, and into the airport terminal. What is going to happen next?

The airport is no longer swamped with scurrying soldiers and frenetic humanitarian aid workers. It is now bustling with civilian passengers, including businessmen and vacationers. There are no longer project coordinators, chiefs of staff, heads of missions, or UN peacekeepers decorated with powder blue berets. And *Médecins Sans Frontières* T-shirts are nowhere to be seen. There is actually nothing distinguishing this airport from any other international airport in the world: security is boldly present for all to see, customs has the usual bureau-cratic formalities, and customs officers are the typical garden variety without facial friendliness or welcoming smiles. The officer before me is no different. A tinge of spicy arrogance defines him, and I ask myself how I got into his line. But here I am. He suspiciously asks why I have come to Rwanda. I tell him I came to see their prized gorillas, Rwanda's number one tourist attraction. He is not convinced. He takes my passport and examines every page, stamp and sticker with a fine-tooth comb. After a few minutes of intense scrutiny, he says, "This is not your passport." He asserts that the picture on page one does not match my face and asks me for an alternative piece of identification. I show him my driver's license. Finally, after grilling me with countless additional questions, he reluctantly gives me a visa to enter the country. I was not expecting such a *warm* and *endearing* welcome. To be honest, I sort of hoped for a hero's welcome. I was surprised to be seen as an enemy of the State. Let this not be my story's sequel. Let this one have a Hollywood ending.

I quickly make my way through the international arrivals terminal and find myself outside, in front of a crowd of hundreds of people eagerly waiting to meet their loved ones. There is a man in a suit standing in front of them all, looking at me, humble and humbled. He smiles. I smile. And then we hug. No words are needed. I hold my tears the best I can, but there is wetness despite my valiant effort to keep them in check. *"Bonjour, Laurent,"* I say. *"Bonjour, Dr. Cary,"* he says. Laurent was my medical assistant. He was also my shoulder, backbone, crutch, and confidant during the toughest times on the medical ward in Mabanza. I haven't seen him for 25 years, except for a small passport-size photo that I carried in my wallet all this time. I held him close in my heart this past quarter-century because he was special and held me tight when I was unraveling during the early days of my mission to Rwanda in 1994. Laurent is now miraculously a physician—a surgeon—working with Doctors Without Borders, serving the poor. He tells me he decided to become a doctor after being inspired by working with me and seeing patients together.

"I was deeply moved by your sacrifice, putting yourself in harm's way and risking your life to come to my country when we most needed a helping hand," he shares. "And so, I had a debt to you to pay forward. Today, I continue your work and give my hand to support those in need," he adds.

I am taken off guard by his touching words and work to find my breath. We hug again—for a long time—then Laurent introduces me to his wife. She smiles at me with an affection not often given to a stranger and says, "Thank you. Thank you for what you did for our people." I am then introduced to their son, a young man who looks at me admiringly, as if I were some sort of superstar. It appears I have been a topic of many discussions over the years, and so there is awe in his face to finally meet the illustrious "Dr. Cary." He was born after the genocide and knows nothing of those times, but honors me for coming to help his people and his country. This time, I can't hold back my tears. Laurent then takes my hand and walks me through Rwanda.

KIGALI

Kigali is no longer a ghost town with tumbleweed rolling across dirt roads. No, it is a sprawling metropolis with high-rise buildings, luxury hotels, and houses in every conceivable corner. The internet is easily accessible. Roads are paved. Cell phones are in everyone's hands. Indoor malls showcase young entrepreneurs, and outdoor markets are filled with everything you want and need and then some. Most impressive is the city's cleanliness. Swiss spotlessness would be humbled by Rwanda's immaculateness. City workers trim and tend flower-beds, water lawns, and meticulously manicure the streets and sidewalks. There is not a speck of trash anywhere except in refuse containers. There are no bottles, cans, paper, cigarette butts, or anything else out of place. No wonder Rwanda is now considered the Singapore of Africa.

Also impressive is the country's security situation. There is practically no crime—no rape, theft, kidnapping, carjacking or robberies. There are also no gunshots, guerrilla incursions, or military checkpoints like in the past. Anyone—men, women, children, young and old—can walk anywhere at any time, day or night, safely without fear of aggression. Today, Rwanda is reported to be the safest country in Africa and the ninth safest country in the world.

There are more astonishing achievements over the past 25 years worth noting. Rwanda has a robust economy with an impressive annual growth rate, universal healthcare for its citizens, and free education through high school. There has been a significant decline in extreme poverty: literacy rates have increased substantially; infant mortality has dropped from more than 10% in the early 1990s to under 3% today, and the average life expectancy has risen from 26 to 69 years.

And then there is the most notable of all achievements: Rwanda no longer has any Hutus, Tutsis or Twas. There are only Rwandans. When you ask someone if they are Hutu or Tutsi, they respond, *"Ndi umunyarwanda* [I am Rwandan]." By official decree, it is illegal to advance genocidal ideology in any way, shape or form. Saying you are Hutu, Tutsi or Twa is considered to be "divisionism," which is strictly prohibited. Anything that could potentially cultivate hatred is forbidden. Anything that could be considered toxic or divisive to the integrity of the country is not allowed. Anything threatening the cohesiveness of the Rwandan people is banned. Hatred does not have a chance under such strict vigilance. As two-thirds of the population is under 25 years old, or, in other words, born after the genocide, there is a real possibility that the sky is finally their limit.

It's curious to me how the youth pass by, engrossed in their tweets, Instagrams, and Facebook pals, never once wondering about what's odd with their surroundings. Once upon a time, blood, hair, skulls, excrement, and decayed body parts littered their gardens and public parks. Today, there is not a trace of anything offensive or repugnant. Everything has since been cleared and sanitized. Today's youth are part of what is now called the "New Generation." When I ask this new generation about the past, they say, "The past is past. We move forward" —seven words they heard from their teachers in school and now recite like a holy mantra without reflection. These words have become a real part of them and how they choose to live today. It is the only way they can live, given what happened to their people. How else do you deal with decimation? "What was no longer is," they say with authority and confidence. "We move forward. We move forward. We move forward," they chant, like a national anthem.

A popular motto that often comes up in conversations with young people is "This is the century of peace." My hope is that this new generation will cherish each other and coexist in peace. Their future is now in *their* hands.

The government appears to be dotting its "I"s and crossing its "T"s to build national unity and foster reconciliation. When people feel unheard or neglected, they lose affection for their government. When people feel marginalized, unrepresented or dismissed, they feel separate from the whole. When there is great disparity between the haves and have-nots, jealousy and resentment monopolize people's better judgment. Invariably, this all leads to civil unrest. The government understands this and works to integrate and advance everyone equally, hence their focus on strengthening education and establishing social programs to help the disadvantaged.

The government is also keen to build people's self-esteem and promote self-reliance. Accordingly, it refrains from giving handouts, which are known to create dependency. Instead, the government has instituted initiatives that encourage people's independence through personal ownership. One such initiative that is currently in practice involves the breeding of cows. In Rwanda, cows have traditionally been an essential and integral part of the household. They are a sign of a family's prosperity and raise people's social status in their community. Cows are invaluable assets as well because they provide a sustainable and continuous source of milk for nourishment, manure for fertilizer, and offspring for barter or cash. The government scheme involves giving needy families a cow to raise and breed. When this cow has her first offspring, the family gives it to another family in need. In this way, people learn to stand on their own two feet and take personal responsibility for their advancement. In addition, they actively participate in the upliftment of others in their community. Overall, the formula for the current governance is about people helping people, which is essential to building a strong and unified society.

The current government is committed to elevating Rwanda to new heights. The standard African status quo is no longer the country's gold standard; something new and improved is. If people are to stand tall with their shoulders back and heads held high, they need to be proud and leave poverty mindsets behind. Therefore, by official government decree, secondhand shoe and clothing imports have been prohibited, plastic bags have been banned, littering has been declared illegal, and grass-thatched roofs (which are so common in Africa) have been outlawed in an initiative called "*Urabeho Nyakatsi* [bye, bye grass roofs]."

The government also enthusiastically cultivates civility and solidarity in the community, which has transformed the people and the country. This transformation is remarkable and sets the Rwandan nation apart from its neighbors on the continent. For example, people respect traffic signals; drivers yield to pedestrians crossing the road; passengers stand politely in single-file lines waiting to board buses; motorcyclists wear helmets; and everyone wears shoes—walking barefoot, I'm told, is illegal. To build a strong and harmonious community, one day a month, people are required to gather and work together for the betterment of the entire community, a concept known as *Umuganda* in Kinyarwanda. Community activities include cleaning the environment, cultivating fields, or any other initiative that benefits the collective whole. Furthermore, twice a month, main roads are closed to traffic so people can claim their neighborhoods, move about freely, and foster a sense of unity in the community.

Rwanda has emerged from a deep, dark abyss and stands tall today on *mille collines*—a thousand hills. Proof of the country's success goes beyond words. Fields are in full bloom, people have food on their plates, the economy is booming, entrepreneurship is exploding, and the people live in peace.

Laurent and I talk nonstop for hours, like grammar school friends exploring life for the first time. He shares that he also kept a diary about the genocide.

"Life is not good when I see people suffering from injustice and other man-made disasters," he says. "When will I publish what I have? When is the appropriate time?" he asks.

"Laurent, I have a lot to say on this subject," I answer. "Like you, I have struggled with the destiny of my own diary. Part of me wants to hide it permanently or trash it. But I know it must be shared to give perspective and legitimacy to a part of our human history that must never be forgotten. Some people would prefer to have the genocide disappear without a trace. It cannot. We must protect its existence, preserve its pain, immortalize its memory, and always remember those who perished," I assert passionately. "Regarding your own diary, I implore you to bring it forward. When is the right time to give it to the people? Now. The world needs it now. If any word you write or experience you share can affect another person's life in a positive way, then it is worth the time, energy and angst publishing it. I know it's frightening. I know people can be brutally harsh and critical, but again, if one word can bring about goodness, then it must be signed, sealed, and delivered to the people." I carry on with my soliloquy. "I don't seek fame or notoriety from publishing my diary. I'm doing it because it's the right thing to do. Many deny that the Rwandan genocide ever happened. Others make false claims about it. And some buy into the notion that it is what the good God wants—'*Si le bon Dieu veut.*'

"You must tell your story. You must share what you saw during that terrible time." I insist. And finally, I conclude, "You never shared with me what you experienced during the genocide. In spite of us being very close, you have yet to let me in. I sense that even today it is hard for you to extract from your archives what you saw, heard, smelled and felt. Such intense emotion must be given flight and allowed to fly in order to touch the people. Surely, their hearts will swell, and they will pause when they hear your story. People hate. People taunt. People kill. The same people love and bring new life into the world. Give them the chance to choose. The love you have for people is immense. The love you have for God is bold and beautiful. Give humanity a chance to experience your world full of kindness and compassion. Make your voice their voice."

Changing the subject, I say to Laurent, "By the way, did you ever cry when the genocide happened? Or were you too stunned for tears to fall?"

He answers, "I am still crying, indeed, and still having flashbacks of my many 1994 memories, like it was of today."

MABANZA

Laurent takes me to Mabanza, the place where I was first stationed in 1994. It is also the place where we first met each other. Driving to Mabanza from Kigali was once a four-hour nightmare over potholes that could have easily caused a major concussion. Today, the road is paved and well maintained. This time, the journey takes just under two hours. What a nice development. While the road has improved, I must say, the people we pass on the side of the road live as before—hard lives. Twenty-five years ago, people carried the sum total of their life possessions in their hands, on their heads, and on their backs. The same remains true today. It was hard to see this back then, and continues to be hard for me today. People are still poor and struggling. Those with a bit more transport their goods on the backs of bikes, which they push up steep hills—too steep for any age. Both the young and old do it not because they can, but because they have no choice.

Rwanda boasts high economic growth, but many people still carry 5-gallon containers of water home from a distant water source and toil a soil that, though fertile, takes all and everything they've got to hand-cultivate. Beads of sweat from every pore pour like rainstorms in this unforgiving heat from a sun that beats them up without reprieve. This sun is no one's friend here, and without umbrellas, shade, or other protection to shield themselves from it, they suffer. Unfortunately, this part of Rwanda has not changed significantly from the previous century. Another remnant of the past that has not changed is the shame I feel having more than others. When I look at the people here, I still have to look away from them. Having so much when they have so little disturbs me. It's just too painful to see their struggle and the inequity between us.

People walk along the side of the road. Many have scars across their faces and necks, and deformities in their skulls, which are clearly inflicted by the crushing blow of a machete. It is shocking to see the number of people missing limbs. The genocide is over, but their pain and suffering are unending.

Mabanza! We finally arrive. Instantly, a flurry of thoughts and memories inundates me—some good and some not so good. I hold my judgment and try my best to just take in the surroundings. The place is completely unrecognizable. I ask Laurent if he has mistaken the location. This can't be the place where I first worked with MSF 25 years ago. He assures me it is. There is nothing familiar—not a hill, not a stone, road, building or field; absolutely nothing is as it was. Even the town's official name has changed. Mabanza has been renamed Rubengera.

Laurent takes me to the house where I once lived with the other expatriates to help me orient myself. The house doesn't look familiar either. I ask him again if he is certain that this is the same place from years ago. He assures me again that it is.

I have to go inside. Reluctantly, I approach the house and knock on the front door. No one answers, so I knock again and then again. A man comes from behind the house and greets us suspiciously. I introduce Laurent and myself, and after some pleasantries, I ask him if I can see his house. He agrees. Once inside, I am convinced it's the house. Everything is as it was: the family room, kitchen, bathroom, my bedroom, and the backyard. The only thing missing is the small wooden gate that once separated me from the rest of Rwanda on the outside. Otherwise, it is all here, including the memories. I remember the smiles on the faces of the house staff meeting me for the first time. I remember the sounds of the cook killing a goat by my bedroom window. I remember the way I used to sneak out through the kitchen over the wooden gate in the dark of night with pots of food to feed the displaced people scattered everywhere the eye could see. None of my memories have changed or faded.

The man of the house is reluctant to engage or share his story with me. After a while, however, he takes me to the side and tremulously shares that he lost 36 people in his family during the genocide, including his mother, father and siblings. He is now suspicious of everyone and trusts no one. He is wary of speaking openly in the presence of another Rwandan, but gives me his phone number to continue our conversation. He is sadly living in consuming fear of there being another genocide. I understand his fear, and he knows it. After an acknowledged closeness between us, I bid the frightened man farewell and hope that his fears prove to be unwarranted. I think to myself that it is absolutely impossible for another genocide to erupt in the future. But isn't that what the Jews thought as they were herded into the gas chambers, expecting a refreshing shower? Despite all the safeguards put in place to prevent it, another horrific genocide is absolutely possible. There remain thousands of people beyond Rwanda's borders, and perhaps even within her borders, who want to finish the job. As I leave, I decide not to take pictures of the house. There are too many painful memories within these walls.

The next place to visit should be the hospital, but I do not want or need to see it. What I saw there and what I will always see there are my patients dying from AIDS, cholera, malaria, Shigella, diarrhea and malnutrition. What I see and will always see is the cruelty of that wretched nurse who set out to destroy me, sacrificing innocent people along her path of destruction in order to achieve her objective. I do not want to be reminded of those times. Perhaps I could compromise a bit and visit the hospital steps. There were many people on those steps worth remembering, like the two women I was forced to dump there because Nurse Ratshit ordered me to expel them from the ward. And then there was my beloved Joseph. His stepmother dumped him on the same steps as if he were a pile of poop, then walked away and never looked back. Those steps either went up to hell in the hospital or down to hell six feet under the ground. Both directions eventually led to the same place. No, on second thought, I don't need to see the hospital or its steps.

I wonder where the hill is—the one that I walked up with Joseph in my arms. And where is that field with all those skulls and bones and the bagel-shaped grass headgear once used by the Tutsi women who tried to flee from death, only to be captured and decapitated? In the end, what happened to all those pieces of people? I don't even know where to begin to look. But it doesn't matter. Just thinking of the field, I can see, hear, feel and smell Joseph in my arms.

Mabanza is no more. Once home to thousands of displaced people, today they are all missing. Once teeming with soldiers proudly camouflaged in phlegm-green uniforms accessorized with weapons, the landscape is missing them too. And what about the camp of handmade huts covered with turquoise plastic sheeting that tried its best to shield the people from the cold, rain, wind and mud? It is nowhere to be found either. Nothing remains of what was. Instead, there are businesses and schools, fields filled with banana bushes, and new houses with color-coordinated paint. People move about freely. Everyone dresses in clean clothing, and every foot walks proudly in a shoe or sandal, unlike the bare ones that had no choice back in the day. No one forages for food. No one is on all fours, picking out single beans embedded in the dirt for something more than nothing to eat. And no one is without a smile on their face as they greet me. People look sincerely happy. What a difference this all is to what once was. What an impressive affirmation of the world's capacity to recover and renew! What a remarkable testament to people's resilience and ability to forgive and move on—to live and let live!

Mabanza was not all bad. There actually were some nice things that happened here, like working together with Laurent and Samuel, my wonderful medical assistants. They were both sources of inspiration and stability for me. They were my rocks, my safe places. I could always go to them and feel protected, respected, and human again. Both commiserated with me and understood how hard it was being under the broomstick of the villainous, wicked nurse. Both were confused about who was in fact running the hospital and who was ultimately in charge. Was it the doctor or was it the nurse? They felt my frustration and encouraged me to let go, hold on, trust and have faith. What exceptional people they were! What good memories they gave me to hold onto and cherish.

Speaking of Samuel, I am told he lives only minutes down the road from Rubengera, so Laurent takes me to his doorstep. When we arrive, Samuel is immediately in my arms, smiling and wondering if it is true.

"Is it really you, Dr. Cary?" he asks excitedly. "Could you really have returned to see me after all these years, coming from so far to have this moment?"

Samuel is no longer single. Today, he is married and has two children. He is also no longer a medical assistant but a head nurse at a local hospital. He says life was good to him. I don't believe him. Some pieces of his life's puzzle just don't fit together. Some chapters in his scrapbook don't make sense. Something isn't right. Starting with his house, it is barely a house—let's say it's something in the making. The walls are unpainted, there is practically no furniture, and some rooms are empty, except for a few moldy mattresses and some pieces of clothing. In all fairness to him, he does own the house, and it does have electricity. But there is only a single, low-wattage LED light bulb that barely gives enough light to see each other. Something isn't quite kosher about the surroundings.

I ask Samuel about his life. He answers with stories about his wife and two children. I continue to poke. He shares how he had tough times after we worked together in 1994. "Lots of struggles and hard work," he says reluctantly. But something is still missing from his account of the past. He is now 49 years old with a wife and two young children, but his timeline just doesn't add up. What am I missing? What is he missing or omitting from his diary? My curiosity won't let me settle for any omissions, so I ask, emphatically, "What happened to you after I left 25 years ago?" I don't give him any leeway to stray from answering me.

"Well," he hems and haws, "my father ..." He pauses. "My father was in the *Administration* and fled to Zaire after the genocide." I'm not sure exactly, but "Administration" seems to suggest that his father was part of the previous Hutu-led government that exercised its power to facilitate the genocide. Why else would he have fled across the border?

"The authorities wanted him to return to Rwanda to face trial, but he stayed there," Samuel continues. "They took me in his place and put me in prison for six and a half years," he painfully admits.

I am aghast. With more prodding from my side, Samuel finally shares that his father was indeed a part of the previous Rwandan government that orchestrated the genocide. He says his father had no blood on his hands, but he was complicit and, therefore, held accountable along with all the others in the government. When his father and mother escaped to Zaire, the authorities in Rwanda sought justice and wanted to try him for his role in the genocide. Unable to reach him, they took the next best in line, his son, Samuel. The authorities reasoned that Samuel's father would immediately return to Rwanda to free his son. But he didn't.

"I was beaten and tortured in prison until the Red Cross started visiting prisoners," he reports. "After they came, things improved, and I wasn't beaten as much." He continues, "After six and a half years, my father finally agreed to return to Rwanda and face trial. He was put in prison and died there. My mother died somewhere along the way during their time in Zaire."

Once Samuel was released from prison, he spent the next many years rebuilding himself and his life. Those incarcerated six and a half years set him back decades.

Samuel's story is hard to hear. When we worked together, I knew him to be an amazing man with a heart of gold and platinum and a spirit of silver and satin. Remarkably, despite those years of abuse and neglect, Samuel remains the same sensitive soul. He is a vegetarian out of respect for animals, a gentle father, and a contributing member of his community. My heart breaks for him. He is an unfortunate victim of a tragic injustice. I will do what I can to help him. I have heard it said that everything has a silver lining. Well, Samuel is a silver lining. It's time for his silver to shine again.

Though Samuel is employed as the head nurse in a hospital, he makes only $6.50 a day. Some might say this is a lot of money in Rwanda, but I can tell you it is not. I don't know how he will ever be able to rebuild and repay his debts. He needs some silver. And he also needs some cloud cover to protect himself from the occasional storms that life giveth and taketh. I wish I were an enormous, white puffy cumulus cloud right about now. Actually, come to think of it, I can be. I once came as a pot of mashed potatoes and a cornucopia of other consumables. I was a plate of onions and tomatoes, rice, rabbit stew, and whatever else I could scrounge up in the kitchen when the other expats finally retired for the evening. I was a mouse in the house, scavenging for whatever could be of service to someone planted precipitously on a plain terrain under a dark sky. Sometimes I came as a blanket, a jerry can, a bar of soap, a bowl of beans and rice, and sometimes I was just a hug or a hand to hold. Of course, I can be a cumulus cloud and make a difference. If Kabera could get his tooth and his smile back, then Samuel could get his smile back too. How blessed am I to liaise with angels whose feathers take flight. How blessed am I to be able to connect with the storks who generously bring baby bundles to those needing a boost from above. I am endowed with treasure troves and privileges to parade miracles to those who have either forgotten or worn holes in the soles of their sandals, looking for hope. Cumulus clouds, here I come!

Despite Samuel's poverty and tough times, he prepares a buffet of delicious food for us. He then introduces Laurent and me to his lovely family, and we all greet one another with the traditional greeting: three cheek cuddles and a finishing arm shake. When the formalities are complete, we sit down and dine together in an unfinished, stark room with mud walls and a single LED light bulb that struggles to show us who is present to celebrate this magnificent moment together.

RUHENGERI

Ruhengeri has officially been renamed Musanze. I recall the very day I first arrived here and Anne brought me a warm bowl of soup. I immediately felt that I had finally come home. Now, many years later, I return to see what has become of this home and the people who were once my family.

Laurent and I arrive at the city's central bus terminal and are warmly welcomed by Gaspard, my previous medical ward assistant. He has a smile that extends from one side of his face to the other. It is good to see him again. We pick up the pieces from when we were last together, a quarter of a century ago. It is as if I never left—just a continuation of what was.

Gaspard has come to take us to see the hospital where we once worked together. I'm quite excited. As we head toward the hospital, I ask him if he knows where Odette is buried. I was hoping to visit her grave, as I heard she had passed away. News of her passing came last year, and I was devastated to learn that such a wonderful woman had passed. Why didn't I return to Rwanda sooner? I may have been able to see her if I had. She was such a saint, a goddess, and an angel all wrapped up in one. Gaspard agrees to take me to her. Some minutes later, he stops in front of a small, modest house.

"*Voilà*, [here it is]," he says.

How odd. I did not know people were buried in residential quarters. "Whose house is this?" I ask.

"Odette's."

"But she's dead."

"No, she's alive," he smiles.

Imagine the immediate resurrection of my dear Odette, who was my rock and security blanket disguised as a head nurse in the hospital way back when. Odette is alive? I can't believe it. I'm too excited and filled with gratitude to see her once again. What a gift Rwanda has given me today.

I knock on the front door. My heart thumps. How would our reunion go? Would she even remember me after all this time? A woman in a wheelchair comes to the door and warmly welcomes us. Gaspard hugs her and then introduces Laurent and me. The woman is so pleased to see me. But who is she? I whisper in Gaspard's ear, "Where is Odette, and who is this?"

"Odette!" he replies.

"Dr. Cary," the woman says, thoroughly elated to see me.

We hug, but my hug is only half a hug. I am not convinced of this person's identity. I think there is some mistake. The woman before me looks nothing like the powerhouse of the woman I once knew. This woman is frail, wasted and meek.

From the corner of my mouth, I whisper, "Gaspard, are you sure this is Odette? You know, the Odette who was the head nurse of the internal medicine ward?"

Gaspard reassures me that this woman is the head nurse from the ward. I just can't believe it. To determine if this is true, I ask the kind woman about specific events that happened on the ward back in 1994. To my surprise, she remembers everything and everyone, and then some. Despite her ill health and frail appearance, her mind is sharp and her memory is strong. I then see a picture of a couple on the wall in her front room. The woman in the picture is really Odette with her late husband, taken back in the early 1990s. The woman before me is indeed Odette. Oh, life can be brutal.

Twenty-five years ago, Odette was a towering figure with a prominent presence that no one dared to counter. She was robust and rotund, raw and very real. No one messed with her. Though I was the head of the internal medicine service, and it was considered "my ward," Odette kept me under her wing and protected me like a momma protects her own newborn. Today, she is a broken woman confined to a wheelchair in a small room, essentially left to fend for herself.

I sit beside Odette and hold her. We reminisce. Laurent steps aside and watches the two of us go at it, like two chickens pecking away at grains of whatever thrown onto a field. We go around and around in our minds, looking for every bit of everything that we can possibly remember. "Remember the time when…And what about…Can you believe…Oh, yes, and then…" is essentially our conversation. Our memories kept it all with remarkable detail. Laurent understands nothing, but he enjoys two souls perched side by side, enjoying just being together for a moment. We all went through tough times back then. And now Odette goes through even tougher times. What a special moment to be with her again. What a gift to have this nanosecond together. When I leave, I hold her tight and close to me, knowing this will be the last time we see each other.

From Odette's house, Gaspard takes Laurent and me to the hospital. To my surprise, I walk right past it; the landscaping makes it unrecognizable. The entrance is the same, kind of, but nothing else looks familiar about the place. The hospital compound's layout has completely changed, and many new structures have been constructed. The field behind the fence that was behind the kitchen—the place where I was going to hide when Base Camp was being attacked—is no longer there. A basketball court took its place. The internal medicine ward appears to be unchanged from the outside, but things probably have changed on the inside. I don't know for sure because I still haven't decided if I want to visit the ward. To be honest, I am not compelled to see it for some inexplicable reason. I think I may still be in shock. It is hard for me to process things very clearly at the moment, as was the case in Mabanza, or should I say "Rubengera." Like in Rubengera, nothing here is familiar to me. This place is totally unrecognizable. Why am I so disturbed by the changes? What difference does it make if I recognize the place or not? I think it's because there is not a trace of what *Médecins Sans Frontières* did during those tumultuous times of the past. There is no plaque honoring the volunteers for their sacrifice. There is no official monument acknowledging the international community's steadfast efforts and generous support for the Rwandan people. No one here today even knows that we were here. It is as if we were never here. It is as if we have been completely erased.

Gaspard takes me to meet Ambroise, a nurse I worked with on the ward. I wanted to apologize to him for being so tough with the staff in the past, but there was no need; he has only fond memories of the time we spent together. After talking briefly about the things we remembered, he fills me in on his current life. Minutes later, there is not much to talk about. We hug goodbye and move on with our lives.

I ask Gaspard if he knows the whereabouts of Kabera, the guy missing a tooth. I had given him money to buy a new tooth and get his smile back. I want so much to see his smile. Unfortunately, no one knows or remembers him. I do hope he was able to procure a beautiful tooth and smiles broadly for all to see. The world needs more smiles.

From the hospital, we go to visit Base Camp, MSF's main compound. I remember it was about a mile down the road from the hospital and took twenty minutes to walk there. Today, it isn't. I can barely make the distance. Previously, I would walk the road at least four times a day. Today, I struggle to make the journey even one time. I could swear the road was straight. But I am mistaken. It is not straight at all. It winds here and there. Did they move the road or the compound? Maybe the road was lengthened or rerouted somehow. Or am I just older, without the same strength and stamina that I had in those younger years? From the outside, our once-upon-a-time Base Camp is dull and dreary, lifeless and badly in need of a paint job and some serious rehabilitation. I don't want to go inside or take a photo of this place either. While there were many great times, there were also quite traumatic times, like when the military stormed the compound with machine guns and when the UN peacekeepers shared their film of their findings of the genocide. It took my breath away then, and still takes my breath away 25 years later.

From Base Camp, I set out to find the house where I lived. The house was about 7 to 10 minutes away by foot, just across the road, tucked discreetly between the lush green trees and banana bushes. I see neither. The trees and bananas are gone. And nothing near or far resembles anything lush either. I walk in circles looking for a house that was my home away from home a long time ago. Pacing back and forth, to the left, to the right, over there, then again here, I believe I can find the house. If only there was something recognizable, like a landmark or some other familiar thing. But to no avail. I ask random people passing by if they know of a residential area in the greens. They don't know what I'm talking about. The little house I once lived in somewhere across the street that was tucked in between the bananas and lush foliage is simply unfindable. After a while of searching, I decide there is no need to see it. It doesn't matter. A part of me ceases to care about the past. Like the adage says, the past has passed.

It is strange to be back in Ruhengeri. To be honest, it is a bit traumatizing. Being here feels like I am experiencing the aftermath of my own death. It is as if I never existed. It is as if everything we were, saw and did has been completely erased. Despite the intensity and magnitude of the work we did here, not a trace of our existence ever made a mark. Ouch! Nothing I remember resembles or remotely corresponds to anything presently around me. Am I having a kind of Rip-Van-Winkle moment, waking up after two decades to find another reality?

I find myself in an existential meltdown. The world marches on without paying attention to the past or anything we ever did in it. Time doesn't stand still. Nothing stands still. Everything is always changing. What is the message in this? We are given a blank canvas at birth. Life is about coloring it wildly, filling it to the edges, and leaving no space untouched. This canvas is our life. It is what we choose to make of it. If we want straight and narrow, put it in. If we want a destiny, put it in or not. If we want full-on, fill it up or not. If we want risky and warrior, go for it. If we want placid and peaceful, go for it too. It is all self-made. We come, we live, we die.

AN UNEXPECTED ENCOUNTER

While traveling through the countryside, I stop in a remote village to explore a small outdoor market. As I mosey around looking at the villagers' goods, all eyes are on me. *Umuzungu* don't typically come to this part of the country, so I am a sight to behold. Judging from some of the people's looks, I may be the first White man they have ever seen.

I'm not sure what the people are saying, but I seem to be the subject of their banter. I ask a number of people if they speak English or French. They look at me blankly. No one can. When I give up trying to communicate with them, a man approaches and greets me warmly in English. I am pleasantly surprised and eager to speak with him. He doesn't appear to be formally educated or literate, so the fact that he speaks English piques my curiosity.

"Where did you learn English?" I ask.

"In prison," he replies.

"You learned English in prison?"

"Yes," he says proudly.

I continue, somewhat surprised, "Why were you in prison?"

"I killed many people," he answers without reservation.

"You killed *many* people?" I say, doubting his claim. He can't be serious.

"Yes," he says nonchalantly, as if everyone has killed many people.

"Who did you kill?"

"Tutsis."

"Tutsis?"

"Hmm," he grunts.

"Tutsis?" I repeat, this time accentuating the final "s" to clarify if it was one or many Tutsis.

"Hmm," he again grunts affirmingly, nodding his head with clear and honest confirmation.

He has obviously been asked the same questions before.

"Why did you kill the Tutsis?" I ask naïvely.

"They (the orchestrators of the genocide) convinced us that our enemies were the Tutsis, and if we didn't kill them, they would kill us."

Finding the entire conversation a bit bizarre, I ask, "How many Tutsis?"

"Oh, many," he responds, with no sense of wrongdoing.

"How many?" I press.

He raises his right hand, and pretending to hold a machete, he slashes it aimlessly in all directions, saying, "Oh, many."

"Many" was apparently the number of people that his blade could execute in the same style and speed as his pantomime. He gives me a visual of the number of people he randomly put to death with his imaginary handheld weapon. As he mimes his personal, reckless, man-made guillotine, he seems to revel in the speed at which he was able to finish the job. He says he was instructed to kill as many *inyenzi* as possible. He did his job quickly and thoroughly and seems proud of his ability to deliver.

I am appalled, yet at the same time, intrigued by this man. On the one hand, he is kind, polite and gentle. On the other hand, he was a monster and a serial killer. It is hard to believe that two such diametrically opposed people could be one and the same. I never met or talked with a convicted killer before. How could such a kind-hearted man kill? It is completely incomprehensible to me.

"Do the people in your community know that you killed *many* people?" I continue cross-examining him, as if in a courtroom.

"Hmm," he says. In other words, affirmative.

"The people in this village know you killed members of their families, and you live alongside them today?" I ask, not expecting him to answer.

"They forgave me," he answers. "I went to the families of all the people I killed and asked for their forgiveness. They forgave me."

They forgave him. How could anyone forgive this?

The man invites me to his home to see his achievements since his release from a 10-year prison sentence. At first, I am reluctant to go with him for fear that he would hurt me. But then I agree to see his house, which is more like a hut. He introduces me to his wife and then shows me his chickens and rabbits. The animals are few, but they are what he has, and he's proud of them. He then takes me to a small plot of land he was given by the government to grow some vegetables, which he sells to earn a living. In this way, he can support his family.

The man steps away from me for a moment and harvests a few vegetables from his garden. He returns and says, "This is for you," as he hands me a bunch of fresh veggies.

"Oh, thank you, but I can't possibly take these. You need these vegetables to feed your family to keep them strong."

The man categorically refuses to have it any other way. As a compromise, I agree to take a single beetroot from his bunch of goodies. I'm so touched by him.

I return to my interrogation. "How did you kill people?"

"The militia and military told me to do it, so I did," he says nonchalantly.

He adds that he feels quite bad about what he did and that he's grateful the families of the people he killed accepted him and are now his friends again. This is truly amazing. These people's capacity to forgive is beyond belief. I'm speechless.

I take the man's telephone number in case we wish to stay in touch. And then I hug him and leave with my beetroot.

THE MEMORIALS

Prior to the genocide, tourists came to Rwanda to see the country's famed gorillas in the wild. Tours included trips to national forests, safaris, and game reserves, as well as treks to bird sanctuaries. Today, in addition to the above-mentioned sights, Rwandan tourism includes excursions to genocide memorials. There are several of them around the country. While each one is unique, they share the same spilled blood. Excavated human remains from mass graves are among the relics on display. Exhumed shattered skulls and femurs from infants are hardly tourist *sights* to behold, but they are an essential part of the Rwandan landscape nonetheless. The memorials are difficult places to visit, but they are a part of the people's history and our collective human experience.

Kigali Genocide Memorial

The Kigali Genocide Memorial is a veritable cemetery with the remains of 250,000 victims of hate. None of them died from natural causes. All of them died from unnatural causes. They all died prematurely, some before taking their first step, some before reaching adolescence, some before their first kiss, some before their first baby. All are lives lost before their time.

A cemetery is usually a peaceful place, a place where you lay loved ones to rest. This cemetery is far from peaceful. It is a "rest-less" place that inflames the senses and begs for a response. Will the response be an angry one that will fill more graves, or will it be one of forgiveness and reconciliation? Only we know the answer to this question because we write the script. This time, it is out of God's hands and in our own. *"Si le bon Dieu veut,"* people say when tragedy strikes. *"Si le bon Dieu veut* [if the good God wants]." In other words, if it is the will of God that some tragedy strikes, then we are obliged to surrender and accept this. Well, I can say with certainty that genocide is not God's will. *Le bon Dieu ne le veut pas* [The good God does not want it].

It took me two full days to go through all the memorial's exhibits. It will take me a lifetime to process the information and lifetimes to deal with the sensations that have surfaced. I read every word on every placard under every picture. The more I read, the more questions I had. The more questions I had, the more I realized how little I knew and understood. The more I realized how little I knew and understood, the more I realized it was all bigger than life, beyond comprehension, and unlike anything human.

The First Floor

On the first floor of the memorial, there is a maze of walls with placards telling bits and pieces of an unfolding story. Every word is poignant. Every picture is provocative. Every detail is evocative. I learn a lot. The following are some facts and figures I glean from the walls:

The word "genocide" was coined by Raphael Lemkin, a Jewish man who fled for his life after being targeted for extermination by the nazis. Their primary objective was to annihilate every single Jewish person in the world. "*Genos*" is ancient Greek for race or family, and "*cidere*" is Latin for killing. So, genocide means killing an entire race or family. In other words—my words—it is the total eradication of the genes of a particular group of people from the human genome.

According to Rwanda's Ministry of Local Government and Social Affairs, 1,074,017 people were killed from October 1991 to December 1994, of which 934,218 of them were identified by name. Of those killed, 93.6% were Tutsis and 6.4% were Hutus married to Tutsis, people resembling Tutsis, Hutus who hid Tutsis, and Hutus opposed to killing Tutsis, as well as Twas. Seventy percent of the Tutsi population was killed along with 30% of the Twa population. Also worth noting is that young people, less than 24 years old, were the main victims of the genocide, representing 53.7% of those murdered. Another disturbing fact is that most people were killed by machetes in the hands of friends, neighbors and strangers.

Some more telling statistics about the genocide:

- 581 tons of machetes were imported to Rwanda to arm Hutus for the genocide.

- 250,000 to 500,000 women were raped.

- 20,000 children were born to the raped women.

- 67% of the women who were raped got infected with HIV from their rapists. At the time of the genocide, there was no effective treatment for it. In other words, getting HIV was a death sentence.

• Men with HIV intentionally raped Tutsi women to infect them with the virus as part of the plan to exterminate them.

• 95,000 children were orphaned.

• More than 50% of the children who survived had to drop out of school because of poverty.

• 700,000 Tutsi refugees living in exile returned to their homeland—Rwanda—after the genocide.

• 2 million Hutus fled the country, fearing retribution after the RPF took control.

• 25 years after the genocide, there are still about 7,000 corpses found every year.

• 1.9 million Hutus were tried post-genocide.

The Second Floor

On the second floor, the children have a place to tell their stories. Their stories, however, are few, brief and incomplete. After all, what could they have on their resumes when their age was still in single digits? The children's exhibit features a number of very large photographs of the faces of young victims with very small plaques beneath them noting each child's age, something noteworthy about their character, and their favorite food. There is nothing more of, from or about the children.

The exhibit also has walls covered with hundreds of small photos of more children who perished. Families gave these photos to the memorial to have their loved ones honored and memorialized forever. On some of the photos, there are short notes that family and friends attached with the words "Will never forget you." These notes remind me of the little notes tucked into the crevices of the *Wailing Wall* in Jerusalem. The Wailing Wall is the name given to the last remaining segment of the holiest Jewish temple complex that was destroyed by the Romans nearly 2,000 years ago. People come from around the world to pray and mourn the loss of loved ones at this wall. Like in Jerusalem, people from around the world visit Rwanda's memorials and stand reverently before this wall of small photos and wail for the loss of their loved ones.

The Basement

The basement is the final resting place most fitting for the remains—below ground. Skulls, femurs, tibias and trinkets are laid to rest in numerous showcases. They are finally at peace. Also on display are rosary beads, a little shoe, and a small pipe. Clothes from the dead hang from the ceiling as if alive in real time—immobile and paused permanently. These simple shirts and pants arc strikingly evocative bccause they were and are. An eerie feeling overcomes me as I stand before one of the shirts and a frayed pair of pants suspended in this dark basement. Something is hauntingly missing. There was life previously there, in that shirt and in those pants. It was, and now it isn't. Was it a he or a she, a mother or father? What happened to him or her? What is their story? Who found the clothes and was there a person in them, or had the dogs already eaten the flesh? Or did the body decay, leaving nothing but bones and fragments of fabric behind? A piece of pants is a powerful testament. These particular pieces of pants are an ever more powerful testimony. They need no words to tell their stories. The clothing makes this place brutally real. In a mysterious and inexplicable way, the hanging tattered shirts and pants seem to cover invisible life forms that continue their presence. It is hard to explain, but it is this way for me.

We are asked not to take any photos of the exhibits without permission. Why should these images be locked away in a memorial in Kigali, Rwanda and hidden from the world? The Rwandan genocide is a global problem. It does not belong to Rwanda. It is a collective nightmare for everyone in the world to take to bed with them. I want the images in this memorial to remind me of the hazards of hate. In this way, if I find myself straying away from love, I can correct myself and try again to be kind, compassionate, forgiving and more loving.

Having had enough of the basement, I make my way back upstairs to the first floor. With too many questions swirling and so many emotions stirred, I spend the next two hours talking to a woman at the reception area. She is a genocide survivor. She is real. She is honest. She is reflective and sincere and brave. I am a pupil again in grade school riveted by her struggle. She shares only a small part of it with me and emphasizes the importance of forgiveness.

"How did you forgive people who killed your family?" I ask her, as I have asked so many others before her.

"If you don't forgive, you imprison yourself," she explains. "I cannot hate a person. For what? Forgiveness helps heal me and enables me to move on. Forgiveness helps the children inherit a better country. With the help of God, we will make it. We choose to live in peace and harmony."

Speaking with a survivor is liberating. Seeing her move on with her life gives me a sense of closure. If she could move on, so could I. If she could forgive and show compassion for those who wronged her and her family and everything she held dear, then I could do the same. The woman then invites me to view a video that features two survivors sharing their stories of the genocide. I am happy to do so.

In the video, two genocide survivors revisit the past. As I listen to their reflections, I note there is something markedly different about these people. At first, I can't figure out what is different, but I find I can barely control my emotions. In fact, I can't stop heaving. Even my breath is interrupted. Why am I so profoundly affected by this five-minute video? Because the people are crying uncontrollably. They are bawling. They, too, struggle to find enough breath to carry their cry. I have not seen such a raw and unbridled display of emotions before in Rwanda. Despite the traumas my patients and their families endured, there was always a reserved stoicism that took hold of them. They either had no tears, held them back, had none left, or lost them during the genocide. Regardless of all the death, disease, hunger, and destitution that were so common during and after hatred had its way here, few people ever showed much emotion, at least in front of me. Not seeing people's emotional turmoil did make it easier for me to cope with the catastrophes that came to the ward on a daily basis, but now I'm unprepared as I see two people in this video find their tears and finally allow them to stream like a waterfall. Suddenly, I find myself engulfed with them in a genocide.

I have to leave this place. I need a timeout to regroup. A bench in the memorial's garden is my companion for a while. I sit quietly and stare blankly at the surroundings. This pause pacifies me like a nipple pacifies a baby. Once composed, I leave the memorial grounds through the main gate. As I walk away, I am abruptly interrupted by a flashback of a disturbing image of a document that I saw hours before on one of the walls of the many exhibits in the memorial. Did my mind intentionally try to protect me from it and now have second thoughts? I do an about-face and return to the memorial to confirm that what I saw was real. I scour the walls until I find the document. It is indeed real—brutally real. The document is known as the "Genocide Fax." It is a communication from Major General Roméo Dallaire, the commander of the UN peacekeeping forces in Rwanda (UNAMIR), to Maurice Baril, the head of the Military Division of the Department of Peacekeeping Operations of the United Nations in New York. It was sent on January 11, 1994, at 1:45 AM—three months before the genocide. The communication from Major Dallaire seeks protection for a credible informant, "Jean-Pierre" (Jean-Pierre Abubakar Turatsinze).

"The Genocide Fax"

FROM: DALLAIRE/UNAMIR/KIGALI

FAX NO: MOST IMMEDIATE-CODE CABLE

SUBJECT: REQUEST FOR PROTECTION OF INFORMANT

ATTN: MGEN BARIL

1. Force commander put in contact with informant by very very important government politician. Informant is a top level trainer in the cadre of Interahamwe-armed militia of MRND. [MRND stands for the *Mouvement Républicain National pour la Démocratie et le Développement*, which was the ruling political party in Rwanda at the time.]

2. He informed us he was in charge of last Saturday's demonstrations which aims were to target deputies of opposition parties coming to ceremonies and Belgian soldiers. They hoped to provoke the RPF BN to engage (being fired upon) the demonstrators and provoke a civil war. Deputies were to be assassinated upon entry or exit from Parliament. Belgian troops were to be provoked and if Belgian soldiers restored to force a number of them were to be killed and thus guarantee Belgian withdrawal from Rwanda.

3. Informant confirmed 48 RGF PARA CDO [RGF stands for the Rwandan Government Forces] and a few members of the Gendarmerie participated in demonstrations in plain clothes. Also at least one Minister of the MRND and the *Sous-Prefect* of Kigali were in the demonstration. RGF and Interahamwe provided radio communications.

4. Informant is a former security member of the president. He also stated he is paid RF150,000 per month by the MRND party to train Interahamwe. Direct link is to chief of staff RGF and president of the MRND for financial and material support.

5. Interahamwe has trained 1700 men in RGF military camps outside the capital. The 1700 are scattered in groups of 40 throughout Kigali. Since UNAMIR deployed he has trained 300 personnel in three week training sessions at RGF camps. Training focus was discipline, weapons, explosives, close combat and tactics.

6. Principal aim of Interahamwe in the past was to protect Kigali from RPF. Since UNAMIR mandate he has been ordered to register all Tutsi in Kigali. He suspects it is for their extermination. Example he gave was that in 20 minutes his personnel could kill up to 1,000 Tutsis.

7. Informant states he disagrees with anti-Tutsi extermination. He supports opposition to RPF but cannot support killing of innocent persons. He also stated that he believes the president does not have full control over all elements of his old party /faction.

8. Informant is prepared to provide location of major weapons cache with at least 135 weapons. He already has distributed 110 weapons including 35 with ammunition and can give us details of their location. Type of weapons are G3 and AK47 provided by RGF. He was ready to go to the arms cache tonight—if we gave him the following guarantee. He requests that he and his family (his wife and four children) be placed under our protection.

9. It is our intention to take action within the next 36 hours with a possible H-HR of Wednesday at dawn (local). Informant states that hostilities may commence again if political deadlock ends. Violence could take place day of the ceremonies or the day after. Therefore, Wednesday will give greatest chance of success and also be most timely to provide significant input to on-going political negotiations.

10. It is recommended that informant be granted protection and evacuated out of Rwanda. This HQ does not have previous UN experience in such matters and urgently requests guidance. No contact has as yet been made to any embassy in order to inquire if they are prepared to protect him for a period of time by granting diplomatic immunity in their embassy in Kigali before moving him and his family out of the country.

11. Force commander will be meeting with the very very important political person tomorrow morning in order to ensure that this individual is conscious of all parameters of his involvement. Force commander does have certain reservations on the suddenness of the change of heart of the informant to come clean with this information. Recce of armed cache and detailed planning of raid to go on late tomorrow. Possibility of a trap not fully excluded, as this may be a setup against this very very important political person. Force commander to inform SRSG first thing in morning to ensure his support.

13. *Peux Ce Que Veux. Allons-y* [When there is a will, there is a way. Let's go).

And the answer in an outgoing cable January 11, 1994:

To: BOOH-BOOH, UNAMIR, KIGALI

    [Jacques-Roger Booh-Booh was the head of United

    Nations Assistance Mission for Rwanda (UNAMIR)]

FROM: ANNAN, UNATIONS, NEW YORK

    [Kofi Annan was the Secretary-General of the UN.]

DATE: 10 JANUARY 1994

NUMBER: 74

SUBJECT   Contact with informant

1. REF Dallaire cable CNR 12 of 11 January on which he is to brief you early Tuesday morning.

2. Information is cause for concern but there are certain inconsistencies. We must handle this information with caution.

3. We await your considered assessment and recommendations. No reconnaissance or other action, including response to request for protection, should be taken by UNAMIR until clear guidance is received from headquarters.

Regards.

I leave the memorial decimated. The tale told on hundreds of placards on the walls of the memorial points an accusatory finger at the colonial powers for staging and orchestrating the Rwandan genocide. It started with the invasion of the African continent in the 1400s. It continued with the colonial powers' arbitrary and divisive partition of the land and its people. It continued with German occupation in the late 1800s and then with the emboldened League of Nations that usurped Africa's inalienable right to self-govern in the early 1920s. It continued with Belgium's brutal reign of Congo and Ruanda-Urundi, dividing and conquering the people along random ethnic lines, mandating identity cards, and favoring one group of people over another. It continued with France competing for dominance in the region by weaponizing despots and militias that controlled and culled the masses. Then, on January 10, 1994, three months prior to the genocide, a man, "Jean-Pierre," on the inside of the killing machine, tells the United Nations of the program to exterminate the Tutsi people. And what do they do? They walk away.

Were any Belgian soldiers killed, as warned by Jean-Pierre? Yes, in an unfortunate turn of events, ten Belgian soldiers were attacked while guarding the prime minister's residence. According to reports, the soldiers' Achilles tendons were slashed, and then they were castrated and choked to death on their own genitalia. Did the remaining Belgian soldiers participating in UNAMIR then withdraw from the country? Yes.

And finally, what happened to Jean-Pierre, the informant? Was he given protection? No, he wasn't given protection. He allegedly joined the RPF and was "killed in battle." No one really knows what happened to him. And no one cares either.

I walk out of the memorial feeling ashamed to be White. While we White people didn't hold the machetes that dealt the final blows that killed over a million people, we indirectly have blood on our hands because over the centuries we created the conditions for the perfect storm, then disappeared when the battle began. No wonder when I arrived in Rwanda this time, the customs officer saw me as an enemy of their State.

Nyange Genocide Memorial

Each genocide memorial has its particular story to tell. This is Nyange's story. When Tutsi extermination reached Nyange, a locale in the country's Western Province, the trusted local priest of the Nyange Parish, Father Seromba, assured the panic-stricken Tutsi parishioners a safe haven in his church. Tutsis had previously been protected in churches in the three prior Tutsi slaughters in 1959, 1963 and 1973. In those times, Hutus respected the sanctity of the church and left those inside unharmed. Expecting the same protection this time, Tutsis fled to Father Seromba's holy sanctuary. Tragically, to everyone's surprise, instead of being protected, the people encountered something else. As two thousand Tutsis sought refuge in their beloved Lord's house, they found themselves barricaded inside, surrounded by dozens of Interahamwe Hutu extremists, who then butchered them. Days after the massacre, a number of Tutsis were still alive, buried among the dead. According to reports, Father Seromba had the church bulldozed and razed to the ground to ensure that no one was left alive to bear witness to what he had done. He then had the bodies buried in trenches that were specially dug to hide any evidence of the massacre.

I come to the memorial to pay my respects to the people who died in Nyange. When I arrive, I am warmly welcomed by a woman who guides visitors through the memorial. There are no other visitors, so I have her all to myself. As she tells me about the history of the memorial and all that happened here, her eyes become glazed. Barely old enough to remember the genocide, she has something of her own that needs to be shared. I sense the burden she holds is an important one to share, so I respectfully ask to hear it. Twenty-five years ago, I had many questions, but I could not ask them because people's wounds were still too raw and painful. Since the genocide, people have worked hard to forgive and heal themselves. I feel now is the time to ask my questions, to know the truth, to fill in the blanks, and to document the hazards of hate for future generations to remember what they will inevitably forget.

"Who are you? What is your story?" I ask.

"I am a Tutsi. I am a Rwandan," the woman confidently responds. "My Rwandan identity is more important now. We are all Rwandan first, but I am also Tutsi, and my history and the consequences of my identity are because I am Tutsi," she continues, carefully weighing each and every word: "I was seven years old when the genocide started. We ran to the church for protection, but it was already filled to capacity by the time we arrived. With nowhere to run, some children were taken by some people. I was one of the lucky ones to have been taken. Unfortunately, my family was not as lucky. My parents, grandparents, and essentially everyone in my family were killed. I was put in an orphanage and looked after by the State. It became my parents and cared well for me. The State supported me through college and continues to help me as a householder and mother of two children."

"How did it happen? How did the genocide happen?" I ask.

She looks at me blankly, unable to answer the question.

"How do people turn into killers?" I continue.

She shrugs her shoulders.

"Can it happen again?"

She wants to say no but knows it is possible. She lowers her head, remembering what was and how tragic it would be if it happened again.

"What happened to the children born of rape?" I press.

"They have a rapist Hutu father and a Tutsi mother," she responds quickly without censoring herself. "Imagine being the offspring of rape—the offspring of hate. The innocent child doesn't have a chance. Mother doesn't like him and often looks upon the child with disdain. The community does the same. Many of the offspring of rape were born with HIV, too. They endure unending trauma," she concludes.

"How do you deal with the Tutsi-Rwandan identities?"

"The government doesn't want anyone to mention Hutu or Tutsi. Rwandans are one people. Everyone advances in life according to their hard work and accomplishments, not on the basis of ethnicity, as in the past," she reports. "But how do you explain to a curious child where his granny is if you don't mention her ethnicity and the consequences of it? If she does not know that her granny was a Tutsi and that she was killed for being a Tutsi, then how will anything make sense to her?" she questions. So, I say we are Tutsis and also Rwandan—Rwandan first."

She did her best to answer my many questions, but much was left to the imagination to figure out.

The woman says no more and takes me to the basement to see the main exhibit. The room is somewhat dark, but there is enough light to illuminate things clearly. There are about 25 coffins and some glass showcases, like the ones you find filled with jewelry in a department store. One showcase is filled with hundreds of femurs of all different sizes. The sizes are especially disturbing because among the many bones are femurs of children—small, innocent, once life-filled children. Another showcase is filled with dozens of skulls. Many of the skulls are cracked from the assault of a machete. Some of them have been hacked repeatedly. These skulls seem to talk and tell their stories. You can almost feel the butchery in real time just looking at them. The blades had to have come down with a hate-filled force to break through the skulls as they did. The killers must have been adroit with a blade in hand because the cracks are well defined, about the width of a single blade. They most certainly struck their victims' skulls repeatedly to ensure that death was delivered definitively. I have seen skulls before, most notably in concentration camps in Germany and in the killing fields in Cambodia. I have also seen them scattered in fields when I was last here 25 years ago. They were everywhere—some whole and intact, and others cracked into pieces, making them unrecognizable. I cannot help but wonder if the fragments of skulls resulted from the repeated hacking blows of a machete, the use of hand grenades, or from the stomping of boots intent on doing their job thoroughly and completely. Skulls seem to be the insignia of man's pride and prejudice. They go together.

The woman tells me the remains of 7,000 people are in this basement, but I don't see how this figure adds up. There are only about 25 coffins and a few showcases with hundreds of femurs, fibulas, clavicles and pelvises. I try to mentally make sense of her calculations. Hundreds, for sure, but certainly not thousands, I conclude. She seems to read my mind, or perhaps my dubious facial expressions that challenge her figures, and proceeds to address my skepticism non-verbally. Approaching one of the many coffins, she respectfully removes a white crocheted covering that is used to beautify it. She then slowly opens the lid to reveal the skulls and bones of hundreds of people. How many? The answer is clear: there are as many bones of as many people that can fit inside a standard human coffin. I quickly understand that the coffins are storage chests for human remains. They are not standard in any way. They are receptacles for pieces of people—once real, live people— who are now just random bones of random people just sharing the space, which is now their final resting place. None of the bones are assembled because they were found bone by bone, above and below the ground in fields, rivers, lakes, trenches, and on the side of roads.

The woman closes the first coffin and then walks over to another one. She does the same—she respectfully removes another white crocheted covering and proceeds to open it. This coffin is also filled to the brim with pieces of people— the lost generation. Every one of the coffins is home to pieces of people—thousands of people. Her calculations are not only correct, but they are part of a much bigger whole. Every year, thousands of pieces of people are found and brought to the memorial. In fact, as recently as March 2019—a month before the 25th anniversary of the genocide—the remains of an additional 84,437 people were also laid to rest at the memorial … finally. These remains required 81 coffins to house and to hold them. This basement is essentially a morgue, and the memorial is a cemetery to honor the dead and remind the masses of their historical hatred. Will it stop? Has it even ended?

On March 18, 1997, the Interahamwe militia along with the ousted pro-Hutu government forces, both intent on continuing their campaign of extermination, breached the Rwandan border from neighboring Zaire and attacked Nyange Secondary School. Students were ordered to separate themselves along ethnic lines, with Hutus on one side of the classroom and Tutsis on the other. The students categorically refused to comply. "*Twese turi abanyarwanda* [We are all Rwandans]," a female student proclaimed. She was then shot dead along with several other classmates. These seven brave martyrs for peace should be mentioned for posterity: Sylvestre Bizimana (22), Marie-Chantal Mujawa-mahoro (22), Valens Ndemeye (25), Béatrice Mukambaraga (23), Séraphine Mukarutwaza (22), Héléne Benimana (18), and Ferdinand Niyongira (23), who died years later from his wounds. Let these national heroes be hailed for their courage and heroism, and let their names be etched in stone, so that all should know for eternity that they were the founding fledglings of Rwanda's peace movement.

Did the hate stop? Did it then end? In 1998, another militia attack occurred. Two teachers were killed in the same village.

And whatever happened to Father Seromba? In July 1994, when the Hutu government fell, he fled to Italy with the help of Catholic monks. He lived under an alias and continued working as a priest for the church. In 2001, the UN Tribunal for Rwanda appealed to the Italian government to extradite him. Only after considerable international pressure did the government and the Vatican agree to do so in 2002. Father Seromba was tried, convicted, and sentenced to 15 years in prison in 2006. In 2008, however, he appealed the verdict and was granted a retrial. The appeal tribunal upheld his previous conviction and determined that there was ample additional relevant evidence to warrant a more substantial sentence—life in prison.

Murambi Genocide Memorial Center

Pandemonium breaks out in Kigali as thousands of Hutu extremists begin wielding thousands of machetes, slashing as many Tutsis to death as their blades can kill. People run for their lives in all directions. The wave of slaughter moves like a tsunami across the country, reaching every city, town, village and Tutsi household. Three hours down the road, Tutsis run for their lives as death looms around them as far as the eye can see. People flee to their church, thinking they will be safe there. But when they arrive, they are directed by their local authorities and bishop to seek refuge at a technical school just up the hill. They are told French troops will be there to protect them.

An estimated 50,000 Tutsis ran for their lives up that hill, expecting protection. Once there, however, they found no French troops. They found, instead, that they were tricked and essentially corralled in a slaughterhouse. With no way out, the people waited for help to arrive—anyone to rescue them. The authorities in charge had other plans for their captives. They cut the water lines and allowed no food to reach those trapped. The Tutsis were going to be starved to death.

Surrounded by madmen who, like vampires, wanted their blood, the Tutsis threw bricks, sticks and stones to defend themselves. Early on, they were able to successfully ward off the attackers, but without food or water for days, they became physically exhausted and could no longer resist the onslaught. The killer Hutus slaughtered all the Tutsis like pigs and threw them into massive pits, which they then covered with earth, which they then covered with concrete to create a volleyball court in order to hide any evidence of their crime.

In 1995, the thousands of hidden bodies were discovered in mass graves. The bodies were so tightly packed that they were essentially airtight. As a result, the corpses did not decay— they mummified. Completely intact with hair and skin, the mummified bodies are now on display in the classrooms of the technical school. No longer hidden, they talk loudly to all.

If you dare to visit the crematoria at the infamous Dachau concentration camp, you will find yourself assaulted by the stench of burned flesh in and around the ovens there. The stench is so vile that you can't inhale. You can't breathe. You can't think. You can't talk. You can't believe. This stench is something you will remember for the rest of your life. If you dare to visit the classrooms at Murambi's Genocide Memorial, you will also find yourself assaulted by a stench—the stench of mummified human corpses. You can't inhale. You can't breathe. You can't think. You can't talk. You can't believe. This stench is something you will remember for the rest of your life.

The mummified corpses tell their tale. They are not only lifeless, but timeless. These once-upon-a-time people manage to share volumes about themselves. Since the bodies did not decompose, they remain in the position they were in at the moment of slaughter. As hard as it is to see the people in this mummified state, one's eyes cannot look away from them, all sprawled out for everyone to see. In one of the rooms, there is a child cowering, waiting for his destiny as he is hacked to death. You see it clearly in the curvature of his spine, the position of his shoulders, and the strain on his neck. There is also a woman whose hands and arms are wrapped around her head as she waits for the final blow of the blade. A man surrenders with his legs spread-eagle, denying his killer the pleasure of a fight. He didn't want to die, but he knew he was going to die that morning. "*Si le bon Dieu veut* [if the good God wants]." Their stories are hard to hear and harder to see. The slaughter started at 3 AM and was completed by 11 AM. Fifty thousand people were massacred in these eight hours. Imagine the screaming. Imagine the pain. Imagine the blood. Imagine the sound of machetes cracking 50,000 skulls.

Murambi's Genocide Memorial defies gravity and makes time stand still. It is timeless and captures a snapshot of an event that no longer lives, yet no longer dies. It is forever. It is something that defies the cycle of life and death and captivates and incarcerates the mind of any spectator. The grotesqueness of the genocide is far beyond what the human mind and heart can hold. No words can do it justice. No chronical can codify its chapters. No poem can be granted poetic license to capture any part of it. No tears can do their duty.

When you walk through the exit of a genocide memorial, you realize you are forever imprisoned by shame for being part of the human race, which has brazenly shown time and time again its inherent capacity to hate and destroy. Why do we do it? Do what? Hate. Why do we hate? What do we gain by hating? What pleasure do we get from hating?

The Rwandan genocide was man at his very worst. Hatred touched everyone—from the killers to the killed, to the loved ones who survived. They now wait patiently for their mothers, fathers, sisters, brothers, friends and lovers to come home. From spectators to innocent bystanders on the side of a road at the time of slaughter, no one was immune to the hazards of hate—not Hutu, not Tutsi, not Twa, not man, woman, child or fetus—no one and nothing was spared. In fact, every person on every continent in the world lost someone in their family as a result of this genocide because way, way, back, back, back, we all had the same mother and father.

The Rwandan genocide was also man at his best. Love touched everyone, from neighbors who risked their lives to save a life to aid workers who risked their lives to make a difference. Donors gave, surgeons operated, doctors cared, humanitarians served, and love was abundant. Sometimes it came as a plate of leftover food, a jerry can of water or a pot of potatoes, a few Rwandan francs, a vaccination, jacket, shirt, hug or hand to hold. Love was truly abundant; no one was immune to its magnificence. No person's heart or soul was spared. Why do we do it? Do what? Love. That's a good question. Is it not our true nature to love? And if it is, and it is so pleasing to love, why don't we do it and only it? Why the hate? Hmm. Why do people choose to hate and hurt others?

What we choose to see and be is a choice. Whose choice is it? The choice is ours.

THE CHOICE

The Rwandan genocide laid to rest more than one million people. The exact figure will never be known because the crocodiles feasted furiously on corpses dumped in tributaries and erased the victims from public record. Now, what do we do? Do we celebrate with the survivors, commiserate with those who lost generations, kill those who killed, segregate ourselves from the perpetrators, or continue to annihilate, as seems to be our human condition nowadays? Or perhaps we could forgive? The choice is ours.

For Rwanda to be the best version of itself, the Rwandan people have to be the best version of themselves. For the Rwandan people to be the best version of themselves, they need to be united, for *a people united can never be divided.* Division weakens and destroys. Unity builds and strengthens. The choice to divide or unite is ours.

To smile or frown is a choice. To accept or reject is a choice. To compliment or criticize is a choice. To give or take is a choice. To help or hurt is a choice. To love or hate is a choice. The choice is ours.

When I was young, I was bullied. I was different from the others, and there was not a moment in my youth that allowed me to feel anything other than *other*. I was separated from the whole, told I was wrong, convinced I was bad, stereotyped as sick, tossed to the side, and given no choice but to remain there. I was told I was contrary, a non-conformist, an anomaly, an aberration, an embarrassment. Yes, I was different, but isn't different beautiful too? The choice to believe I am beautiful or not is mine. Who decides? I decide. And so I choose to believe I am beautiful.

Throughout the toughest times in my life, I learned first-hand a simple truth: we are perfect just as we are. If our skin is black, white, yellow, red, chocolate, vanilla or *café au lait*, we are perfect just as we are. Whether we are thin or rotund, tall or short, African or Asian, rich or poor, gay or straight, Hutu, Twa, Tutsi or Rwandan, we are perfect just as we are. For sure, sometimes we get it right and sometimes we get it wrong. And being imperfect is perfect too.

The origin of the Rwandan people remains an unsolved mystery. Some say there is only one ethnicity in Rwanda. Others say there are three separate ethnicities in Rwanda. While no one has yet been able to definitively determine the truth, there is one truth that is undeniably irrefutable: All Rwandans are people, and all people originally came from the same mom and dad, so we are, in essence, all related to one another. We are family!

Today, we are blessed because we have choice. We can reject or accept one another. We can divide and conquer or unite and love each other. The choice is ours. Whose choice is it? The choice is *ours*.

JOSEPH

And finally, what happened to Joseph, my little raisin in the sun? The answer to this question goes back to 1996, a year after I left Rwanda. Miraculously, a letter arrived that year in the post. It was from Rwanda—from Laurent. Thrilled to have received something from that remarkable time and place that changed my life in so many ways, I opened the envelope carefully, as if delivering a newborn baby. What happened to Joseph? Let Laurent tell you his story:

Mon cher Docteur Cary,

I pray this letter finds you well and that God benevolently blesses you and your mother and father and family. I wish to tell you of the happy occasion of my marriage. I was married in the suit that you gave me. It was a grand event with much joy. Thank you again. My wife is now pregnant, and God willing, we will begin to see light again in our small, turmoiled Rwanda. After your departure, life has remained hard. Much pain fills our lives, but God willing, we will heal.

I wanted to write earlier and tell you of this news, but I did not wish to make you unhappy. Three days after you visited Joseph at the orphanage, I went to adopt him. I knew you loved him, and I knew that he loved you. He was a very special child. Unfortunately, Joseph died two days after you saw him. He was not ill. He quietly died of a broken heart. – Laurent

IN HONOR OF JOSEPH

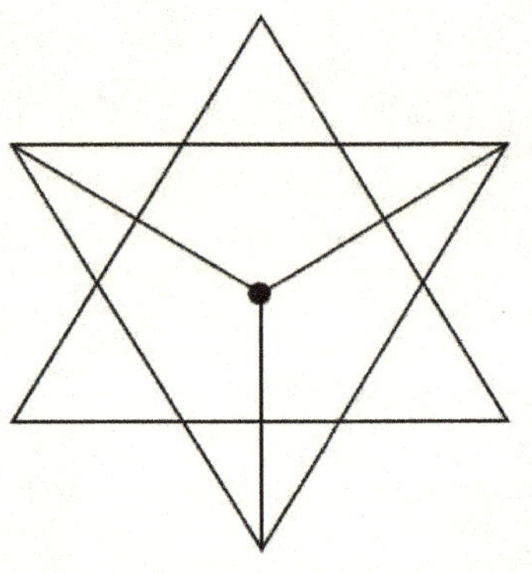